CELEBRATE

CELEBRATE

A Year of Festivities for Families and Friends

PIPPA MIDDLETON

With photography by David Loftus
and illustrations by Gill Heeley

VIKING

VIKING

Published by the Penguin Group

Penguin Group (USA) Inc., 375 Hudson Street, New York,
New York 10014, U.S.A.

Penguin Group (Canada), 90 Eglinton Avenue East, Suite 700,
Toronto, Ontario, Canada M4P 2Y3 (a division of Pearson Penguin Canada Inc.)

Penguin Books Ltd, 80 Strand, London WC2R 0RL, England

Penguin Ireland, 25 St. Stephen's Green, Dublin 2, Ireland
(a division of Penguin Books Ltd)

Penguin Books Australia Ltd, 707 Collins Street, Melbourne, Victoria 3008, Australia
(a division of Pearson Australia Group Pty Ltd)

Penguin Books India Pvt Ltd, 11 Community Centre, Panchsheel Park,
New Delhi – 110 017, India

Penguin Group (NZ), 67 Apollo Drive, Rosedale, Auckland 0632, New Zealand
(a division of Pearson New Zealand Ltd)

Penguin Books (South Africa) (Pty) Ltd, Rosebank Office Park, 181 Jan Smuts Avenue,
Parktown North, 2193, South Africa

Penguin Books Ltd, Registered Offices:
80 Strand, London WC2R 0RL, England

First published in 2012 by Viking Penguin,
a member of Penguin Group (USA) Inc.

1 2 3 4 5 6 7 8 9 10

ISBN: 978-0-670-02635-7

Printed and bound in Italy by Graphicom srl
Color reproduction by Altaimage Ltd

Set in Gill and Mrs Eaves

ALWAYS LEARNING   **PEARSON**

To my family, for all their love
and support over the years.

CONTENTS

INTRODUCTION

It's a bit startling to achieve global recognition (if that's the right word) before the age of thirty, on account of your sister, your brother-in-law and your bottom.

One day, I might be able to make sense of this. In the meantime, I think it's fair to say that it has its upside and its downside. I certainly have opportunities many can only dream of, but in most ways I'm a typical girl in her twenties trying to forge a career and represent herself in what can sometimes seem rather strange circumstances.

I am by nature an optimist, so I tend to concentrate on the advantages. One of the most attractive has been the chance to publish *Celebrate*.

I've always loved to write, so it seemed natural to try to combine this passion along with my enjoyment for entertaining, an enthusiasm I hope to share with others.

I don't think there's a right way or a wrong way to celebrate. But I do strongly believe in the importance of bringing friends and family together. I have been lucky enough to grow up in a very close-knit family and this has played a central role in my life. The nurturing of friendship, family and home feels more important than ever to me in a world that sometimes appears to be moving so fast that we forget what really matters.

This book is designed to be a comprehensive guide to home entertaining, based on my experience in my family's party business, Party Pieces, and previous work for London-based events company, Table Talk. It is a useful and practical journey into British-themed occasions and I hope it offers welcome inspiration and ideas, most of which needn't leave you alarmingly out of pocket. While some of the events, crafts and dishes may be unfamiliar to an American audience, I am thrilled to share my favorite British traditions and hope you'll find them as lovely as I do. Entertaining on any scale can be stressful and daunting so this is all about finding ways to manage and enjoy the process.

I hope you will see this as a feel-good book with ideas to look forward to each month, providing threads of lasting, happy memories, be it around a table lit with candles in winter, outside on a blanket in summer or in the autumn, perched on a leaf-covered bench, hot drink in hand.

I have very fond memories of many of the events celebrated in this book and each seasonal introduction seeks to give you an insight into why I feel it should be there. I hope there's something here for everyone, whatever their age. In some cases I've harvested fascinating tidbits of history, which shed a little light on why we celebrate certain occasions in the first place.

The book is structured around the seasonal cycle and focuses on tradition, ritual and rhythm, providing a glimmer of anticipation and hope—like that warm feeling on your back on the first sunny day of the year or spotting the first signs of spring.

I know many of you will have picked up this book out of nothing more than curiosity. I can assure you that it feels even stranger to me than it probably does to you to have seen so much written about me when I have done so little to paint a picture of myself. This is my first chance to do that, and I've enjoyed every minute of it.

I hope you find *Celebrate* fun to read, practical to use and inspiring to look at. I've tried to make it as all-embracing as possible—but I'm having new ideas all the time, which I look forward to sharing with you in the future.

Thank you very much for your support.

Pippa Middleton, 2012

AUTUMN

HALLOWEEN
SUNDAY LUNCHES
COZY SUPPER PARTIES

Autumn is a celebration of gathering and of golden
light. Leaves turn to all shades of bronze, chestnuts
carpet the dewy ground. The weather brings cooler
days and fresh misty mornings. It marks the end
of summer and a new start. Hedgerows boast ruby
fruits among spindles and spikes, root vegetables
swell and flavorsome game appears in butchers'
windows, wholesome and plump. Stews, roasts and
pies fill our plates.

Light as feathers the witches fly,
The horn of the moon is plain to see;
By a firefly under a jonquil flower
A goblin toasts a bumble-bee.

"Camomile Tea,"
Katherine Mansfield

HALLOWEEN

Halloween is a chance to celebrate the macabre and brings out the impish spirit in us all. Ghost stories and fairy tales depict creatures howling at the full moon, bats flitting across troubled skies and pumpkin lanterns glowing on windowsills to ward off bad spirits – scenes that evoke fright and mystery. On this night, trick-or-treaters take to the streets: ghosts rub shoulders with trolls and hobgoblins, witches ride their broomsticks and Frankenstein's monsters seem to emerge out of nowhere.

Many of the elements of today's celebration have their origins in Celtic Ireland and the festival of *Samhain*, and are heralded by the falling leaves of autumn, which signify death. Spirits of those who had died in the previous year were thought to return to Earth in search of living bodies to inhabit. The Celts would disguise themselves in ghoulish costumes, hoping that the spirits would mistake them for one of their own kind and pass them by.

Halloween lends itself to a family celebration: adults get involved with the preparations, helping children carve pumpkins, create costumes and have fun with face painting and traditional games. As a child, I felt that Halloween was a time when creatures of the night suddenly came to life – we would turn off all the lights in the house and let flickering candlelight conjure up scary shadows and create the effect of imaginary figures lurking in dark corners. It was also a time for sugary treats – we feasted on creepy edible morsels, Halloween-themed chocolates and spookily named concoctions, which often looked better than they tasted.

Nowadays, I frequently celebrate Halloween over a supper with friends. It's a wonderful excuse to let your imagination run riot with gory-looking food and special effects: stir witchy cauldrons of pumpkin soup, hang homemade spiders inside window nooks, string cobwebs on tables and haunt gardens, attics and stairways with ghosts made from sheets.

Shops are well stocked with fancy dress and decorations in a palette of garish colors – pumpkin orange, bat black and the sinister purple of unspeakable potions. Mix and match store-bought items with things you have at home and make your celebration as elaborate or as low-key as you like, depending on how much time you have, the size of your venue and its location. It needn't cost a fortune, just a simply carved pumpkin lit up among glimmering candles will go a long way to producing the right atmosphere.

EXTEND A SPOOKY WELCOME

At Halloween your home should look the part on the outside to greet your guests and any passing spooks and spirits. Decorate your windows with stained-glass bats (page 17). String outdoor fairy lights around trees and shrubs, and light the pathway with a few paper lanterns. A scarecrow under a tree and lit with a flashlight will set the scene from a distance. A few mournful ghosts floating around will add to the effect. Simply blow up white balloons, tie each one to a bamboo cane and drape a white sheet over it. Tie around the "neck" with string and use a black marker to draw the face. Stick the canes in the ground where you want each ghost to stand.

You can buy cobweb-effect decorations, but they are easy enough to make yourself using plenty of cotton batting. Swathe liberally over tree branches, doorknobs, in doorways and on light fixtures, and hang pompom spiders from them. These are made using black pompoms (page 154) for the spiders' bodies and pipe cleaners for legs. You can add some googly eyes for extra scare tactics. Scrawl a menacing message on a sign for the front door to prepare the unwary for what lies within. You might like to welcome guests into a pitch-black hallway or garage, devoid of electric lighting, with only candles and flashlights available to help them find their way inside. It's amazing how creepy even the most familiar places can seem when plunged into darkness.

Arrange glowing pumpkins in a prominent position where they will light up windows and the front door, welcoming wandering souls and frightening off supernatural beings. As well as the classic scary face, you can also carve out stars, names, numbers and other

HALLOWEEN CRAFTS

The jack-o'-lantern (or pumpkin) is now the most recognizable symbol of Halloween, but it's not the only fun craft to do in the run-up to the event. For a gothic touch, cover a cauldron or saucepan with aluminum foil and fill with candy.

CANDY WREATH

A twist on the classic door wreath, you can make this trick-or-treat version with wrapped candies, such as toffees, or any other kind of treat that comes in shiny paper.

I: Curve a 3-foot length of gardening wire into a circle, weaving the two ends together to fasten. 2: Using 3-foot of fishing thread knot together 3 wrapped candies and tie the thread tightly around the circled wire. 3: Repeat with 3 candies at a time. 4: Each time you knot the candies on, bunch them up to create a full-looking wreath.

SPOOKY BOTTLES

Stack some aged "spell books" beside these candlesticks dripping with blood for a maximum eerie effect.

I: Prepare the label for your bottle by printing or handwriting with a marker pen an evocative description of the contents (i.e., "Witches' Wine," "Bats' Blood," "Spooky Syrup"). 2: Cut into label shape, burn the edges, dab with a wet teabag and sprinkle with coffee grounds. Leave to dry and then glue to your bottle with craft glue. 3: Place a white candle in the neck of the bottle, then light a red candle and allow it to drip over the white candle and the bottle. The messier it gets, the better! Experiment with other colored candles, such as slime-green or purple, if you prefer.

STAINED-GLASS BATS

Add the finishing touches to your room with Halloween bat window decorations, or vary the template and cut out star, moon, or pumpkin shapes.

I: Draw around a plate on black construction paper. In the center of your circle, position a bat template and draw around the outlines of the bat. 2: Cut around the bat and the circle. 3: Stick some colorful tissue paper to the back of the silhouette with craft glue, or use colorful sweet wrappers instead (in which case use a glue stick).

SET THE SCENE

Transform your dining table into a Halloween focal point. If the weather is good enough you can place your table outside for an autumn tea. Spread a multi-colored knitted blanket as a tablecloth or overlap scarves in brilliant oranges, yellows and reds to add warmth and texture. Long-necked butternut squash and plump root vegetables (carved or covered with glitter using craft glue) fit the autumnal theme and add variety to the table.

LOLLIPOP-STUDDED PUMPKIN

A great table centerpiece, the lollipops can be handed out as going-home treats. You can also skewer pumpkins with other nibbles, such as cocktail sausages, tomatoes and mini mozzarella balls, or chunks of fresh fruit.

Cut a white paper napkin or a piece of paper towel into quarters. 2: Place one piece of napkin over the head of the lollipop and tie tightly at the neck with a piece of white cotton thread. Draw on eyes with a black marker pen. 3: Repeat until you have enough lollipop "ghosts" to cover your pumpkin.

A HARVEST HALLOWEEN TABLE

If you want your table to have a grown-up, pagan feel to it, go for a Halloween Harvest look using the colors of the season. Scatter your table with leaves, clusters of chestnuts, acorns and other seedpods—go on a nature walk with children to collect various bits and pieces in advance. This style of decoration is perfect for a bare wooden table. Alternatively, cover your table with a dark-colored cloth or burlap (which you can buy in department stores and fabric stores).

Pewter, stone and slate offer a stark contrast to rich autumn shades, so, where possible, use these natural materials—slate looks particularly good as place mats or dinner plates. Inject an element of magic and mayhem with a scattering of edible (or plastic) creepy crawlies and make silhouetted place cards, handwritten in silver pen, or cut out a colony of bat silhouettes using black construction paper and fix them on the wall. Light lots of candles, dripping with red blood (page 17), stack up old "spell" books and close curtains, blinds or shutters to conjure up a moody atmosphere. Autumn branches and ferns in tall vases with hanging spiders make simple, structural centerpieces. Intersperse with branches of Chinese lanterns with their papery orange husks, or use other orange-hued flowers, such as mango calla lillies, burgundy sunflowers, russet hydrangeas or gerbera daisies and dahlias.

There is no such thing as overdoing it when it comes to Halloween, but there's no need to buy lots of expensive decorations: make simple crafts or be inventive and adapt household items to transform the party room into a cavern of ghoulish wonders.

ALL HALLOWS' FEAST

Whatever you choose to eat on Halloween, dress your food for the occasion and add some hair-raising dishes to your table. Children will love to get involved, so help them to make delicious cookies or a jelly bowl crawling with worms. You could also let them mash up blackberries for a flavored butter with the gory appearance of entrails to seep into English muffins or spread liberally on toast.

Dishes with spooky names will both feed the imagination and satisfy the stomach, so prepare your guests to eat toad-in-the-hole, witches' fingers and devil's food cake. You can accessorize dishes with a trickle of tomato ketchup "blood" and black plastic spiders perched on serving trays or in drinks.

WORM-RIDDEN GELATIN BOWL

Have some gummy worms "escaping" to make everyone's toes curl. Add in any other spooky gummy sweets you can find.

The night before you want to serve this, make a layer of lime gelatin according to the packet instructions in a clear glass bowl. Add a few gummy "worms" before putting into the fridge overnight to set. The next morning, make up some grape gelatin and pour over the first set layer, adding more worms. Put back into the fridge to set. The steps can be repeated again with different colors of gelatin to create an impressive layer effect.

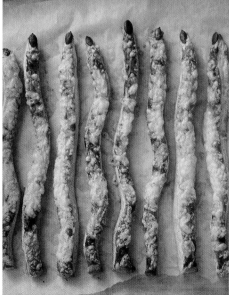

HALLOWEEN COOKIES Makes 16

These cookies use white chocolate and cranberries to represent ghosts and blood, dark chocolate and raisins for bats and witches. Shape them using Halloween-themed cookie cutters if you like. The raw dough mixture can be frozen once wrapped in plastic wrap. Simply defrost thoroughly before rolling out.

Preheat the oven to 350°F and line a baking tray with parchment paper. In a large bowl, beat 2 sticks plus 2 tablespoons of softened unsalted butter and ¾ cup of superfine sugar together until creamy. Stir in 1 teaspoon of baking powder, 2½ tablespoons of golden syrup or honey and 3 egg yolks. Gently mix in 4 cups of all-purpose flour to form a dough.

Split the dough in two and put half into a second bowl. Add ½ cup of white-chocolate chips and 3 tablespoons of dried cranberries to one half, and ½ cup of dark-chocolate chips and 3 tablespoons of raisins to the other half. Mix each batch. Place one dough on the work surface, working with your fingertips to bring it together, and shape into a sausage. Repeat for the second dough. Wrap each dough in plastic wrap and place in the fridge to rest for 30 minutes. Once chilled, cut each sausage in half, for ease of handling. Roll out each half to about ½-inch thickness, then cut out your cookies using a cutter. Place the cookies onto your baking tray and cook in the preheated oven for 10 to 12 minutes, until golden brown.

BLACKBERRY BUTTER Makes 2 jam jars

Gently heat 10 ounces of blackberries, 2 tablespoons of lemon juice and 4 tablespoons of confectioner's sugar in a small pan for 5 to 6 minutes, until the berries look soft. Allow to cool completely. Soften 2½ sticks of unsalted butter and, using an electric mixer or food processor, beat the blackberries into the butter to create a lovely ripple effect. Spoon into jars and use on English muffins. This can be stored in the fridge for up to 4 days, or frozen for 1 month.

TIPS: *The soup can be frozen for up to 3 months in a sealed container.* • *Fry sage leaves in a little oil to create sage crisps for a soup garnish, or try adding drops of pumpkin-seed oil to the finished dish.* • *If you don't have enough pumpkin flesh, bulk it up with chunks of butternut squash. Alternatively, you can always cheat by adding store-bought cartons of puréed butternut squash or carrot soup.*

PUMPKIN SOUP

Served in its own raw or baked "carcass," this soup is one of my favorites for this time of year. Hollowing out the pumpkins always proves a challenge—many an evening has been spent carving them in front of the TV—but the final result is well worth the effort. Witches' fingers cheese straws are great to dip into the soup, or as a predinner nibble with drinks, served in steins.

SERVES 8

For the soup

8 to 10 small sugar pumpkins, or 1 large pumpkin

7 tablespoons unsalted butter

3 medium onions, peeled and finely chopped

4 garlic cloves, peeled and crushed or finely chopped

a large pinch of dried chili flakes

¾ teaspoon freshly grated nutmeg

sea salt and freshly ground black pepper

7 cups chicken or vegetable stock

To serve

heavy cream

toasted pumpkin seeds

Cut the tops off the pumpkins and set aside. Remove the seeds and fibers from the middle of each and discard. Using a sharp knife and a spoon, carefully hollow out the pumpkins. Scoop out the flesh and roughly chop.

In a large pan with a lid, melt the butter over low heat, then add the onion and garlic. Cook gently for 10 to 15 minutes, until softened and golden brown. Add the chopped pumpkin, the chili flakes and the nutmeg, then season with salt and pepper. Increase the heat to medium and cover with the lid. Sauté for 6 to 8 minutes.

Pour in the stock, bring to a boil, then simmer for 40 to 45 minutes, stirring occasionally. Remove the pan from the heat and allow the soup to cool slightly. Whisk until smooth. To serve, fill the hollowed-out pumpkins with soup (these can be raw or baked with their lids on at 350°F for 20 to 25 minutes, drizzled with a little olive oil). Swirl over a little cream and scatter with toasted pumpkin seeds. Pass cheese straws at the table for dipping.

WITCHES' FINGERS CHEESE STRAWS Makes 24

Cut 13 ounces of thawed, frozen puff pastry in half, and roll each half out on a lightly floured surface into a strip about 9 inches long. Brush with 2 beaten egg yolks mixed with a little water, sprinkle with 1 teaspoon of paprika and ¼ cup of grated cheddar cheese. Cut the pastry into ¾-inch-wide strips with a sharp knife—uneven strips make the knobbliest fingers. Press a pumpkin seed onto the tip of each to make a "fingernail." Bake on a lined baking sheet for 10 to 15 minutes at 400°F or until lightly browned. Remove to racks to cool. These can be frozen, unbaked, for up to 3 months in a sealed container. If cooking from frozen, add 3 to 5 minutes to the cooking time.

MUSHROOM CAPPUCCINO

After a damp afternoon spent kicking up the autumn leaves, this velvety, earthy soup will warm you up. Transform it into a magic potion with a cloud of foam and serve in little china cups. A drizzle of truffle oil will really lift the flavor. Serve with garlic croutons or garlic bread to keep evil spirits at bay.

SERVES 8

1½ pounds mixed mushrooms (Cremini and Portobello), wiped clean and chopped

12 scallions, trimmed and chopped

4 garlic cloves, peeled and chopped

2 tablespoons olive oil

2 tablespoons butter

1 quart chicken or vegetable stock

1 cup skim milk

¼ teaspoon ground white pepper

To serve

½ ounce dried porcini or chanterelle mushrooms, finely chopped

sea salt and black peppercorns

¾ cup skim milk

In a large pan, sauté the mushrooms, scallions, and garlic in the olive oil and butter over high heat for 3 to 4 minutes. Pour in the stock, cover the pan and continue to cook for another 3 to 4 minutes. Add the milk and white pepper, then blend the soup with an immersion blender until very smooth. Keep hot. (At this stage the soup can be frozen for up to 3 months.)

To serve, grind the dried mushrooms, sea salt and peppercorns into a fine powder using a pestle and mortar or food processor and set this aside. Heat the milk until very hot, then use a milk frother or electric mixer to create billows of light foam. Fill two-thirds of each serving cup with hot soup, spoon a little of the froth on top and sprinkle with the ground mushroom powder.

 Chablis would complement this.

TIPS: *This makes a lovely starter, but double the quantities if you're serving it in soup bowls. • To make garlic croutons, cut 2 slices of crusty bread into small cubes, toss them in 2 tablespoons of olive oil with 1 clove of crushed garlic and season with salt and freshly ground black pepper. Fry over medium heat until golden brown all over.*

TOAD-IN-THE-HOLE WITH ONION GRAVY

Although it's a supper staple throughout the year, this is perfect for Halloween—when better to put a toad on somebody's plate? Buy the sausages from a local butcher and choose interesting flavors for variety. The batter is flavored with rosemary, but you could also try a few pinches of paprika or replace the mustard powder with a tablespoon of whole-grain mustard. Serve with a rich onion gravy.

SERVES 8

16 pork sausages

16 slices prosciutto

2 tablespoons olive oil

3½ cups all-purpose flour

8 eggs

2 cups milk

1 teaspoon mustard powder, or to taste

2 tablespoons chopped fresh rosemary

salt and freshly ground black pepper, to taste

For the onion gravy

2 tablespoons olive oil

2 large onions, peeled and finely sliced

4 teaspoons Dijon mustard

1 quart beef stock

Preheat the oven to 400°F. Wrap the sausages in prosciutto. Pour the oil into the bottom of two large 9 x 13 x 1½-inch-deep baking dishes and arrange the sausages in a single layer in each pan. Place in the preheated oven and bake for 10 minutes.

In a bowl, whisk together the flour, eggs and half of the milk. Gradually mix in the rest of the milk until smooth. Add the mustard powder and rosemary. Season with salt and pepper.

Remove the pans from the oven. Ladle the batter over the sausages until they are three-quarters covered. Return to the oven, and bake for 20 to 25 minutes, until risen and golden brown.

To make the onion gravy, heat the olive oil in a heavy-bottomed saucepan. Add the sliced onion and cook over low heat until soft, golden and caramelized. Stir in the mustard and pour in the stock. Bring the mixture to a boil, and simmer for 10 minutes or until the liquid has thickened and reduced by half.

 Rich and savory red wine like a Rioja works well with this dish.

BUTTERNUT SQUASH LASAGNA

A large dish of this lasagna will bring the season to the table. This recipe may be vegetarian but it's so delicious that many a carnivore will consider converting. Serve with a mixed green salad.

SERVES 8

olive oil

1½ large onions, peeled and thinly sliced

2½ pound butternut squash, peeled, seeded and sliced into ⅛-inch-thick crescents

1 large bunch sage leaves, half left whole, half chopped

4 large garlic cloves, peeled and sliced

1 pound fresh spinach

generous grating of nutmeg

sea salt and freshly ground black pepper

1 pound dried lasagna noodles

two 4-ounce balls of mozzarella

For the béchamel sauce

1 stick unsalted butter

1 cup all-purpose flour

3 cups milk

¾ cup grated Parmesan, plus ½ cup extra, for sprinkling between layers

Preheat the oven to 400°F. Drizzle a little oil into a large baking dish, add the onion, butternut squash, chopped sage and garlic, then roast in the oven for 15 to 20 minutes until soft.

To make the béchamel sauce, melt the butter in a medium saucepan, then add the flour until you have a paste and cook for 1 to 2 minutes. Slowly add the milk, constantly stirring until it forms a thick sauce and add the ¾ cup of Parmesan.

In a separate pan heat a little oil and add the spinach, nutmeg and salt and pepper. Cook for a couple of minutes until the spinach has wilted, squeezing out any excess water.

Bring a pan of salted water to a boil, drizzle a little oil into it and cook the lasagna noodles for 5 minutes, to soften them. Put a layer of pasta into a 9 x 13-inch earthenware baking dish, top with a layer of the butternut squash mixture, a layer of béchamel sauce, some spinach and a sprinkling of Parmesan. Repeat the layers, ending up with a final layer of pasta. Spread the remaining béchamel sauce on top. Rip the mozzarella into pieces and scatter these over the top with any remaining grated Parmesan. Place in the preheated oven for 25 to 30 minutes until the mozzarella bubbles and browns. Garnish with the whole sage leaves flash-fried in a little butter.

 *Aromatic and full-bodied whites like Chenin Blanc or a white Rhône.*

TIP: *This can be kept in the fridge for two days if covered in plastic wrap or frozen for up to 3 months. Defrost fully before cooking.*

DEVIL'S FOOD CAKE

This chocolate cake reminds me of holidays in the Lake District when I was a child. A friend who lived there would make this cake and leave it in an old Roses tin for us to enjoy during our stay. It's comforting, not too rich and stays moist for ages (a treat for the rest of the week). Serve big wedges with a thick blood-red raspberry coulis to complete it as a dessert.

SERVES 8–10

6 tablespoons unsalted butter

1⅓ cups superfine sugar

2 medium eggs, lightly beaten

½ cup cocoa powder, plus 2 tablespoons

1 cup water

1⅓ cups self-rising flour

For the icing

1 stick unsalted butter

2 cups confectioner's sugar

2 tablespoons cocoa powder, plus extra for dusting

2 tablespoons milk

For the raspberry coulis

10 ounces raspberries

lemon juice, to taste

3 tablespoons confectioner's sugar

Preheat the oven to 300°F. Grease and line two 8-inch layer cake pans with parchment paper. Cream the butter and superfine sugar together until soft and fluffy. Then gradually add the beaten eggs, mixing well after each addition. Blend the cocoa powder with the water. Add alternately with the flour into the butter mixture, until all is blended smoothly. Divide the cake batter between the two pans and bake in the center of the oven for 25 minutes until firm and just coming away from the side of the pans. Leave to cool on a rack. (At this stage the cakes can be frozen for up to a month.)

To make the icing, beat the butter and confectioner's sugar together until light and fluffy. Add the cocoa powder and milk and beat until combined. Sandwich the cakes together using half of the icing, then use the remainder to top the cake. Decorate with a simple dusting of cocoa powder.

For the coulis, blend the raspberries, lemon juice and sugar until smooth, then strain to remove any seeds.

TIP : *To make chocolate curls to decorate the cake, melt 3½ ounces of dark chocolate (70% cocoa solids), then pour onto a flat surface (such as a baking sheet) and spread it out thinly. Cool until set, then carefully drag a sharp knife from one end of the chocolate to the other to form curls.*

SOUL CAKES *In the Middle Ages, "soul cakes" made of bread, currants and spices were laid out, along with glasses of wine, as an offering to the souls in Purgatory. On All Hallows' Eve and All Souls' Day, families sent their children out "souling": walking from house to house begging for these cakes. For each cake received, they would say a prayer for the souls of the donor's dead relatives.*

CREEPY COCKTAILS

BLACKBERRY COLLINS Serves 4

Blend 3½ ounces of blackberries with 1 tablespoon of confectioner's sugar to make a blackberry purée. Strain this through a sieve into a wide shallow bowl. Pour a little superfine sugar into another bowl, then dip the rims of 4 tall glasses into the purée and then into the sugar. Fill the glasses with crushed ice. Add the blackberry purée to a cocktail shaker, with ½ cup of blackberry liqueur or cassis and ¾ cup of gin. Shake well with ice cubes before carefully pouring into your sugar-rimmed glasses. Stir in a little soda water and finish with a couple of blackberries.

BLOOD AND SAND Serves 1 (make to order)

It's all in the name. Fill a cocktail shaker with ice and pour in 1 ounce of Scotch whisky, 1 ounce of blood orange juice, 1 tablespoon of Italian sweet vermouth and 1 tablespoon of cherry liqueur. Shake and pour into chilled martini glasses or Champagne coupes. Garnish with an orange twist.

ESPRESSO MARTINI Serves 1 (make to order)

This cocktail can be served after dinner in lieu of dessert. Make each to order to get the best flavor and froth. Put just a few cubes of ice in a cocktail shaker and pour in ¼ cup of vodka, 2 ounces of good-quality coffee liqueur (such as Kahlua), 1 ounce of espresso and a dash of sugar syrup (page 80). Shake well and strain into a chilled martini glass. Garnish with coffee beans and dust with cinnamon.

SHIRLEY TEMPLE Serves 1 (make to order)

For this alcohol-free option, adding grenadine syrup at the end gives the effect of blood trickling down the edges of the glass. Make these up individually to achieve the best layering effect. Fill a tall glass with ice and add old-fashioned lemonade (or use the juice of 1 large lemon and ½ cup of soda water) until it is three-quarters full. Top off the glass with orange juice and add a few teaspoons of grenadine syrup. Garnish with a slice of orange and a maraschino cherry on a toothpick or skewer.

> **RAISING A TOAST** *Lambswool, a cocktail of mulled ale with sugar, spices and the pulp of roasted apples, served with spiced pieces of brown toast floating on the surface, was historically drunk at Halloween. (The custom of floating toast on drinks is said to be the origin of people raising a toast.)*

FUN AND GAMES

For parties, make sure all your guests are in character. Provide a dress-up box and face paints, then organize a variety of activities and games. Stage rounds of bobbing for apples and eating doughnuts dangling from a tree, or for a quieter activity set up a leaf-rubbing table. And don't forget to spook the children by telling them ghost stories to heighten the atmosphere.

DRESSING UP AND FACE PAINTING

Generations of adults and children have devised increasingly imaginative ways of dressing up as scary and supernatural creatures. My Halloween costumes as a child were usually homemade mismatches from the dress-up box. Traditional characters include witches, ghosts, skeletons, vampires and cats. In more recent years, these Halloween regulars have been joined by zombies, aliens and superheroes from popular sci-fi and horror films.

A black sweater and leggings or pants can be embellished to create a whole host of different characters. Try adding:

- *A cape and an arrowhead tail for a devil costume.*
- *Ears and a tail for a black cat.*
- *A pointy hat, fake hair and a broom for a witch's outfit.*
- *A pair of white gloves and a ghoulish mask for a skeleton look.*
- *A headband with corks stuck to it and sprayed silver (as bolts) for Frankenstein's monster.*

Another easy idea is to use old white torn-up sheets to create a ghost or a mummy (add an extra wrapping of toilet paper for the full effect). A flour bag or muslin bag with slits for eyes, nose and mouth can also be the basis for a dressing-up costume—think scary escaped convict . . .

Face paint, makeup and grisly accessories are vital for a convincing costume. Have plenty of white and red face paint for zombies, some horns for your little devils, and orange face paints and stripy scarves for pumpkins. Beards and brows can be applied using soot from a cork burned in a candle flame. Make sure you have some false teeth for vampires, black eye pencil for scars and cat features, and red lipstick for blood. You can buy fake body tattoos for a bit of fun, and face paint stencils if you'd like a professional touch.

PUMPKIN BOWLING

This is a seasonal take on ten-pin bowling. In the run-up to Halloween, save ten small drink bottles for pins. You can give them the appearance of ghosts by pouring in 2 inches of white gloss paint and a drop of thinner and shaking. Add faces to the outsides with black marker pen. You'll also need small pumpkins with short stems for bowling balls. If you can't find any, oranges work just as well.

Add some gravel or water to each bottle so they don't topple over too easily. Arrange them in a triangle and mark out the boundaries of your "alley" with twigs and branches or string if you are indoors, plus a starting line. Then, following the rules of ten-pin bowling, each player gets two goes at bowling to try to knock down as many ghost "pins" as possible.

THE MUMMY CHASE

You'll need a garden to play this game, or a quiet street and understanding neighbors, plus a stockpile of toilet paper.

Divide the players into teams. Each team nominates a mummy. Give each team a couple of toilet paper rolls and put on some Halloween-themed music. As the music plays, team members must wrap their mummy from head to toe, leaving just a small gap for the eyes and nose. Teams must use up all of their rolls.

Once the mummification is complete, everyone goes outside. Set up a starting and finish line for a race between the mummies, who must complete it without their wrappings coming off. If the paper starts to unravel mid-race, the mummies must return to the starting line, where their teammates can perform emergency repairs. The first mummy to cross the finish line with bandages intact is declared the winner.

BOBBING FOR APPLES

This has many variations, but here I've turned bobbing for apples into a team relay for enhanced exhilaration. Play this outside, or have a lot of towels on hand to mop up the mess! Blindfolding the players can be hilarious, and remember, the deeper the container, the harder it is to bite the apple.

Fill two large tubs with water and enough apples for each team member, then place each bowl on a chair about 12 inches apart. Divide the players into two teams and stand behind the starting line about 6 feet away from the tubs. On the command "Go!," the first players on each team run up to the tubs and try to get an apple out of the water by kneeling or standing in front of the tub and using their teeth. No hands allowed! As soon as an apple is out of the water and dropped on the floor, the successful player races back and tags the next player. The winning team is the first to empty their tub. To keep things moving, set a limit of a minute per person.

LEAF RUBBING

This is a lovely activity to make the most of the splendors of the season. Set up a table with colored wax crayons and paper, and send the children on a hunt to find autumnal leaves in interesting shapes and textures. Lay the paper over the foliage and rub using the sides of the crayons to create skeletal pictures of nature.

THE WITCH'S LAIR

Sometimes you want a game that's more of an experience than a contest. One Halloween game I particularly remember playing with friends involved taking turns to delve into bowls of unusual objects and "guess the body part." In advance of your party, gather a selection of "body parts." Here are some suggestions, but let your imagination run riot:

- **Eyeballs:** *peeled or oil-covered grapes, olives, lychees.*
- **Guts and veins:** *cooked spaghetti or vermicelli noodles, sausages with most of the sausage meat removed from the casings or marshmallows soaked in water, strung together and coated with oil.*
- **Brain:** *overcooked cauliflower.*
- **Heart:** *a skinned beef tomato.*
- **Toenails:** *shells from pistachio nuts or walnuts.*

Decant your body parts into separate bowls and hide them out of sight of your guests or cover the bowls with tea towels. When it's time to play, gather your guests and blindfold them. Tell them a Halloween story about a local witch who has been collecting body parts to use in her potions. Lead your blindfolded victims to the "body parts" and share with them the grisly items the witch has left behind, guiding hands into the bowls and asking your victims to identify what they're touching. Invariably, the game ends in howls of horror and disgust.

GHOULISH GAMES AND GHOST STORIES

THE DOUGHNUT TREE

This is best played outside, before it gets too dark and cold, but if you play indoors, line the floor with plenty of newspapers. If you have time to prepare the tree in advance, hang other spooky decorations from it to conjure up a witchy atmosphere.

You'll need a tree with accessible branches. Hang up a ring doughnut for each player, spacing them out and dangling them from various heights to accommodate both the short and the tall. (If you're playing indoors hang them from a length of string across the room.) Players stand by the doughnuts and when the umpire shouts "Eat!" everyone must devour their doughnut as quickly as possible without using their hands. The first player to finish wins. Umpires must demand to see an empty mouth as proof of victory.

GHOST STORIES

Share stories as the light begins to fade, with just a flashlight for illumination. Get an enthusiastic storyteller to read from a classic children's book: some brilliant reads include the *Dr. Seuss* books, Grimm's fairy tales, *Frankenstein*, *Dracula*, *The Worst Witch* and Roald Dahl's ghost stories. Or you could let everyone take turns adding a few sentences to a story and see where it leads. Serve hot blackcurrant squash (vampire's blood) and Halloween cookies (page 23) and tell your younger guests that they've been prepared using a secret "spell" to ratchet up the tension and multiply the chills running down their spines.

When mighty Roast Beef was the Englishman's food,
It ennobled our brains and enriched our blood.
Our soldiers were brave and our courtiers were good
Oh! the Roast Beef of old England,
And old English Roast Beef!

"The Roast Beef of Old England,"
Henry Fielding

SUNDAY LUNCHES

A Sunday roast with all the trimmings is something to look forward to when the summer months are coming to an end and we move from refreshing salads and sizzling barbecues in the fresh air to indoor feasts. As the nights draw in, the kitchen once again becomes the nucleus of the household, wafting tantalizing aromas of roasting meat and baking, attracting everyone in the house and echoing the natural instinct in us all to batten down the hatches and prepare for the cold months ahead.

The Sunday roast has a long and distinguished history in Britain; customarily a piece of meat was rotated before an open fire or else dropped off at the baker's on the way to church to cook slowly in the cooling bread ovens (bread wasn't baked on Sundays). It was seen as a weekly treat; Sunday was the only rest day after a six-day working week, and this meal gave families the opportunity to sit down together. Modern life has reinvented the nature of Sundays, however many shops are open, and some people now work while others choose to go out for the day, leaving little time to dedicate to cooking and being domestic.

Cooking a roast is a traditional domestic ritual that does require some time, but it can be a great focus for a casual celebration, perhaps centered around a family get-together, birthday or other special event. It's worth putting in the effort to make an occasion of it and having a sit-down lunch as a regular feature of your home life. Sunday lunch offers the perfect slot in the weekend to rejoice in the company of those close to you, to push the pause button and to take stock before the madness begins again the following week. In my boarding-school days, a family Sunday lunch gave us a good reason to come back from school, even just for the day—we would be fed the full works, dessert and all, to prepare us for the school week ahead (a great way to fend off the dreaded Sunday-night blues).

What I like about this ritual is the fact that it's essentially unfussy—there's nothing to dress up, not even the food. It should be an occasion, like the Christmas meal, where everyone pitches in to help—setting the table, carving, clearing up and chatting together, so you'll need to pay less attention to the finer details. It's also a great way to feed many people with relatively little effort. With a clever choice of cut and various preparation shortcuts, the perfect roast can be something you almost forget about in the oven. You can even cheat with a few of the ingredients if you simply haven't got time to prepare things yourself. Remember: it's all about being gathered around the table, talking and enjoying the meal together.

RELAXED SUNDAYS

What you choose to cook for your Sunday lunch depends on what plans you have over the weekend. Visit your local butcher and experiment with different cuts of meat and seasonal game—don't worry about getting a piece a little bigger than you need as roasts make for delicious leftovers for the rest of the week. The traditional choice is a classic roast but it can be quite a feat bringing all the components to the table at the same time (particularly the gravy). If you're planning a walk before lunch, consider slow cooking or pot roasting. You might want to encourage your children to get involved and help plan the menu; this way they can feel part of the occasion and will, hopefully, inherit a love for this time-honored ritual.

Starters are rarely necessary as this meal is often substantial enough to keep everyone full throughout the afternoon, but some spiced nuts (page 67) and vegetable chips are great to pick at between bouts of table setting and vegetable prepping. Serve a few pitchers of Bloody or Virgin Marys alongside. Use colorful autumn leaves as place cards for the table. Stick a pretty feather on it with craft glue and staple it to a piece of card or burlap. Use a gold pen to write the name.

HOW TO CARVE A ROAST

Carving a roast at the table makes a real ceremony of the meal. Always let the meat stand for 10 to 20 minutes after you take it out of the oven, depending on how large the roast is, to keep in the juices and make carving easier. This also gives you time to get the trimmings ready and make the gravy. When it comes to carving, make sure you have a very sharp, long-handled knife and a pronged fork (with a guard) to hold the meat. Use a carving board with a lip or well around the edges to catch the tasty juices—you can add these to the gravy. Carve the meat using long, sweeping motions and firm pressure; avoid sawing or pressing down too hard as this will create distorted or ragged-edged slices. Have a warmed platter ready for the carved slices and cover them with foil until you need them. Don't forget to serve some of the crispy ends, skin and brown meat, as these are often the tastiest morsels.

LEG OF LAMB

Cut a few slices in the same direction as the bone to create a flat base. Hold the protruding bone of the lamb steady with your fork, start at the shank end and slice down toward the bone at a slight angle (across the grain). Turn the knife slightly to free each slice from the bone as you go, or do it at the end by turning the knife parallel to the bone and freeing all the slices at once. Turn the leg over and do the same on the other side.

RIB OF BEEF

Steady the joint with the fork and carve downward with the thick end parallel to the rib bones, starting on the right side if you are right-handed and on the left if left-handed. Cut vertically along the bone. I like thicker slices for beef, but carve to your preference.

CHICKEN

You can cut up your chicken into portions consisting of the drumstick, thigh, breast and wing. With the legs pointing away from you, pull the whole leg away from the body and cut through the skin and joint. Then separate the drumstick from the thigh by cutting down through the joint (if it's turkey, you can carve slices off the drumstick first, slicing at an angle). Remove the wing by cutting it at the joint with the body. Turn the chicken so the neck is facing you and cut each breast away from the breastbone either in slices or as a whole slab—you can then carve the whole breast on the diagonal. Don't forget to remove the "oysters" under the carcass—these tasty little nuggets are the carver's reward!

POT ROAST
TARRAGON CHICKEN

This is a great way to cook a whole chicken while keeping the meat juicy. This recipe serves four people but is easily doubled if you have room in the oven. The chicken can be shredded in its sauce (simmer it until thickened if it's too runny) and will make a great pie filling.

SERVES 4

3½-pound free-range whole chicken

salt and freshly ground black pepper

1 lemon, halved

2 tablespoons olive oil

2 medium onions, peeled and cut into wedges

2 celery stalks, roughly chopped

2 garlic cloves, kept whole, but squashed

½ cup white wine

1 cup chicken stock

½ bunch fresh tarragon

For the sauce

11 ounces button mushrooms, brushed clean and halved

2 tablespoons butter

7 ounces crème fraîche

1 to 2 tablespoons whole-grain mustard (optional)

2 tablespoons chopped fresh tarragon leaves

Preheat the oven to 350°F. Season the chicken with salt and pepper and stuff the lemon halves into the cavity. Heat the oil in a large Dutch oven over medium to high heat. Add the seasoned chicken and brown on all sides. Transfer to a plate. Into the same pan, toss the onion, celery and garlic. Sauté for 2 to 3 minutes. Sit the chicken back in the pan on top of the vegetables. Pour in the wine and chicken stock before adding the tarragon. Bring the liquid to a boil, put the lid on and then cook in the oven for 1 hour 10 minutes. To test doneness, insert a skewer in the thigh and the juices will run clear.

Remove the chicken from the pan and transfer to a plate. Strain the onions, tarragon and celery through a sieve. Let the remaining liquid sit for a few minutes before skimming any fat from the surface. In another pan, brown the mushrooms in the butter, remove from the pan and set aside. Pour in the reserved liquid gradually, then whisk in the crème fraîche, mustard (if using) and tarragon. Stir well until combined and cook until starting to thicken before finally adding the mushrooms. Serve the chicken whole at the table in the pot and carve, or cut the rested chicken into pieces and serve in a dish with the sauce poured over the top. This is lovely served with the roast potatoes on page 54.

 Hunter Valley Semillon Sauvignon Blanc or a Pinot Noir.

ROASTING TIMES FOR CHICKEN

For a traditional, oven-roasted chicken, allow 20 minutes per pound at 375°F, plus 10 to 20 minutes at 425°F, uncovered, at the end to crisp the skin. Check and baste the meat frequently and adjust the timings for your particular oven.

ROASTING TIMES FOR BEEF ON THE BONE

For rare, allow 12 minutes per pound, plus 15 minutes. For medium, allow 16 minutes per pound, plus 20 minutes. For well done, allow 20 minutes per pound, plus 25 minutes. Check and baste the meat frequently and adjust the timings for your particular oven.

TRADITIONAL ROAST RIB OF BEEF

The ultimate Sunday lunch dish, roast beef and Yorkshire pudding is a quintessential British combination, well known from the middle of the eighteenth century, when the French started referring to the English as "les rosbifs." Rib of beef is one of the tastiest cuts as it's cooked on the bone, which also makes for a flavorful gravy. Ask the butcher to trim the bones for a neat finish. I like to cheat a little and use store-bought fresh or frozen Yorkshire pudding. Remember to remove the meat from the fridge half an hour before cooking to allow it to come to room temperature.

SERVES 8

---

3 to 4 bone-trimmed beef rib roast, approximately 6½ pounds

4 to 6 tablespoons Dijon mustard

salt and freshly ground black pepper

For the horseradish sauce

½ cup extra-spicy prepared horseradish or horseradish sauce

4 tablespoons crème fraîche

a squeeze of lemon juice

For the gravy

4 tablespoons all-purpose flour

3½ cups good-quality beef stock

⅔ cup red wine

Preheat the oven to 425°F. Place the rib roast in a large flameproof roasting pan and spread the mustard all over the meat. Season well with salt and pepper. Roast in the oven for 20 minutes and then reduce the oven to 350°F and roast for the remaining calculated cooking time (see box opposite). Baste occasionally with the roasting juices. Once the meat is cooked to your preference, remove it from the oven, transfer to a board and cover with foil. Pour the roasting juices into a pitcher, leaving the fat behind in the pan. Allow the meat to rest for at least 25 to 30 minutes. Combine the horseradish sauce, crème fraîche and lemon juice in a bowl. Season to taste.

To make the gravy, drain all but 3 to 4 tablespoons of fat from the roasting pan. Place the pan on the stove over medium heat and stir in the flour. Once combined, gradually whisk in the stock and red wine. Continue to whisk until smooth and simmer until thickened. Season with salt and pepper to taste and add the reserved roasting juices, and strain before serving.

 A red Claret.

SLOW ROAST LEG OF LAMB

The ultimate lazy roast, and delicious served with whole roasted bulbs of garlic (page 67). To add extra flavor and tenderize the meat, marinate it in the red wine, herbs and garlic overnight before cooking as instructed. You can also use this recipe with lamb shanks, if you prefer (see tip below).

SERVES 8

5- to 5½-pound bone-in leg of lamb

salt and freshly ground black pepper

2 tablespoons olive oil

4 red onions, peeled and cut into wedges

4 carrots, peeled and cut into chunks

4 garlic cloves, peeled and crushed

3 bay leaves

3 sprigs rosemary

one 750ml bottle red wine

1¾ cups lamb or beef stock

8 plums, cut in half and pitted

1 tablespoon butter, softened

1 tablespoon all-purpose flour

1 to 2 tablespoons red currant jelly

Preheat the oven to 325°F. Season the lamb with salt and pepper. Heat the oil in a pan and cook the onions and carrots for a few minutes until softened. Place the lamb in a very large thick-bottomed, lightly oiled roasting pan. Add the softened vegetables, garlic, bay leaves and rosemary. Pour in the wine and stock, cover tightly with foil and cook in the preheated oven for 3 hours, basting occasionally with the cooking juices. Remove the foil and cook, uncovered, for another 30 minutes, then add the plums and cook for another 20 to 25 minutes until the lamb is tender, almost falling off the bone, and the liquid has reduced slightly.

Remove the lamb, vegetables and plums from the pan, set aside and keep warm. Remove and discard the bay leaves. Place the roasting pan on the stove over high heat. Mix together the butter and flour in a small bowl until it forms a smooth paste, then whisk into the sauce in the pan. Simmer for 10 minutes or until the sauce has thickened and reduced. Stir in the red currant jelly and season to taste. Return the lamb, vegetables and plums to the sauce and warm through.

 *A red Ribera del Duero.*

TIP: *Substitute the leg of lamb with 8 seasoned lamb shanks. Brown them in a little olive oil in a large Dutch oven. Remove from the pot, add the onions and carrots and cook for a few minutes until soft. Stir in the garlic, bay leaves and rosemary and return the shanks to the pan. Pour in the wine and stock, bring to a boil, then reduce to a simmer for 8 to 10 minutes. Cover with a lid, transfer to the preheated oven and cook for 2 hours. Add the plums and cook, uncovered, for another 20 to 25 minutes. To finish the recipe, continue as per the leg of lamb recipe above.*

...AND TWO VEG (OR MORE)

Depending on what vegetables are in season, serve them freshly boiled or steamed on the side. They can be cooked at the last minute and neatly arranged on a platter. Alternatively, parboil them ahead of time, chill in ice cold water and reheat in butter or oil and herbs when needed. Look out for mini versions of vegetables when in season, such as carrots, leeks, zucchini and asparagus, which look tidy and don't require peeling or chopping. Aside from the classic sides here, you could serve Honeyed Parsnips and Carrots (page 123), or a Potato Dauphinoise (page 237), which can be made ahead of time.

GARLIC AND ROSEMARY ROAST POTATOES Serves 8

Preheat the oven to 450°F. Peel 4 pounds of Yukon Gold or other floury potatoes, and cut any large potatoes in half so that they are all a uniform size. Put them in a pan of cold salted water, bring to a boil and cook for 6 minutes. Drain, return the potatoes to the pan and shake them with the lid on to "fluff" them up, then allow to cool.

Place 3 tablespoons each of goose fat and vegetable oil in a heavy-based roasting pan; heat in the oven for 5 to 10 minutes, until the oil is almost smoking. Add the potatoes with 4 roughly chopped sprigs of rosemary and 12 fat garlic cloves with their skins on, and season well. Make sure everything is well coated in the oil and not too crowded in the pan. Cook for 40 to 45 minutes until golden and crispy, turning the potatoes every 10 minutes.

HASSELBACK POTATOES Serves 8

Preheat the oven to 400°F. Parboil 8 unpeeled medium-size baking potatoes for 10 minutes, then drain. Using a sharp knife, make slices crosswise across each potato about ⅛ inch to ¼ inch apart, but don't cut all the way through the potato (see the photograph on page 75). When all the potatoes have been sliced, place them cut side up in a shallow baking dish or small roasting pan. Drizzle 2 tablespoons of melted butter over the potatoes, then season with salt and pepper.

Bake for 15 to 20 minutes. Remove the potatoes from the oven and drizzle another 2 tablespoons of melted butter over them. Sprinkle 4 tablespoons of finely grated Pecorino cheese and 2 tablespoons of bread crumbs on top of the potatoes and season with a little more salt and pepper. Return to the oven and bake for another 20 minutes, or until nicely browned.

CAULIFLOWER AND BROCCOLI CHEESE Serves 8

Preheat the oven to 350°F. Cut a large cauliflower and a large head of broccoli into florets. Boil the cauliflower in salted water for 4 to 5 minutes, until just tender. Add the broccoli midway through the cooking as it takes less time to cook.

For the cheese sauce, melt 3 tablespoons of butter in a medium saucepan. Add 3 tablespoons of all-purpose flour and 1 teaspoon of mustard powder, stir well and cook for 1 to 2 minutes. Gradually whisk in 2¾ cups of milk and cook over low heat for 6 to 8 minutes, stirring frequently, until the sauce begins to thicken. Stir in a generous pinch of freshly grated nutmeg. Remove from the heat and mix in 7 ounces of aged cheddar and ½ cup of Parmesan (both finely grated), until the cheese has melted and the sauce is smooth. Arrange the cauliflower and broccoli in a 9 x 12-inch ovenproof dish. Pour the sauce over the vegetables, making sure everything is evenly coated. Sprinkle more Parmesan and nutmeg over the top, then bake for 30 to 35 minutes, until golden brown and bubbling.

RED CABBAGE Serves 8

In a large pan, melt 2 tablespoons of butter and sauté 1 red onion, peeled and thinly sliced, until softened. Remove and discard the core from a red cabbage, shred the rest finely, then add to the pan along with 4 tablespoons of red wine vinegar, 5 tablespoons of dark brown sugar and a cinnamon stick. Stir together for a few minutes, then pour in the juice and zest of 1 orange and ½ cup of water. Season with plenty of salt and freshly ground black pepper. Bring to a boil, then reduce the heat, cover with a lid and simmer for 35 to 40 minutes until the cabbage is tender and the liquid has evaporated. Garnish with orange zest.

FAVORITE BRITISH DESSERTS

Traditional desserts are a key element of a Sunday lunch. I've included some of my favorites, but for a more continental option, drown vanilla ice cream in a shot of espresso to make an *affogato*, an instant dessert that's a quick and light end to a meal.

STICKY TOFFEE PUDDING Serves 8

The cake can be frozen for up to a month tightly wrapped in plastic wrap. Reheat with toffee sauce drizzled over.

Preheat the oven to 350°F. Lightly grease a 9 x 10-inch rectangular baking pan. Mix 3½ ounces of chopped dates, 1 teaspoon each of vanilla extract and baking soda with 2 cups of water. In a separate bowl, cream 4 tablespoons of softened unsalted butter and ¾ cup of packed soft light brown sugar together until pale and fluffy, then gradually beat in 1 egg. Sift 2 cups of self-rising flour and gradually add this to the creamed mixture with 1 teaspoon of pumpkin pie spice and ½ teaspoon of ground cinnamon, then add the date mixture, stirring to combine. Pour into the baking pan, and bake for 40 minutes until it's spongy to the touch. To make the sauce, put ½ cup of heavy cream in a pan with 2 tablespoons of unsalted butter and ¼ cup of dark brown sugar. For extra spice, add 3 teaspoons of chopped fresh ginger. Stir over low heat until the sugar is dissolved. Serve the pudding with the sauce poured over followed by a drizzle of cream.

APPLE AND BLACKBERRY CRUMBLE Serves 8

Fruit crumble always goes down well. Apple and blackberry wins the filling contest for me, but peach and banana, blueberry or rhubarb are all delicious. Make up a batch of crumble and store in an airtight container.

Preheat the oven to 350°F. Lightly grease a 2-quart ovenproof dish or 8 individual ramekins. Melt 1 stick of unsalted butter in a large nonstick pan. Add 1¾ pounds of peeled, cored and roughly chopped Granny Smith apples with ½ cup of superfine sugar, ½ cup of apple juice and the finely grated zest of 1 lemon and cook for 6 to 8 minutes, stirring frequently, until the apples are softened. Add 8 ounces of blackberries and toss together, adding more sugar if necessary, then transfer the mixture to the prepared dish. Sift 1¼ cups of all-purpose flour into a large bowl and add 5 tablespoons of cold unsalted butter cut into cubes. Rub the butter into the flour until the mixture resembles fine bread crumbs. Stir in ¾ cup of packed light brown sugar, ¾ cup of old-fashioned rolled oats, ½ cup of roughly chopped almonds and 2 teaspoons of ground cinnamon. Spoon the topping over the filling, sprinkle a little more light brown sugar over the top and bake for 30 minutes or until the top is golden brown. Serve with custard sauce or heavy cream.

APPLE PIES IN POTS

This is a classic autumnal staple, a dessert that everyone loves and that can be served in 8 small individual ramekins, cups or bowls, or as 12 mini apple pies. You can also make these with a lattice topping—just cut the rolled-out pastry into strips and lay it over the pie filling in a crisscross pattern, then trim to size. Make the filling ahead and freeze for up to a month.

MAKES 8 POTS

For the filling
7 tablespoons butter
½ cup soft light brown sugar
5 McIntosh Apples, peeled, cored and chopped
7 Granny Smith apples, peeled, cored and chopped
I teaspoon ground cinnamon
zest and juice of ½ a lemon

For the pastry
flour, for dusting
28 ounces ready-made piecrust

For the glaze
2 egg yolks, beaten
a splash of milk
superfine sugar, to sprinkle

Preheat the oven to 350°F. Melt the butter in a large pan over medium heat. Add the sugar and mix until slightly golden. Add the apples, cinnamon and lemon zest and juice. Cook the apples on low-medium heat for 10 to 15 minutes until soft but with a little bite. Add a splash of water and allow to cool.

Dust a little flour on your work surface and rolling pin. Flatten the pastry out on the surface then, working from the center outwards, roll the pastry out into a large circle, until it is ⅛ inch thick. Cut out 8 circles of pastry for the top crusts, cutting each one larger than your chosen ramekins or bowls. (To make mini pies, see below.)

Fill 8 ramekins, cups or bowls with the cooled pie filling, and then cover with the top crusts. Use your fingers to crimp and pinch the pastry to seal the pies. Mix the beaten egg with the milk and brush this glaze over the top of each pie, followed by a sprinkling of sugar. Bake for 20 to 25 minutes until the pastry is golden and brown.

TIPS: *To make one large pie, follow the recipe above but divide the pastry into two when rolling out. Line a 8-in pie plate with half the pastry, add pie weights and bake blind for 8 minutes at 375°F. Remove the weights and bake for a further 4 minutes to brown the pastry. Add the filling, then cover with the remaining top crust, glaze and bake for 20 to 25 minutes as above.* • *Squeeze the lemon juice over the apples after you've cored them if you have other preparation to do, as this will prevent them discoloring.*

MINI APPLE PIES
Grease a 12-hole shallow muffin pan, cut out 12 circles of pastry using a cutter and press into each hole. Divide the filling between them, cut top crusts or lattice strips from the pastry, place on top, then glaze and bake as above.

FUN AND GAMES

Games are not only fun but are also useful for keeping children at the table. A Sunday lunch merits a good walk afterward to at least attempt to burn off some of the excess calories. Give each child an egg carton in which to collect nature's treasures, or even a matchbox, and tell them to find as many objects as they can fit in.

FICTIONARY DICTIONARY

Scan the dictionary for a suitably obscure word and read it out loud. Everybody invents a definition and writes it down on a piece of paper. Write down the real definition, collect the papers from the group and read them all out loud. Everyone votes for the definition they think is true and the person who fools the most people is the winner.

COIN RUGBY

This is a game for two players sitting opposite each other. To start, someone balances a quarter on their edge of the table so that half is resting on the table while the other half is hanging off the edge. From this position, the player has three moves to slide the coin across to the other side of the table, where it should end up hanging half over the edge again. The first move should be with a flattened palm—the player simply hits the overhanging coin farther onto the table. The second and third moves can be flicks or nudges but sustained contact with the coin in the form of a push or a drag is forbidden. If the player doesn't manage to achieve overhang at the other side of the table in his three goes, then it is the other player's turn to play. If, however, he does succeed, then he can attempt to score a "try." To do this, he must flick the overhanging coin into the air with one of his fingers and then catch it with the same hand. A point is awarded for a successful try.

BOUCHON

For this family favorite, players sit around a table with a number of corks in the center, one fewer cork than there are players. Appoint a game "leader" and decide how many "lives" players will have before they are eliminated. From a full pack of cards select four cards of the same number or rank for each player, i.e., for four players select all the fours, aces, eights and jacks. Shuffle this selection and deal each player four cards. To start a round, each player places one of their cards facedown on the table. When the leader says "pass", cards are passed one at a time to the left while they are received from the right. The aim is to collect four cards of the same kind. Once someone has achieved this, he takes a cork and calls out "Bouchon" ("cork" in French). The other players must snatch a cork as quickly as possible. The one who fails to do so loses a "life". When a player is eliminated remove one set of four-of-a-kind cards from the pack and one cork from the pile and carry on with the game with one fewer player, and so on …

STOP THE BUS

Ask everyone to draw a simple grid on a piece of paper with columns for categories such as colors, parts of the body, breeds of dog, etc. The first column must be blank and labeled "Bus Route". Randomly select a letter of the alphabet — this becomes the Bus Route and should be entered on the first line of each player's grid in the Bus Route column. One of the players "Starts the Bus" and the idea is to fill each column with an entry that begins with this chosen letter. The first player to complete every column shouts "Stop the Bus". Everyone stops writing and reads out their answers. Players are awarded 2 points for a unique entry, 1 point for a nonunique entry and no points for a blank entry. Select another random letter for the next round. After a set number of rounds, add up the final scores to determine the winner.

That the speed of eating should be moderate, dinner being the last affair of the day, and that the guests behave like travelers who aim to arrive at the same destination.

La Physiologie du Goût,
Jean Anthelme Brillat-Savarin

COZY SUPPER PARTIES

Not tied to a specific calendar event, informal suppers span the seasons and cover a multitude of occasions, from a low-key birthday to a house-warming event or simply because it's a Friday evening and you can enjoy some respite at the end of a busy week. See this chapter as a celebration of the everyday and the chance to reconnect with important friends, something that seems increasingly difficult with the pressures of work and family life.

Historically, the dinner party was a largely nineteenth-century creation, which reflected broader changes in society. But this sort of evening isn't about the "pomp" and pretentiousness often associated with a dinner party, nor is it about fancy decorations and presenting a procession of expensive gourmet delights. It's about creating a welcoming and private space for people to unwind after a day's work. You could be sitting at a dining table, a kitchen counter, perched on a stool or relaxed on the sofa for a TV dinner in front of a big sporting game. As with traditional Sunday lunch, the focus here is on breaking bread, sharing good food and wine in an intimate and more personal way, not about slaving over a hot stove for hours on end. Good friends shouldn't and won't expect this—the company and atmosphere should reign above all else.

For these sorts of low-key occasions, often the foods that everyone enjoys the most are old friends themselves, familiar and reliable. Nothing could be more welcoming than walking into a home that smells of glorious comfort food (by this I'm talking about pies and stews bubbling in the oven). Lots of friends I know serve the same "signature" dishes when they have people for supper, often because they don't have lots of time and their recipes are guaranteed to work. Similarly, these fail-safe dishes often mean you can prepare them on autopilot and ideally freeze them ahead of time, so when guests are over you're not fussing about the food in the kitchen and being kept from the company for too long. A personal touch, such as a thoughtful place setting, an unusual dessert from the supermarket if you've run out of time or a fun after-dinner game, are quick and inexpensive ways to make the evening your own. But these are added extras, only if the occasion calls for it.

SET THE SCENE

A relaxed supper with friends needn't be a tablecloth occasion. Keep everything low key: a bare wooden table with a simple table runner, bistro-type glasses and plenty of candlelight. Buy a bunch of fresh flowers for a side table and scented candles for the bathroom.

LINENS

Keep linens simple. If you want to use one to cover an unlovely table or, conversely, you have a good dining table you need to protect, opt for a classic white cloth, or a darker one if you're worried about stains. If cloth napkins are a bit creased, just put them on the table in the morning and spray the creases with water. By the evening the creases should be gone. If it's a particular festive occasion supermarkets have plenty of colorful paper napkins that might brighten up the table—it's a dinner with friends after all, so no need to get too fancy.

GLASSES

If you want to serve red and white wine and don't have sets of glasses for both, it doesn't matter. Also remember that mismatched glassware can look very pretty. To make wine glasses shine, polish them at the table with a hot damp tea towel followed by a dry one. If you use a dishwasher, ensure that you add a rinse aid to maintain the shine of glasses. For a rustic dinner, small water tumblers can be charming for red wine, but if you want something similar with a more delicate rim, stemless glasses by Riedel are a personal favorite of mine.

Don't forget to put a pitcher of water and glasses on the table or a nearby side table if there's no room. It sounds so obvious, but it's often overlooked! Add a ribbon of cucumber to the water to infuse it, or a sprig of mint, or slices of lemon or lime. Keep sparkling water in its bottle in the fridge and simply refill glasses when necessary.

PLACE SETTINGS

You can be creative here without spending too much time or money; it's particularly nice to make the effort if the supper is for a special occasion or birthday. Fruit with stems tied with brown gift tags, leaves, photographs, thick construction paper, even Scrabble letters can be used for informal place settings, or cut grooves into the long edges of used corks and slot in place cards. For quirky place mats, use art catalogs or editions of a glossy magazine, or make your own personalized mats by printing and laminating favorite photographs.

GREET YOUR GUESTS

Offering something other than wine as an aperitif when your guests arrive will help everyone relax and unwind. Set up a help-yourself gin and tonic or martini bar (page 69), with an ice bucket, knife and small board for slicing lemons and limes, or perhaps a dry sherry and spiced nuts.

NIBBLES AND STARTERS TO SHARE

Your friends will need something to graze on to keep hunger pangs at bay, especially if they've arrived straight from the office or with empty stomachs. Grissini (breadsticks) wrapped in prosciutto and asparagus tips in season make simple yet delicious nibbles. Vegetable chips are more interesting than the standard potato variety, along with salted cashews or almonds, but good-quality salted potato chips with dips are still extremely popular. If you find martinis a bit strong for an aperitif, marinate green olives in a martini mix instead, for a hint of the taste without the powerful hit.

Starters, if you decide to serve them, should be quick and simple. A Camembert baked in its box or a whole Vacherin Mont d'Or with some crudités and breadsticks is lovely (see page 313). A board of charcuterie and antipasti can be put together in minutes and shared from the middle of the table with good crusty bread or homemade soda bread (see page 189) and small bowls of olive oil and balsamic vinegar for dipping. Or drizzle some whole heads of garlic with olive oil and sea salt, then roast at 375°F for 30 to 40 minutes until soft, and serve halved with French baguettes.

SPICED NUTS Serves 8

Heat a large, nonstick frying pan over medium heat and dry roast 14 ounces of mixed plain nuts (hazelnuts, pecans, whole almonds, cashews and walnuts) for 5 to 6 minutes, until golden. Transfer to a large bowl. Melt 3 tablespoons of butter in the hot pan and add 3 tablespoons of packed dark brown sugar, stirring gently until the sugar dissolves. Mix ¼ teaspoon each of ground cumin, cayenne pepper and pumpkin pie spice with a pinch of chili flakes and ¼ teaspoon of sea salt. Return the nuts to the pan, add the spices and stir to coat evenly with the sticky mixture. Pour onto a tray lined with parchment paper, and leave to cool and harden before serving.

Manzanilla or Fino Sherry, a red Chilean Merlot or Rioja or a white Chenin Blanc.

MADE-TO-MEASURE MARTINIS

It can be fun to set up a bar dedicated to martinis where guests can mix their own concoctions. On a small side table set out the basic ingredients: bottles of vodka, gin and dry vermouth that have been chilled in the freezer; a small pitcher of chilled "dirty" water (the olive brine); dishes of sliced cucumber, olives and citrus fruit for garnishes—lemons, oranges and limes are classics, or try grapefruit rind (for garnish ideas see page 80). Make sure you have a cocktail shaker, strainer and stirrer, as well as plenty of ice. Your guests can opt for shaken, stirred, poured, clean or "dirty." Typically, a martini should be stirred, not shaken, as the gin can "bruise" and become bitter, but of course James Bond has popularized what was traditionally known as a "Bradford" martini. Chill martini glasses to give them that lovely opaque look by putting them in the freezer along with your gin and vodka. To keep the glasses cool on the bar, fill them with iced water. It's likely that one friend might like to take charge if they know what they're doing and make them for everyone. Have a menu card handy with notes on how to mix a dry or wet martini or some variations so guests can experiment.

THE BEST VODKA MARTINI Serves 1 (make to order)

There has been so much written about this legendary cocktail in a seemingly endless quest for the perfect mix. For gin-based versions, the classic garnish is an olive or three, or a cocktail onion (this is called a Gibson). I prefer a vodka martini, simply garnished with lemon. For refreshing alternatives, try a passion fruit martini (page 137), a pear martini (page 109), or a White Lady (page 230).

Slice pieces of rind from a lemon into 1-inch-x-½-inch wide strips (one per drink). Fold the rind in half lengthwise over a frozen martini glass to catch any escaping juice and rub the folded edge around the rim of the glass before placing it inside.

Fill a cocktail shaker with ice. Pour a capful of vermouth into the shaker and put the lid on. Shake gently and strain away any excess vermouth so that the ice is only covered in it (there should be no liquid left in the shaker). Pour 3 ounces of frozen vodka into the shaker with the ice. Shake vigorously for 10 to 20 seconds. Strain into the glass and serve immediately. Garnish with a lemon twist.

TIP: *The lick of vermouth will take the edge off the vodka so you don't get that horrible shudder when you sip it, but too much makes the martini too sweet. Try varying the amounts of the ingredients and you'll see what I mean. It is a glass of vodka after all, and there's a fine line between sublime and undrinkable.*

STEAK, GUINNESS AND KIDNEY PIE

This pie evokes the rustic charm of traditional village pubs. An essential comfort food, it's ideal for feeding friends over to watch a soccer or football game. If you don't like kidneys, just add more steak or mushrooms.

SERVES 8

3 pounds beef chuck, trimmed of fat and cut into cubes

1 pound ox or lamb kidneys, cleaned and cubed

salt and freshly ground black pepper

6 tablespoons all-purpose flour

6 tablespoons sunflower oil

2 tablespoons butter

11 ounces small button mushrooms

2 onions, halved and thinly sliced

2 cloves garlic, peeled and crushed

2 celery stalks, chopped

2 carrots, peeled and chopped

4 large sprigs thyme

1 tablespoon sugar

1¾ cups Guinness

1¾ cups beef stock

2 tablespoons Worcestershire sauce

3 bay leaves

For the pastry

4 large egg yolks beaten with 1 tablespoon water, for glazing

18-ounce pack of frozen puff pastry, thawed but cold

flour, for dusting

Season the beef and kidneys well, then coat in the flour. Heat 4 tablespoons of the sunflower oil in a large Dutch oven or saucepan and brown the meat in batches. Remove and set aside. Add another tablespoon of the oil and half the butter into the pan and brown the mushrooms, scraping up the residue in the pan from the meat, then remove and set aside with the beef. Add the last of the oil and butter to the pan and cook the onions over medium heat until soft, then add the garlic, celery, carrots, thyme and sugar and sweat for another 5 minutes.

Return the meat and mushrooms to the pan, pour in the Guinness, stock and Worcestershire sauce and add the bay leaves. Partially cover with a lid and simmer for 1½ hours, stirring occasionally to ensure nothing sticks to the bottom. Remove the lid and continue to simmer uncovered for another 30 minutes, until the meat is tender and the sauce has thickened. Season well.

Preheat the oven to 400°F. Spoon the beef mixture into a 4-quart pie dish (or into 8 individual pie dishes). Brush the edges of the pie dish with a little of the beaten egg and roll out the pastry on a lightly floured surface until it is just larger than the dish. Arrange the pastry over the dish and trim off any excess so it fits the dish nicely, pressing the edges down to secure. Use any trimmings to decorate the pie as you wish, and secure them to the top of the pastry with a little of the egg wash.

Brush the top of the pastry with the remaining egg wash and cut a small cross in the middle of the pastry to allow the steam to escape and keep the pastry crispy. (You can use a pie funnel in the center if you have one.) Put the dish in the middle of the oven for 25 to 30 minutes, until the pastry is golden. Allow to stand for a few minutes before serving.

A French regional red, or real ale.

TIPS: *Other fillings, such as game, are also very popular, or for a chicken pie filling, see page 48 • You can freeze the finished uncooked pie for up to 3 months. It is best baked straight from frozen, but you need to add 15 minutes cooking time.*

FISH PIE

Mashed potatoes are a classic topping for this pie, but for something lighter use a mix of bread crumbs and Parmesan or simply a scattering of good-quality crushed potato chips for a crunchier texture. Try adding a couple of handfuls of washed spinach to your filling just before topping with the mashed potatoes. You could substitute haddock or pollack for the cod (a fish with similar white flesh) or use scallops instead of shrimp and serve with garden peas. You can make this the night before.

SERVES 8

8 eggs

1¾ pounds cod filet, skinned and bones removed

1¾ pounds undyed smoked haddock filet, skinned and bones removed

6 cups milk, plus extra for the mash

4 bay leaves

2 lemons, cut into slices

16 black peppercorns

5½ pounds Yukon Gold potatoes, peeled and halved

salt and freshly ground black pepper

For the white sauce

1 stick butter, plus extra for the mashed potatoes

1 cup all-purpose flour

a large pinch of freshly grated nutmeg

a large handful of chopped flat-leaf parsley

14 ounces raw tiger shrimp, peeled and deveined

Preheat the oven to 350°F. Bring a pan of water to a boil and cook the eggs for 8 minutes. Run under cold water, peel and cut into quarters. Set aside.

Place the cod and smoked haddock in a saucepan, cover with the milk and add the bay leaves, lemon slices and peppercorns. Bring to a slow simmer for 4 to 5 minutes. Remove the fish with a slotted spoon and set aside. Strain the milk into a large pitcher and reserve. Cook the potatoes in boiling water for 12 to 15 minutes until tender. Drain in a colander, return to the pan and mash. Season well, add a pat of butter, a splash of milk and beat until smooth.

To make the white sauce, melt the butter in a medium saucepan. Add the flour, stir well and cook for 2 to 4 minutes. Gradually whisk in approximately 5 cups of the reserved milk from poaching the fish and cook over low heat for 6 to 8 minutes, stirring frequently, until the sauce begins to thicken. Stir in the nutmeg and the parsley and season to taste.

Pour the sauce into a large ovenproof dish. Scatter the shrimp and flake the fish evenly over the sauce. Divide the eggs over the fish, followed by the rest of the sauce and top with mashed potatoes, fluffing them up with a fork. Dot the pie with butter, and bake in the oven for 30 minutes until the top is golden brown and the sauce is bubbling.

A crisp Chablis suits this creamy dish.

VENISON AND BEET STEW

This is a lovely, dramatic deep burgundy color. I always enjoy cooking stews, particularly with venison in early autumn. This recipe will freeze for 3 months in a sealed container.

SERVES 8

8 tablespoons all-purpose flour

salt and freshly ground black pepper

3 pounds stewing venison, trimmed and cut into 1½-inch pieces

1 cup olive oil, plus a little extra

12 ounces bacon, cut into pieces

16 juniper berries, crushed

4 teaspoons thyme leaves

2 bay leaves

2 teaspoons pink peppercorns

4 garlic cloves, peeled and crushed

8 medium raw beets, peeled and cut into wedges

zest and juice of 2 oranges

1¼ cups red wine

1¼ cups port

1¾ cups beef stock

4 red onions, peeled and cut into wedges

11 ounces whole shallots, peeled

5 tablespoons butter

1½ tablespoons sugar

Preheat the oven to 325°F. Place the flour in a large bowl and season well with salt and pepper. Add the venison pieces and toss to coat evenly. Heat the olive oil in a large Dutch oven and brown the venison pieces, in batches if necessary, until evenly browned. Remove from the pan and set aside. Add the bacon and cook for a few minutes until golden. Stir in the juniper berries, thyme leaves, bay leaves, peppercorns, garlic, beet wedges and orange zest and juice. Cook for several minutes, stirring frequently. Return the venison to the pan.

Add the red wine, port and beef stock. Bring to a boil, then reduce the heat and cover with a lid. Transfer to the oven and cook for 1½ hours, until the sauce has thickened and the venison is tender. (If you are making the stew in advance, reduce the cooking time by 30 minutes so that the meat doesn't overcook when you reheat it.) While the meat is cooking, in a skillet over medium heat, caramelize the onions and shallots in the butter with the sugar, stirring until soft and golden, then add to the stew for the last 30 minutes of cooking. Season to taste. Serve with baked or Hasselback potatoes (page 54) topped with sour cream and chopped chives.

 *A Tuscan red wine.*

> **SEALING THE MEAT** *The word "stew" is said to have come from the old French word "estruier," meaning to enclose, suggesting the importance of sealing the juices in the meat before stewing it and adding flavor.*

DESSERTS

BROWN BREAD ICE CREAM Serves 8

This is best eaten as soon as it comes out of the freezer when the caramelized bread crumbs are at their crunchiest.

Preheat the oven to 400°F. Mix 3½ ounces of brown or whole-wheat bread crumbs with ½ cup of packed soft brown sugar on a baking tray and place in the oven. Bake for 12 to 15 minutes until the sugar has caramelized and the crumbs are golden and crisp, keeping an eye on them and turning them once or twice. In a saucepan, heat 2½ cups of heavy cream to just below boiling point. Meanwhile, separate 2 eggs. Beat the yolks and ½ cup of superfine sugar together and, beating continuously, slowly pour the cream into the eggs to make a custard. Return the mixture to the pan and heat gently, stirring constantly, until the mixture thickens enough to coat the back of a spoon. Leave to cool. Whisk the egg whites until stiff. When the custard is cool, stir in 1 teaspoon of vanilla extract, most of the cooled bread crumbs (reserving some for serving) and the egg whites. Freeze the ice cream for 5 to 6 hours, stirring once after 30 minutes, and again 30 minutes later. Serve garnished with the reserved bread crumbs.

POACHED PEARS IN RED WINE Serves 8

A lovely, light and elegant dessert. It looks great too. You can make these 1 to 2 days ahead.

Place 1 bottle of red wine, 1¼ cups of port, 2 split vanilla beans, 4 whole star anise, 2 cinnamon sticks, 1¼ cups of superfine sugar, 4 tablespoons of honey, and the peel and juice of 2 oranges in a wide saucepan and heat gently until the sugar has dissolved. Peel 8 firm pears carefully, leaving the stems intact. Sit them upright in the saucepan (slice off the bottoms if necessary) and submerge them in the wine. Cover with a lid and simmer very gently for 25 to 30 minutes, until they are a deep red color and tender. Allow the pears to sit in the liquid for 1 hour to let the color develop, then transfer the fruit to 8 serving bowls. Bring the poaching liquid to a boil and simmer for 15 to 20 minutes until syrupy, then strain it and pour over the pears.

BLOOD ORANGE POSSETS Serves 8

These are delicious, but if blood oranges aren't in season, use the juice and zest of 5 oranges and 2 lemons.

Gently heat 3¾ cups of heavy cream and 1¼ cups of sugar in a large pan, stirring to dissolve the sugar. Simmer for 3 to 4 minutes, being careful not to let it boil. Remove from the heat and whisk in the juice and finely grated zest of 7 blood oranges, retaining a little zest to garnish, and the juice and finely grated zest of 2 lemons. Pour into 8 small glasses or ramekins. Allow to cool, then transfer to the fridge for 1 to 2 hours or until set. You can chill these overnight. To serve, garnish with ribbons of orange rind.

EASY ENTERTAINING

Informal cocktail parties are a great way to entertain a crowd for a short time in the early evening. They're always popular, and can be very useful if you want to thank people for invitations you've received throughout the year. Don't be intimidated by the logistics of catering for lots of guests; with some simple tips, cocktail parties can be enjoyable occasions to host as well as attend.

ESSENTIAL SUPPLIES

Keep these items in your kitchen and pantry for parties and celebrations. Some you'll have already, but others are simple and affordable supplies that are useful to stock up on.

- **Cookie cutters and chef's ring molds:** *for shaping cookies, canapé bases and sandwiches.*

- **Serving platters:** *see "Canapé Presentation" (page 81).*

- **Large plastic buckets or bins:** *for chilling drinks when fridge space is limited and emptying dregs from used glasses.*

- **Vases in assorted shapes:** *for flower arrangements (page 262). Column vases can be filled with whole fruits and used as decoration on the bar.*

- **Candles and candle holders:** *scented candles, tapered candles and lots of tea lights to cluster in groups.*

- **Glassware:** *wine and highball glasses as well as Champagne coupes or martini glasses can be rented or bought very inexpensively in bulk from restaurant supply stores.*

- **Plastic wine glasses and Champagne flutes:** *emergency spares in case you run out of clean glassware.*

- **Cocktail napkins, skewers and toothpicks:** *keep a stock of these handy.*

- **Paper plates, bamboo and disposable cutlery:** *bamboo serving ware, mini paper plates and party boxes are all great for "mini meals" for children.*

CANAPÉ PLANNING

Allow 10 to 12 canapés per person for a two-hour drinks-only reception, 6 to 8 if you're serving dinner too. Bolster these with a few bowls of nuts and chips on side tables for early guests. Aim to hand out your first canapés about 20 minutes after your first guests arrive and have plenty of cocktail napkins on hand. Sweet canapés can be a subtle way to signal that the evening is drawing to a close (or just stop refilling glasses and your guests will soon start to disperse!). You can buy all sorts of ready-made items—see "Time-Saving Tricks" (page 81) or there are lots of recipes for homemade canapés throughout the book. Just remember to keep them bite-sized.

DRINKS PARTY DOS AND DON'TS

- Do move any clutter from the space you're entertaining in and push large items of furniture back against the walls (but provide lots of side tables for nibbles and empty glasses).

- Do designate a space for guests' coats. Empty hooks or coat racks so guests can use them, leave a number of spare hangers on stair banisters or open a bedroom for the purpose.

- Do set up a bar area away from the entrance to your party to encourage guests to move into the space. Make sure the bar is well stocked with a little more than you think you'll need (many wine merchants will trade on a sale or return basis). Cover the table you're using with a large tablecloth to hide supplies underneath, provide a slosh bucket for dregs and a trash bag taped to the side of the bar for garbage.

- Do offer drinks on a tray as people arrive to cut wait times at the bar. Have a few soft drinks along with the alcoholic options, and use garnishes of different citrus slices (page 80) to differentiate between drinks.

- Do mark glasses for your guests at smaller gatherings so they don't lose track of their drink (easily done!). Buy glass tags online or make your own to fit the theme of the evening. Write guests' names with glass paint that comes off in the dishwasher, or use ribbons in a rainbow of colors (at Christmas my mum has a ribbon tied to hers because she's always losing her own glass and takes everyone else's!).

- Don't go it alone. Enlist help to make things run smoothly. Get a few friends or family members to help you greet guests and take their coats, refill and clear away glasses, hand out food, man the bar and keep the kitchen tidy.

- Don't offer too wide a selection of drinks that require different sorts of glasses. For example, if you're serving Champagne or sparkling wine in flutes, use only one other type of glass for soft drinks, wine and cocktails.

- Don't forget the ice. Properly chilled drinks make such a difference. Buy bags of ice cubes, or fill trays with water well before your party and make plenty in advance. Clear space in your fridge for wine the night before, and for large quantities of bottles use a sink filled with ice. Adding salt to ice and cold water will lower the temperature and chill bottles more quickly.

- Don't lose the corkscrew. Attach it to the bar on a string (have a few spares).

- Don't underestimate how much food you'll need. Plan quantities per person (see "Canapé Planning," page 78) and stagger when and where you hand them out so you don't run out too early or end up with leftovers.

- Don't worry about accidental spills. If you don't have red-wine stain remover, it's best to remove the stain when it's still wet. Blot with a clean cloth, pour a little white wine over it or soak up the stain with a pinch of salt or talcum powder.

DRINKS AND COCKTAIL KIT

- **Cocktail shaker set:** *with glass tumbler with written measurements, bar spoon for mixing, and strainer.*
- **Bottle openers, corkscrews and foil cutter.**
- **Muddler:** *for crushing sugar or bruising mint and fruit (or use the end of a rolling pin).*
- **Ice, wine buckets, pitchers, and tongs:** *plus a large bowl and a ladle for serving.*
- **Straws, toothpicks and umbrellas:** *various thin, short and long straws.*
- **Small chopping board, knife and garnishes:** *citrus fruits, maraschino cherries and olives.*
- **Sugar syrup:** *store-bought or homemade (see right).*
- **Flavored cordials and fruit liqueurs:** *to spruce up soft drinks, wine and sparkling wine.*
- **Fruit juices and pureés.**

SUGAR SYRUP

This is useful in all sorts of cocktails, as well as for glazing fruits and edible flowers (page 265). Best of all, it doesn't even require a recipe—just boil together 2 parts of water to 1 part of sugar (e.g., 1 cup of water with ½ cup of sugar) until all the sugar is dissolved. Store it in a sterilized bottle in the fridge for up to three months, but it's best to make up a small batch as you need it.

CITRUS GARNISHES

These add visual effect to cocktails and the citrus peel releases the oils held in the rind, adding an extra zesty flavor. Avoid the pith as much as possible and use fresh fruits so that the skin is firm—it won't work with old, soft fruit.

- **Twists or Spirals:** carve around the diameter of an orange, lemon, or lime using a deep-channeled zester, making sure you get a lovely length of peel. For a tight curl, wrap around a straw or chopstick. Drape off the rim of the glass.
- **Knots:** using a narrow zester, peel a medium length of citrus rind and tie it into a knot.
- **Wheels:** use a narrow or deep-channeled zester to score the length of the citrus fruits, leaving even spaces between each. Slice the fruit to create wheels.
- **Rinds:** peel a wide unbroken strip of citrus rind with a potato peeler and gently squeeze to release the oils from the rind, then use as a garnish.

CANAPÉ PRESENTATION

Collect pretty bowls, patterned plates and other interesting serving dishes from markets and vacations. Decorate simple platters with natural items or use themed accessories. Assemble smaller foods on mini forks, or thread onto toothpicks and skewer them into watermelons (page 285) or pumpkins (page 19). Scoop out the insides of a loaf of bread and fill with cocktail sausages, or serve seafood canapés in cleaned oyster and scallop shells.

- **Wooden and porcelain boards:** simple and practical, these are great for summer gatherings, charcuterie and antipasti. Small, handled boards are easier for passing around.

- **Silver trays, round or square table mirrors:** these add a shimmer to foods and are perfect for special occasions, particularly Christmas and New Year's.

- **Natural slate:** dark tones set off delicate canapés; use chalk to label foods.

- **Baskets:** line with cellophane, parchment paper or straw for rustic entertaining.

- **Chinese soup spoons:** use to assemble individual portions on a tray. Particularly good for messier bites where guests can't use their fingers.

- **Paper cones:** buy or make your own. Use them to serve crudités, popcorn and fruits.

- **Mini galvanized buckets and tankards:** stand foods, such as cheese straws, upright in these.

TIME-SAVING TRICKS

These instant nibbles can take you from casual suppers with friends to more formal entertaining.

PANTRY

- *Good-quality potato and vegetable chips, cheese straws, mixed nuts and savory popcorn.*

- *Stuffed olives and other jarred antipasti, such as roasted peppers and artichokes in oil.*

- *Instant canapé bases: croustades, crostini, cheese crackers, mini oat cakes, poppadoms, blinis and mini tart shells.*

- *Store-bought premade sauces: Hollandaise, sweet chili dipping sauce, tartar sauce and mayonnaise.*

- *Quick garnishes, such as red-onion marmalade (page 388), fig jam and inexpensive caviar.*

- *Good-quality white, dark and milk chocolate: use it melted to dip fresh and dried fruit or breadsticks in.*

- *Ready-made petits fours, biscotti, mint thins, ameretti biscuits and Turkish delight.*

FREEZER

- *Ice (crushed and cubed): buy in bulk for delivery from liquor or grocery stores, or make batches of your own.*

- *Store-bought pastry (puff, pie crust, and phyllo): for canapés, tarts, samosas and spring rolls.*

- *Smoked salmon, uncooked cocktail sausages and frozen crescent rolls.*

- *Precooked canapés: test out and stock up on ones you like, such as Indian or Asian selections.*

- *Pizza crusts, pita, rye and other breads, to slice and use for quick canapé bases.*

WINTER

CHRISTMAS
NEW YEAR'S EVE
BURNS NIGHT

Days grow short and icy winds blow; it's time to bundle up. Sharp frosts dust the roofs and bare trees stand dark against a metallic sky. Coldness bites on wintry walks; breath rises in clouds while grass crunches underfoot. The red-breasted robin perches on a branch: a quintessential holiday card image. There's a chance of snowfall and we all hope for a white Christmas.

CHRISTMAS

*"Happy, happy Christmas, that can win us back to the delusions of
our childish days; that can recall to the old man the pleasures of his youth;
that can transport the sailor and the traveler, thousands of miles away, back
to his own fire-side and his quiet home!"*

The Pickwick Papers, *Charles Dickens*

One of the best things about Christmas is the anticipation. There's something in the air throughout December, and it's not just the cold weather. Window displays sparkle with gift ideas and stocking stuffers, lights twinkle above streets, and markets spring up out of nowhere. When I was a child, my December weekends were spent making cards, decorating the tree, hanging the wreath and preparing brandy butter and peppermint creams. Bowls brimming with walnuts, shiny wrapped chocolates and piles of clementines would appear around the house. There was always a distinctive smell, too: pine and cinnamon and the heady scent of mulled wine and pomanders that merged into one festive bouquet.

No matter how much we may adapt other celebrations, come December we tend to repeat our own familiar customs year after year—and this is perhaps key to the magic of Christmas. Looking back, I don't remember the presents I received, nor whether the sprouts were overcooked or the turkey dry. But what I do remember are all the small rituals that we reveled in. It's inevitable that as we get older, Christmases become more complicated, and as one of the biggest events of the social calendar, raised expectations and high stress levels are unavoidable. Families grow, the dynamics change, and as children become adults and parents themselves the innocent thrill of opening a stocking is replaced by the responsibility of ensuring a memorable Christmas for their own children, relatives and friends.

HISTORY AND ORIGINS OF CHRISTMAS *Pagan midwinter festivities were recorded throughout Europe for hundreds of years (probably longer) before the birth of Christ, marking the onset of winter, a time of darkness. The Romans illuminated buildings with bright lights and decorated their houses with evergreens, exchanged presents, feasted, drank, danced and played games. The Germanic peoples of northern Europe celebrated Yule on December 25th, lighting fires to assist in the revival of the waning sun.*

It was against this background that the Christian Nativity feast developed. The early Christians, seeking to spread their faith throughout Europe, chose midwinter to mark the birth of Christ as it was a potent and symbolic time in the year. The result was a festival that combined both pagan and Christian elements. But it was the sentimental Victorians who provided most of the traditions: cards with elaborate snow scenes, Christmas party crackers, an extravagantly decorated tree and the turkey feast that we know and cherish today. They established Christmas as a celebration of the domestic arts, of hospitality and warmth and, above all, of reuniting with friends and family.

THE COUNTDOWN TO CHRISTMAS

You won't have time to do everything from scratch but pick and choose what you can manage making yourself. Clear out your kitchen before the festive period and make separate lists for different stores you might visit: the butcher, wine store, florist, supermarket and department store. Putting the lists on your fridge door will make them easily accessible. The priority is to get all the food planned and organized as far in advance as possible, freezing where you can. With lots of stores closed around this time it's harder to pop out and get last-minute goods, so it's wise to get ahead and you can then put your feet up after Christmas Day.

END OF NOVEMBER: Advent calendar: buy or make (page 91). Cards: gather addresses, buy or make (page 91). Christmas pudding (a British tradition): buy ahead, or make on the last Sunday in November (page 88). Browse online for stocking stuffers and present ideas.

4 WEEKS TO GO: Crafts: buy or make wrapping paper (page 173), tree decorations (page 99) and wreath (page 95). Christmas tableware: use the 4 Cs checklist (crockery, cutlery, candles, centerpiece); check linen and napkins, then buy any extra supplies you need.

3 WEEKS TO GO: Write and send Christmas cards. Order turkey, meat and cheeses to be picked up the week before Christmas.

2 WEEKS TO GO: Plan meals and order nonperishables and drinks for delivery. Christmas tree: buy on second weekend of December. Decorate the tree and house (page 96). Make berry ball (page 95), edible gifts (page 92) and mince pies (page 88).

1 WEEK BEFORE CHRISTMAS: Pick up turkey and buy perishable food, plants and flowers. Prepare ahead: freeze meals for the period between Christmas and New Year's, and any food for New Year's Eve (page 133). Wrap presents and stocking-stuffers.

A FEW DAYS BEFORE CHRISTMAS: Sort seating plans for Christmas meals. Set out a corner for a Christmas puzzle and some other games. Make ahead any food for Christmas Day.

CHRISTMAS EVE: Set out stockings, snacks for Santa and reindeer food (page 110). Last-minute wrapping. Set the table (page 114) and chill relevant drinks. Pour yourself a large glass, and put on Christmas carols.

PREPARE-AHEAD FOOD

The following recipes in this chapter can be frozen or prepared ahead so you won't feel quite as stressed when it comes to entertaining over the Christmas period.

**STORE COOKED FOR
UP TO 6 MONTHS:**

- **Christmas pudding** *(page 88)*: *keep covered in a cool, dark place, and reheat before serving.*

**FREEZE UNCOOKED
FOR UP TO 3 MONTHS:**

- **Mince Pies** *(page 88)*: *bake from frozen, adding 5 minutes to the cooking time.*

- **Cheese Biscuit Dough** *(page 104)*: *allow to stand for 10 minutes, slice into rounds and then bake, adding 5 minutes to the cooking time.*

- **Gingerbread Dough** *(page 92)*: *defrost thoroughly before rolling out.*

- **Pigs in Blankets** *(page 123)*: *defrost thoroughly before cooking.*

- **Stuffing** *(page 123)*: *freeze in balls and bake from frozen, adding 5 minutes to the cooking time.*

- **Brandy Butter** *(page 126)* **and Christmas Butter** *(page 113)*.

**FREEZE COOKED
FOR UP TO 1 MONTH:**

- **Twice-Baked Cheese Soufflé** *(page 119)*: *freeze this after first cooking. Bake from frozen to complete second cooking.*

- **Chocolate Yule Log** *(page 126)*: *freeze the sponge cake only for up to a month. Defrost, unroll, fill and decorate with chocolate ganache.*

- **Giblet Gravy** *(page 122)*: *defrost, reheat until piping hot and add the roasting juices from the turkey on the day of serving.*

- **Bread Sauce and Cranberry Sauce** *(page 122)*: *defrost thoroughly before heating through.*

- **Parsnip Soup Espresso** *(page 106)*: *cook and freeze before adding the milk and cream.*

UP TO 3 DAYS IN ADVANCE:

- **Peppermint Creams** *(page 92)*: *store in an airtight container.*

- **Crostini and toasted bases for Christmas Canapés** *(pages 104, 106)*: *store in an airtight container, then assemble the toppings on the day of serving.*

- **Boxing Day Ham** *(page 130)*: *store cooked but unglazed in the fridge before roasting.*

24 HOURS BEFORE SERVING:

- **Celery Root Remoulade** *(page 106)*.

- **Smoked Fish Pâté** *(page 119)*.

- **Shellfish Tian** *(page 119)*: *prepare the base ahead, but finish on the day of serving.*

- **Brussels Sprouts** *(page 123)*: *blanch and refresh in iced water, store in the fridge and finish cooking on the day of serving.*

ON THE DAY:

- **Canapés** *(pages 104, 106)*: *prepare toppings and assemble.*

- **Drinks and Cocktails** *(page 109)*.

- **Pear, Walnut and Roquefort Salad** *(page 119)*.

- **Roast Turkey** *(page 120)*, **Roast Potatoes** *(page 54)*, **Honeyed Carrots and Parsnips** *(page 123)*.

CHRISTMAS BAKING

CHRISTMAS PUDDING Serves 8-10

A British ritual, Christmas pudding is a lovely dessert with many variations. Traditionally made at the end of November, preparing the pudding mixture a month in advance gives the flavors plenty of time to develop.

In a large bowl, mix together 1⅓ pounds of chopped mixed dried fruit, 4 ounces of candied citrus peel, 1 large peeled and grated cooking apple, 2 teaspoons each of pumpkin pie spice and ground cinnamon, the finely grated zest and juice of 1 lemon, ¾ cup of packed soft brown sugar, 5 ounces of halved glacé cherries, 1 large peeled and grated carrot, 1½ cups of ground almonds, 2 tablespoons of molasses, ⅓ cup of all-purpose flour, ½ cup of shortening, ½ teaspoon of salt, ⅔ cup of brandy or Calvados, ¼ cup of stout or dark ale and 2 beaten eggs. Give them a good stir and leave them for 2 hours or preferably overnight. Pour the mixture into a 1-quart high-sided deep bowl and cover securely with a lid or foil. Put a metal trivet or rack in the bottom of a large saucepan, fill it half full of water and bring it to a simmer. Carefully lower the pudding bowl into the pan and rest it on the trivet. Cover, and adjust the heat to maintain a gentle boil. Steam the pudding, filling the pan as necessary with more water so the bowl is partially submerged, for 7 hours. To reheat the pudding, steam it for 1 to 2 hours until thoroughly warmed through.

MINCE PIES Makes 12-18

For really delicate mince pies, roll the pastry out very thinly. Make a variety of sizes—mini ones are great for passing around at cocktail parties and normal-sized ones are perfect for tea or dessert (warm them in the oven before serving). For a pretty alternative to traditional mince pie tops, use Christmassy cutters like stars or snowflakes.

Preheat the oven to 350°F. Unroll 1 pound of refrigerated pie crusts and use a rolling pin to roll them until very thin, and cut circles with a 2½-inch plain or crimped cutter. Press these into the greased holes of a muffin pan. Divide 14 ounces of ready-made mincemeat (available in jars at specialty food stores or online) between them. Roll out the remaining pastry until thin and use a slightly smaller cutter to cut tops from it. Seal the pies, brush with beaten egg and sprinkle with a little superfine sugar. Bake for 10 to 15 minutes, until golden. Cool in the pan for 5 minutes and then transfer to a wire rack. These will keep for 3 to 4 days in an airtight container.

HOW THE TRADITIONS BEGAN... *Christmas pudding was traditionally made with thirteen ingredients to represent Christ and the twelve apostles. A coin was often added to the ingredients and cooked in the pies (supposedly bringing wealth to whoever found it on Christmas Day). It remains a symbol of Christmas and family pudding recipes are often handed down the generations.*

The earliest type of mince pie was a medieval baked or fried pastry containing chopped meat or fish along with hard-boiled egg, dried fruit and other sweet ingredients. By the sixteenth century "minced" or "shred" pies had become a Christmas specialty and later the meat filling had disappeared from "mincemeat," leaving us with the fruit version we know today.

CHRISTMAS CRAFTS

In the build-up to Christmas it can be fun to make a few things. Christmas is, after all, about the exciting sense of anticipation. Buying cards sold in aid of charity is a good way of supporting worthy causes but children might enjoy making them. Similarly, it's nice to add a personal touch to Christmas wrapping using various ribbons, accessories and even potato printing onto plain paper.

RED ROBIN CHRISTMAS CARDS AND GLITTER CLOTHESPINS

Red robins are symbols of Christmas, but you can experiment with other seasonal motifs and designs. Use images from old cards as well as lace, buttons, felt, cotton balls for snow, paper—the possibilities are endless. Decorated clothespins add a little sparkle to cards pinned onto ribbon. Hang the ribbon on either side of doorways.

1: Cut a bird shape from some pretty paper and glue it to folded construction paper using a glue stick. 2: Glue a button for the eye and colored paper for the red chest and draw feet. 3: To make glitter clothespins use a brush and coat one side of a wooden clothespin with craft glue. Dip it into a shallow plate filled with glitter and shake off the excess, leaving to dry on a sheet of newspaper.

CHRISTMAS CRACKERS

It's lovely to make your own Christmas crackers and find gifts inside that are personalized to the recipient.

1: For each cracker, cut two 12 x 14-inch sheets of crêpe paper and roll around 3 toilet paper tubes (lined up end to end), gluing down the seem to prevent unravelling. 2: Place a gift, joke and a snap into the middle tube and tie a ribbon at either end of it. 3: Remove the 2 outer tubes and fluff up the end of the crêpe. Decorate the top of the cracker with a dried leaf stuck on with glue stick and write your guest's name on it.

A MATCHBOX ADVENT CALENDAR

I first came across this idea when a school friend's mom made her a matchbox advent calendar. It's amazing what you can fit into a matchbox—this is all part of the challenge!

1: Number 25 small boxes. Add a button or a short cotter pin to each drawer as a handle. 2: Fix the boxes together, drawer side out, using double-sided tape. Stack the boxes in 5 tiers, with 25 at the top. 3: Glue a strip of wrapping paper around the edges.

EDIBLE GIFTS

Homemade treats can be served as dessert canapés or handed out as gifts. Buy a few to save time—things like florentines, chocolate-covered orange peel and candy canes—then put the effort into wrapping them in pretty cellophane, boxes and festive tins lined with Christmas tissue paper. Gingerbread houses are fun to make and can sit on windowsills or as a centerpiece for a small table; gingerbread stars look lovely hanging from the Christmas tree.

CHRISTMAS TRUFFLES Makes 12–15

Make the truffles using the cocoa-dusted recipe on page 197 and turn them into mini Christmas desserts. Decorate them using white fondant icing, shaped to look like snow and use an icing pen to stick the fondant to the truffle. Finish with mini red candies for the berries and green icing pens to draw holly.

GINGERBREAD STARS Makes 15–20

Preheat the oven to 350°F, and line 2 baking trays with parchment paper. Melt 9 tablespoons of butter, ½ cup of packed dark brown sugar and 6 tablespoons of golden syrup or honey in a medium saucepan, stirring occasionally. Once the sugar is dissolved, remove from the heat. Sift 3 cups of all-purpose flour into a bowl with 1 teaspoon of baking soda, 2 heaped teaspoons of ground ginger and a good pinch of pumpkin pie spice. Pour the melted ingredients over the dry ingredients, stirring together to make a dough. Cover in plastic wrap and place in the fridge to cool for 20 to 30 minutes.

Turn out the dough onto a lightly floured surface and roll to a thickness of about ⅛ inch. Dip star-shaped cookie cutters into flour before cutting the dough. Place the shapes on the baking sheets and bake for 12 to 14 minutes until light golden brown, then remove from the oven. (If hanging them from the tree, use a skewer or toothpick to make holes in the warm cookies to thread ribbon through.) When completely cool and hardened, finish with glacé icing and decorate. Store in an airtight container for up to a week.

PEPPERMINT CREAMS Makes 40

Whisk 1 large egg white in a clean bowl until it forms stiff peaks. Add a few drops of peppermint extract and 3 cups of confectioner's sugar (add green food coloring if you like) and mix well until it combines to form a stiff paste. Dust your work surface, hands and a rolling pin with confectioner's sugar and roll out the paste to ⅛-inch thick. Cut out shapes, place them on a tray and refrigerate for 3 to 4 hours until set.

EVERGREEN DECORATIONS

A CHRISTMAS WREATH

A wreath can make a welcoming first impression when hung on a front door. Regularly mist with a water sprayer every few days and the wreath will last you well into the new year. Laid flat, it also makes a good table centerpiece.

1: Soak a ring of floral foam in water and attach a loop of ribbon for hanging. Gather your foliage together—rosemary, bay and sage, along with eucalyptus or spruce all work well. Create the shape of your wreath by pushing similar lengths of foliage, as well as some thistles, into the ring until it is evenly covered. 2: Add groups of roses around the wreath, making sure they are spaced evenly so it looks balanced. 3: Finish by adding wired bundles of cinnamon sticks and dried fruit such as apple slices, then hang on the door with a wide bow.

A FESTIVE BERRY BALL

Hang your berry ball above a door or suspend it from a light fixture. You can replace the berries with mistletoe in case a romantic occasion arises. To ensure maximum freshness, water the center of the ball every few days over a sink or outside, keeping it damp. Allow the excess water to drip out before hanging inside again. It should last a couple of weeks.

1: Wrap a ball of floral foam with chicken wire and secure the seams with tie wraps or wire. Soak the ball in water. 2: Using a loop of ribbon, hang the ball up to decorate. Using foliage such as mistletoe, eucalyptus or olive, mark out the top, bottom and sides to create the shape and size of your ball. 3: Continue to fill in the rest of the shape with foliage of similar lengths until the ball is covered. Add clusters of seasonal berries to inject a bit of color.

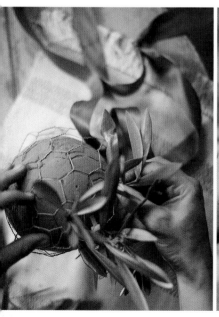  

THE CHRISTMAS TREE

The Christmas tree has its origins in Germany, and first became popular among Europe's nobility in the early nineteenth century, adorned with nuts, dates, apples and sweets and lit by candles. We have Prince Albert to thank for bringing the custom to Britain, where it has evolved into a symbol of the happy family gathering. Even today, the tree remains the main visual attraction in homes during the festive period, so before you buy one, decide in advance where it will look best. Roughly calculate the height of the tree you want, allowing enough space for the tree topper, and for the tree base or pot. Avoid positioning your tree beside a radiator or fireplace, and make sure there are outlets nearby (or use an extension cord) for the Christmas lights.

CHOOSING THE RIGHT TREE

Whether you choose your tree from a nursery or a lot on a street corner, try to pick the tree that looks the freshest and consider which variety will best suit your domestic setup. Families with small children or pets might prefer an evergreen fir as these don't drop their needles; for those who want a traditional-looking tree the Norwegian Spruce is ideal as their fuller branches give you plenty of space for an abundance of decorations.

> • **Norwegian Spruce**: the classic British Christmas tree. As it tends to drop its needles, it is also the most inexpensive variety and shouldn't be bought too far in advance.
>
> • **Nordmann Fir**: is more expensive than the spruce, less likely to lose its needles (which are short and soft), and has more space between its branches, giving it a graceful shape rather like a tiered cake stand. Another variety that retains its needles is the Noble Fir, used for almost all wreaths and other decorative foliage.
>
> • **Blue Spruce**: the most expensive type of Christmas tree. It is a wonderful pale, silvery blue with short, stiff, pointed needles and a strong, fragrant smell.

DECORATING THE TREE

Decorating the Christmas tree is a ceremony for the whole family. Make a weekend of it and get into the Christmas spirit with Mince Pie baking (page 88) and Mulled Wine making (page 109) with carols in the background. When it comes to decorations, individual style is everything. I prefer trees decorated with lots of plain white Christmas lights (no tinsel) and a variety of ornaments (wooden, glass or felt) with a few edible Gingerbread Stars (page 92) or foil-wrapped chocolates. The ceremonial finale is placing the tree topper: a fairy, angel or star. Inevitably children will all want to do it, so to save arguments let them all have a go.

TREE DECORATIONS

CRANBERRY AND POPCORN GARLANDS

Drape these around tree branches or hang above the mantelpiece. Once Christmas is over, leave them outside for the birds to nibble at.

Thread fresh cranberries and popcorn (stale is easier to thread) in sequence onto strong embroidery thread, using a needle if required. When it reaches the desired length, tie a knot to secure.

PAPER BIRDS

Paper birds are easy to make and add a homemade personal touch to your tree (see the picture on page 97).

I: Cut around a bird template on two pieces of construction paper and stick them together using a glue stick. 2: Stick on buttons for the eyes. 3: Cut a slit in the construction paper where the wings should go. Cut a sheet of colored tissue paper to the size you would like the wings, accordion fold it and insert it through the slit, fanning out the tissue paper and gluing in place if necessary. 4: With a hole punch, pierce a hole through the bird and run yarn through it, fastening with a knot.

CLOTHESPIN ANGELS OR FAIRIES

Girls will particularly love to make these; they look so pretty hanging from branches or as a tree topper.

I: Draw a face at the top of an old-fashioned wooden clothespin and wind yarn covered with a small amount of craft glue around the head to make hair. 2: Cut 3 inches of pipe cleaner to create arms and glue to the back of the doll. 3: Cut a 5-inch circle out of a doily, crêpe paper and netting, with a hole in the center of each to put the doll through and secure to the clothespin with masking tape. 4: Using craft glue, glue a loop of ribbon around the bodice and use the remainder to hang the doll. 5: Glue feathers to the back and paint shoes with glitter glue. (See the picture on page 97.)

FABRIC-COVERED ORNAMENTS

A practical way to revive older, tired-looking ornaments, and to make the most of fabric scraps.

I: Cut a circle of fabric big enough to cover the ornament and mold it around, sticking it down with craft glue. 2: Tie a festive ribbon around it and add a loop to hang.

DECK THE HALLS

GREENERY, FRUITS AND FLOWERS

Get creative and bring your house to life from the outside in. Greenery and fruits can instantly transform a home—sprigs of pine, ivy and berries are beautifully effective when they form the base of the decorations for the mantelpiece and banisters; lighten the dark green foliage with clusters of battery-operated Christmas lights. Sprigs of holly look neat above picture frames and mirrors.

Assemble everyday containers that work with your decorations and fill them with long-lasting seasonal flowers and branches such as holly berries and pussy willow. These should last well into the new year. Flowers can be expensive and are often out of season around this time of year, so potted bulbs and houseplants are best. Cyclamen, jasmine, narcissi and amaryllis are fresh alternatives to the ubiquitous poinsettia. Like with the Christmas tree, position them away from radiators and in cooler parts of the house, keeping them well watered.

Stud oranges with cloves to make scented pomanders to sit in bowls. Choose clementines with their leaves still on and clusters of whole nuts (with nut crackers) on side tables for casual grazing. Dried orange slices hanging from ribbons make lovely decorations. Cut some oranges into $1/8$-inch slices, lay them on a rack over a baking sheet and dry them out in the oven on its lowest setting for about 4 hours. You can also use just the dried peel as fire starters because of their natural oils. When they burn, the scent is wonderful.

ADDING A TWINKLE...

DECORATIVE AND SCENTED CANDLES

Candles are perfect for Christmas, traditional and welcoming whether they are on a table, reflected in shiny glassware, twinkling on a mantelpiece or windowsill. Scented candles in accents of orange, clove, cinnamon or sandalwood will add an evocative, spicy fragrance to rooms—a large round one with three wicks will give hours of burning time and last for several months. Wrap the bases of plain white pillar candles with cinnamon sticks: put a rubber band around a white pillar candle and insert cinnamon sticks underneath it, side by side. When the candle is surrounded by the sticks, tie a ribbon around it to hide the rubber band. Or place pillar candles in storm lanterns and decorate around them with sprigs of pine, rosemary, eucalyptus and dried apple slices (they also look lovely filled with faux snow and decorated with red Christmas ribbon). To decorate tea lights, wrap ivy or other wintry leaves around inexpensive tea light holders. To do this, arrange the leaves upside down on newspaper and lightly mist with adhesive spray. Wait for a few seconds and then place on the tea light holder, overlapping the leaves slightly. Tie jute twine around the leaves to keep them in place.

FLICKERING FIRELIGHT

The fireplace is the natural focus of the room. It is, after all, where Father Christmas enters the house, so it's worth dressing up. Hang your stockings or suspend long socks, the toes stuffed with tissue paper, on either side of the mantelpiece. Stand a rattan reindeer (some come with decorative Christmas lights) to guard the fire. If you have a fireplace that's unusable, fill the hearth with an assortment of candles and storm lanterns.

PAPER CHAINS AND ORNAMENTS

Children will enjoy helping to decorate rooms with colorful paper chains. I used to love making these at Christmas and hanging them in my bedroom at home. Assembling them from a store-bought kit is easier and less fussy than creating your own. Christmas tree ornaments need not be confined to the tree—dot them around on tables and in bowls, hang from twigs sprayed white or silver (a great alternative to a full Christmas tree) or tie ribbon to ornaments and hang them at staggered heights from light fixtures.

A SPRINKLING OF GLITTER AND SNOW

A dusting of glitter on pine cones, acorns and seasonal fruits will add a festive twinkle (just use craft glue and glitter). Fake snow can be sprayed from cans onto windows and loose powder (which can be bought online) can be scattered around fireplaces.

FESTIVE CANAPÉS

If you throw only one party a year, it's likely to be in the run-up to Christmas. Whether it's an informal gathering or a more organized affair, it's an occasion you'll need to plan. Stock your freezer in the weeks before Christmas (page 87). Accessorize serving trays with evergreen sprigs, bundles of cinnamon sticks or tree decorations. For more ideas on hosting see page 78.

DEVILS ON HORSEBACK
Makes 24 (allow 3 per person)

Preheat the oven to 400°F. Remove the pits from 24 prunes or use pitted ones. Wrap half a slice of bacon around each. Place on a baking sheet and drizzle 2 tablespoons of olive oil and the juice of 1 small orange over the wrapped prunes. Bake for 8 to 10 minutes, or until the bacon is crisp.

SMOKED SALMON AND BEET CROSTINIS
Makes 24 (allow 3 per person)

Preheat the oven to 350°F. Using a cookie cutter, cut 24 rounds (1 inch to 1½ inches) from thin slices of walnut bread and place on a nonstick baking sheet. Brush with 2 tablespoons of olive oil and bake in the oven for 3 to 4 minutes or until golden brown. Remove and leave to cool. Mix together 2 cooked, peeled, grated beets, 2 teaspoons of horseradish and 1 tablespoon of crème fraîche and season well. Cut 4 ounces of smoked salmon into thin strips. Place a teaspoon of the beet mixture on each toasted round, top with a small twist of smoked salmon, a dollop of crème fraîche, ground black pepper and decorate with a few snipped chives.

CHEESE BISCUITS
Makes 24 (allow 3 per person)

This is a great recipe I learned at the Grange Cookery School. Preheat the oven to 400°F. Grate 2 ounces of strong cheese such as aged cheddar or other leftovers and blend in a food processor with 4 tablespoons of softened butter, ½ cup of all-purpose flour and 1 teaspoon each of dried oregano and coriander seeds until it forms a ball. Using wax paper, roll the dough into a sausage shape about 1 inch in diameter. Roll the sausage in 1 tablespoon of crushed peppercorns or 2 tablespoons of sesame seeds. Slice into ⅛-inch thick rounds and cook on a baking tray lined with parchment paper for 10 minutes or until golden brown. Cool on a wire rack. Top with cream cheese, a few slivers of sun-dried tomato and a basil leaf.

PARSNIP SOUP ESPRESSO

Makes 24 (allow 1-2 per person)

Melt 2 tablespoons of butter in a large saucepan over medium heat. Add 1 peeled and chopped onion and cook for about 5 minutes until soft but not browned. Peel 3 parsnips and 1 medium pear, and chop into ½-inch cubes. Peel and finely chop 2 cloves of garlic, then add the parsnips, pear and garlic to the pan and continue to cook for another 2 minutes. Pour in 2½ cups of chicken stock and 1½ cups of whole milk. Simmer for about 20 minutes, until the parsnips are soft. Remove the pan from the heat and purée the soup with an immersion blender. This recipe makes more than you'll need for 8 guests, but the excess freezes well. Serve warm in espresso cups, garnished with truffle shavings and a few drops of truffle oil.

WELSH RAREBIT AND CRANBERRY TOASTS

Makes 24 (allow 3 per person)

Preheat the broiler to high. Cook 1 tablespoon of butter and 1 tablespoon of all-purpose flour together in a saucepan for a minute or two until it makes a smooth paste. Add 1¾ cups of grated aged cheddar cheese, 1 teaspoon each of mustard and Worcestershire sauce, 3 to 4 tablespoons of dark ale and a dash of Tabasco. Season well and stir constantly over a gentle heat until smooth. Toast 12 thin slices of ciabatta under the broiler until both sides are golden, then cut in half crosswise. Spread some of the cheese mixture on each piece. Return to the broiler for 2 minutes or until golden brown. Garnish with cranberry sauce and parsley sprigs.

BRESAOLA WITH CELERY ROOT REMOULADE

Makes 24 (allow 3 per person)

Peel and coarsely grate a small celery root and mix with 5 tablespoons of mayonnaise, 1 tablespoon of grainy mustard, 3 to 4 teaspoons of lemon juice and season well. Fold 24 slices of bresaola in half (or leave whole if smaller slices), place 2 teaspoons of the remoulade on top and roll up into a parcel. Tie each with a chive to serve.

QUAIL EGG CROUSTADES

Makes 16 (to keep expense down, allow 2 per person)

Preheat the oven to 350°F. Put 16 premade mini pastry shells on a baking tray. Crack a quail egg into each and cook for 4 minutes until the whites have set. Spoon ½ a teaspoon of warmed ready-made Hollandaise over each and garnish with a small piece of pan-fried crispy pancetta.

CHRISTMAS DRINKS

A Christmas canapé party requires suitably festive drinks, mulled wine being a classic, or try a Horse's Neck, a Christmas variation on a Moscow Mule (page 137). Pomegranate ice cubes also add a touch of festive charm to any clear drink. Carefully pick out the seeds from a halved pomegranate. Drop a few in each compartment of an ice-cube tray, fill with water and freeze.

MULLED WINE Serves 8

Peel 4 oranges and set aside the peel. Juice the oranges into a bowl, then stud the orange peels with 20 cloves. Pour 2 bottles of fruity red wine, such as Merlot, into a saucepan with a pinch of ground ginger and 4 cinnamon sticks, then add the orange peel and orange juice. Measure out about 1 cup of soft brown sugar and add a little at a time—the amount of sugar you need depends on how sweet you like your mulled wine, so taste as you go. Simmer gently for 10 minutes until the sugar dissolves (do not allow to boil), and serve warm.

EGGNOG Serves 8

In a saucepan, warm 1 quart of whole or 2 percent milk over low heat. In a pitcher, mix together 6 free range egg yolks, 6 tablespoons of superfine sugar and 1 teaspoon of vanilla extract or the scraped seeds of 1 whole vanilla bean. Add this to the warmed milk along with ⅔ cup of brandy and heat through gently, without boiling, until the mixture thickens enough to coat the back of a spoon. Be very careful here—you don't want to scramble the eggs. The eggnog can be chilled at this stage for a few hours until needed, or served warm. Heat gently for 5 to 7 minutes and grate nutmeg over the eggnog before serving in small cups.

CLASSIC CHAMPAGNE COCKTAIL Serves 1 (make to order)

Place 1 brown sugar cube in the bottom of a Champagne flute and soak it with 2 dashes of Angostura bitters and add ½ ounce of brandy. Top with Champagne or sparkling wine and stir to dissolve the sugar. Garnish with a knot of orange rind. If you are making lots of these, add the sugar cubes, brandy and Angostura bitters to each glass and wet the glass with Champagne. When you top up, this will prevent the Champagne fizzing over.

PEAR MARTINI Serves 1 (make to order)

Shake 1½ ounces of pear vodka with ice cubes and ¼ cup of apple juice, and serve in a martini glass with a squeeze of lime, garnished with a slice of pear or dried apple rings. If you can't get ahold of pear vodka, use plain vodka and canned pears in syrup—use the syrup for the pear flavor and the fruit for garnish. Make in a pitcher for larger numbers.

CHRISTMAS SLOE GIN COCKTAILS

Gin and tonic: Add some festive color and warmth to a classic. Replace regular gin with sloe gin (page 389), serve over ice, add tonic and garnish with a candied orange slice.

Sloe gin fizz: A wintry English take on the classic French Kir Royale. Add sloe gin to the bottom of a Champagne flute and top with Champagne or another sparkling wine.

CHRISTMAS EVE

Christmas Eve is a day to put all the finishing touches to your preparations. Wrap last-minute gifts first thing (try to keep this to a minimum) and, if you can, set the table for Christmas lunch (page 114) to save time the following day. Come late afternoon children's excitement will have reached fever pitch at the prospect of Santa arriving, so keep them occupied with some simple activities. Hide a few foil-wrapped chocolate coins for a Christmas treasure hunt or encourage them to mix up oats and glitter to scatter outside the door or down the garden path to guide the reindeer.

STOCKINGS

Each family has its own special place for hanging stockings, be it on either side of a fireplace, on the mantelpiece or at the end of a bed. Wrapping stocking presents in tissue paper is not only cheaper and faster than using gift wrap, it makes opening them easier, too. Wrist tape dispensers are essential when wrapping lots of stocking fillers. A great tip is to color coordinate presents for each stocking so they don't get mixed up. For more wrapping ideas see page 173.

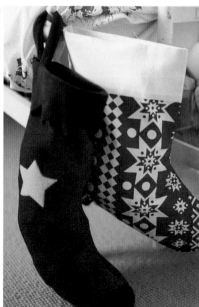

CHRISTMAS DAY

CHRISTMAS MORNING

Christmas morning is a magical time, with stockings first thing amid a flurry of excitement and strewn wrapping paper. Stocking stuffers can be the simplest of things; essentials for me are a tube of jelly beans poking out, oranges and a bag of chocolate coins. If Christmas lunch is planned for much later in the day, serve something satisfying and filling for breakfast, such as smoked salmon with scrambled eggs. For those with a sweeter tooth, raisin bread with Christmas Butter (see below) is delicious, and for kids make Hot Chocolate Spoons (page 379).

CHRISTMAS MENU

Light starters
Twice-Baked Cheese Soufflé *or*
Pear, Walnut and Roquefort Salad *or*
Shellfish Tian *or*
Smoked Trout Pâté Quenelles

Main course
Traditional Roast Turkey
Gravy, Bread Sauce and Cranberry Sauce
Roast Potatoes
Brussels Sprouts, Pancetta and Chestnuts
Honeyed Carrots and Parsnips
Pigs in Blankets and Stuffing

Desserts
Christmas Pudding and Brandy Butter
Chocolate Yule Log
Stilton

Loire Chenin blanc
A good-quality red or white Burgundy
Sauternes, Port or Piedro Ximénez

Christmas Butter: Add 3 ounces of diced cranberries, 3 tablespoons of soft brown sugar, a good pinch each of pumpkin pie spice and cinnamon, the finely grated zest of 2 clementines and 1 ounce of chopped mixed candied citrus peel to 2 sticks of unsalted, softened butter. Mix to combine. Refrigerate in 2 sterile jam jars or wrap in plastic wrap and parchment paper.

CHRISTMAS LUNCH

This lunch comes only once a year, so stick to a traditional menu. It's also a time to bring out special wines. The turkey with all the trimmings is the star attraction, so if you're serving a starter, keep it light or offer festive canapés (page 104) with drinks. Cooking the turkey might be a heroic solo effort but it's a meal everyone can help out with: peeling vegetables, carving the meat, serving and clearing away.

THE CHRISTMAS TABLE

White table linen is an effective backdrop to any Christmas color scheme, but if you have a wooden tabletop in good condition consider leaving it bare or just add a bit of softness to it with a Christmassy-colored table runner.

TRADITIONAL

I prefer a traditional table with strong colors of rich reds and evergreens because it feels warm and nostalgic. Add touches of gold (or silver) to bring a special feel to the table with glassware, china and festive charger plates. Shiny pebbles and wrapped chocolates can be grouped in small bowls or scattered sparingly along the length of the table. If you are using natural foliage to decorate your table, you'll need plenty of light to keep it from looking heavy and gloomy (battery-operated Christmas lights and tea lights are perfect for this). You could turn your door wreath (page 95) into a table centerpiece with the well in the middle filled with candles. Otherwise, stemmed, cut-glass bowls filled with frosted fruits, berries and ornaments as well as decorative storm lanterns can act as prominent features.

Pick out a particular color or texture from your table-center display and mirror this in smaller details such as the napkins, place cards and Christmas crackers. Napkins tied with tartan ribbon will complement holly and berries or attach a bundle of cinnamon sticks and faux berries to each place setting. Name cards can be wedged into pine cones, along with colorful pompom balls, or tied with raffia string to the stalks of festive fruits such as pears, clementines and figs.

CONTEMPORARY

For a more contemporary table, use crisp white linen and silvery-gray accessories as your base color. For the table center, a collection of elegant candlesticks at varying heights interspersed with silver foliage will create a twinkling, magical feel. Clusters of white, glass and silver tea lights (or lace-paper lantern jars, page 180) on table mirrors will catch the light, as will glass or acrylic nuggets and silver foil chocolate coins scattered loosely on the table. A minimalist palette relies on texture and pattern such as cut glassware and embroidered linen, but a splash of red will bring a Scandinavian feel.

Add personal touches, such as Christmassy decorations on place settings or on the backs of chairs. Attach name cards to mini ornament holders or to glass stems using glitter clothespins (page 91). Look out for pretty silvery napkin rings throughout the year, a mismatch feel can be quite charming and means that each guest can save their napkin for subsequent meals.

LIGHT STARTERS

TWICE-BAKED CHEESE SOUFFLÉ Serves 8

Preheat the oven to 350°F. Separate 3 eggs, and put to one side. Melt 3 tablespoons of unsalted butter in a pan, stir in 3 tablespoons of all-purpose flour and mix to a smooth paste. Gradually add 1 cup of whole milk and a pinch of nutmeg, stirring until the sauce thickens. Leave to cool slightly, then beat in the 3 egg yolks, 1 cup of grated cheddar cheese and 2 tablespoons of chopped chives. Using an electric mixer, beat the egg whites to soft peaks. Mix 1 tablespoon of egg white into the sauce, then carefully fold the sauce and eggwhites together with a metal spoon. Spoon the mixture into 8 buttered ramekins, place them in a roasting pan and add hot water to fill pan halfway. Cook for about 20 minutes, until firm. Remove from the pan, cool, running a knife around the edge of each soufflé and turning them out onto a baking sheet. Increase the oven temperature to 425°F. Combine 1½ cups of heavy cream and 1 tablespoon of mustard and top each soufflé with 3 tablespoons of the mixture, sprinkle extra cheese over them, and bake for 15 to 20 minutes, until golden and risen. Serve garnished with chives.

PEAR, WALNUT AND ROQUEFORT SALAD Serves 8

Separate 4 heads each of red and white endive and place the leaves in a large serving bowl. Add 3 peeled and thinly sliced large pears and ½ cup of chopped walnuts, then crumble 7 ounces of Roquefort cheese over the salad. Mix the juice of 1 lemon, 6 tablespoons of extra virgin olive oil and 2 tablespoons of honey together in a pitcher. Drizzle over the salad just before serving.

TWO WAYS WITH SEAFOOD Serves 8

Shellfish tian: Mix 6 tablespoons of mayonnaise, 2 tablespoons of ketchup, a good dash each of Worcestershire sauce, brandy, Tabasco and lemon juice, to taste. Season well. In a separate bowl, combine 14 ounces of fresh picked (or canned) crabmeat, 8 ounces of small Atlantic shrimp, a large bunch of chopped chives and the juice of 1 lemon. Divide the crab mixture between 8 medium metal chefs' ring molds, filling them about two-thirds full. Press down with a spoon to compress, then refrigerate. To serve, unmold each seafood "tower" onto serving plates. Spoon a little sauce over the fish, then finish each with 3 or 4 peeled jumbo shrimp.

Smoked fish pâté: Put 8 ounces of skinless smoked trout, 3½ ounces of crème fraîche, 2 teaspoons of horseradish, 2 tablespoons of cream cheese and the juice of ½ a lemon in a food processor and pulse until smooth. Season well and stir in 2 tablespoons of chopped chives. Shape between 2 tablespoons to form quenelles. Top with caviar and garnish with a sprinkle of cayenne pepper. Delicious with Melba toast.

ROAST TURKEY

There is no doubt that carving a turkey at the table makes for an impressive display but with so many other ingredients to serve, plating up in the kitchen will save time and keep the food warm. Because of their size, turkeys are perfect for feeding larger gatherings. If you're cooking for a small group, a roast goose might make a welcome change.

SERVES 8

1 stick butter, at room temperature

finely grated zest of 1 orange

10 sprigs thyme, 8 picked, 2 left whole

sea salt and freshly ground black pepper

one 9-pound turkey, at room temperature, giblets removed

3 bay leaves

olive oil

1 recipe Sage and Onion Stuffing (page 122)

1 cup red wine, water or cider

TIMING IT RIGHT: *When the turkey is out of the oven and resting, add the potatoes (page 54) and cook for 40 minutes. Add the stuffing balls, parsnips and carrots (page 123) to the oven, and roast for 20 to 25 minutes.*

Preheat the oven to 425°F. In a bowl mix the butter with the orange zest and picked thyme leaves and season well with salt and pepper. Starting from the neck end of the bird, gently push your fingers under the turkey's skin and ease it away from the flesh (be careful not to tear it and make sure it is still attached to the flesh around the edges). Push the flavored butter under the skin, on top of each breast, then smooth it out evenly and smooth the skin back in place. Quarter the zested orange and place it in the turkey cavity with the bay leaves and thyme sprigs. Drizzle the turkey with a little olive oil, rub it over the skin and season well. Place some stuffing (page 122) in the neck of the bird. Roll the rest of the mixture into balls, place on a greased baking sheet and set aside (see box).

Put the prepared turkey in a large roasting pan, and add the red wine, water, or cider around the base. Cover the roasting pan completely with foil, tucking it underneath to create a "tent" over the turkey. Cook the turkey for 30 minutes at 425°F, then turn the oven down to 350°F and cook for 35 minutes per 2 pounds (roughly 2 hours 20 minutes for a 9-pound bird). Turn the oven up to 400°F. Remove the foil and return the turkey to the oven for another 30 minutes to crisp the skin.

To test if the turkey is cooked through, pierce the fattest part of a thigh with a skewer. The juices should run clear. This is an essential test to do as ovens vary. Alternatively, use a meat thermometer, which should read at least 165°F. Rest the turkey, covered loosely with foil, for at least 20 minutes and up to 1 hour.

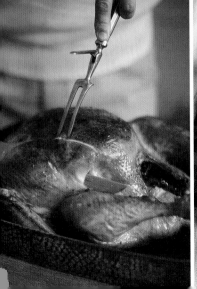

. . . AND ALL THE TRIMMINGS

All the following recipes serve 8. These are all must-have accompaniments to turkey, and most can be prepared ahead (page 87).

PERFECT GRAVY

Roughly chop the giblets from the turkey and brown them in a little olive oil in a saucepan over medium heat, adding 1 chopped onion, 1 chopped carrot and 1 chopped celery stalk. When the vegetables have softened, add 2 tablespoons of all-purpose flour and whisk to combine. Pour in 1 large glass of red wine or Madeira and simmer until the liquid is reduced by half. Add 1 quart of fresh dark chicken stock and 1 bay leaf to the pan, bring to a boil and then reduce the heat and simmer for 30 to 40 minutes. Strain the broth, discarding the giblets and vegetables. Add the juices from the resting turkey to the broth, being careful to remove the excess fat and simmer again until dark and thick. Strain into a gravy boat.

TIP: *Warm up your gravy boat by filling it with very hot water.*

BREAD SAUCE

Warm 3 cups of milk, 2 tablespoons of butter, 1 onion studded with 6 cloves, 6 peppercorns and a bay leaf in a saucepan for 10 minutes. Strain and return the liquid to the pan. Add 5 ounces of fresh white bread crumbs and simmer for 3 to 4 minutes. Add a generous pinch of nutmeg, and season with salt and pepper to taste. This freezes well for up to 6 months.

TIP: *You can stir in some of the roasting juices as a substitute for a little of the milk or to thin the sauce, if required.*

CRANBERRY SAUCE

Put 21 ounces of fresh cranberries in a saucepan with the finely grated zest and juice of 2 oranges and 1 cup of packed light brown sugar. Add a generous splash of port and simmer for 8 to 10 minutes, until the sugar is dissolved, the cranberries have popped their skins and the sauce has thickened. Add more sugar if required.

PERFECT POTATOES

The recipe for roast potatoes on page 54 is an essential accompaniment to turkey. Put your potatoes in the oven as the turkey comes out to rest, and to save time on washing up use disposable aluminum trays. Always make more than you think you will need!

SAGE AND ONION STUFFING

Put a large pan on medium heat and pour in about 2 tablespoons of olive oil. Add 2 peeled and chopped onions and 2 peeled and finely chopped cloves of fresh garlic and cook gently for 5 to 10 minutes, until soft and slightly golden. Add 1 bunch of chopped fresh sage and 5 ounces of fresh white bread crumbs. Remove the pan from the heat and allow to cool. Once cool, mix in 1½ pounds of good-quality bulk fresh sausage, a handful of chopped dried apricots and a beaten egg. Season well, and set aside while you prepare the turkey. Cook according to the instructions on page 120.

BRUSSELS SPROUTS, PANCETTA AND CHESTNUTS

Bring a pan of water to a boil and cook 1 pound of small Brussels sprouts for 5 to 6 minutes until al dente. Drain them and set aside. To keep them green, plunge briefly into ice-cold water to stop the cooking process. Heat 2 tablespoons of unsalted butter in a frying pan and add 3½ ounces of chopped dry-cured bacon or diced pancetta. Fry gently for 2 minutes until it starts to crisp. Add 3 ounces of peeled, cooked, and roughly chopped chestnuts and cook for another minute. Add the sprouts and a squeeze of orange juice and bring to a simmer. Season to taste.

TIP: *Choose small fresh sprouts for the best flavor, and when preparing them, don't peel back too much of the outer skin or make a crisscross on the base as this can make them soggy.*

HONEYED CARROTS AND PARSNIPS

Preheat the oven to 400°F. Peel 2 pounds each of carrots and parsnips, cut into wedges and scatter them in a large roasting pan. For larger parsnips remove the core, which can be bitter. Drizzle 3 tablespoons of olive oil over the vegetables and season them generously with sea salt and freshly ground black pepper. Toss to coat, then roast for 20 to 25 minutes until tender and slightly charred. Drizzle 2 tablespoons of honey over the vegetables, add a pat of butter, toss again to coat and serve.

PIGS IN BLANKETS

Preheat the oven to 400°F. Put 24 mini hotdogs or sausages (allow 3 per person) on a greased baking sheet. Cut 12 slices of pancetta in half, then stretch each piece lightly with the back of a knife. Wrap a pancetta piece around each sausage, making sure the seam is underneath the sausage. Roast for 10 to 15 minutes until the pancetta is cooked and crisp.

TIP: *My favorite Christmas side dish of all, these are also delicious as a festive canapé.*

CHRISTMAS DESSERTS

It's a wonderful piece of theater, when the Christmas Pudding (see recipe on page 88) makes its grand entrance, lit with burning brandy. Serve Brandy Butter or cream alongside it and warm a batch of Mince Pies.

A Chocolate Yule Log might be a welcome alternative to Christmas Pudding, decorated with woodland symbols or covered with a white chocolate icing to create a snowy scene. Bring out a cheeseboard and crackers with a large wheel of cheese to complete the feast.

BRANDY BUTTER Serves 8–10

Mix 2 sticks of softened, unsalted butter, the finely grated zest of 1 orange and ¼ cup of packed soft light brown sugar until thoroughly combined. Gradually add ⅓ cup of brandy while mixing until you have a creamy, smooth paste. This will keep in the fridge for up to 4 days.

CHOCOLATE YULE LOG Serves 8

Preheat the oven to 375°F. Grease and line a 9 x 12-inch jelly roll pan with parchment paper. Separate 4 eggs. Beat the egg whites with an electric mixer until stiff, then gradually add ¼ cup of superfine sugar while whisking continuously. In a separate bowl, beat the egg yolks with ⅓ cup of superfine sugar, add ½ cup of self-rising flour and 2 tablespoons of cocoa powder, then fold in the egg whites. Pour the batter into the pan. Use a spatula to spread the mixture evenly, then bake for about 10 minutes, until the top is springy. Remove from the oven, place a damp tea towel over the top of the tray and set aside to cool. Whip ¾ cup of heavy cream to stiff peaks, then add 1 teaspoon of vanilla extract.

To flavor the cake with cherry liqueur, remove the cooled sponge cake from the pan and turn it upside down on a platter. Soak the cake with ½ cup of cherry-flavored liqueur, then turn it back over onto the parchment paper and spread the whipped cream on top. Otherwise, simply spread the cream all over the top of the cake. Holding the parchment with the longer side toward you, roll the cake up, keeping it nice and tight. To make the icing, beat 1 stick of softened, unsalted butter until smooth and then gradually beat in 1¼ cups of confectioner's sugar and ¾ cup of cocoa powder. If using, add another splash of cherry liqueur and mix well. Add 4 tablespoons of milk a little at a time to thin the icing if necessary, then spread it over the cake with an offset spatula, making markings to resemble bark. Sift confectioner's sugar over, then decorate with chocolate shavings (page 33) and Christmas cake decorations.

FESTIVE FUN

Christmas is still one of the few occasions when you can get everybody playing and, hopefully, enjoying games. I have picked out some traditional games and others that won't be so familiar. Charades is a classic, and inclusive for all. Most people know the rules (or their own versions of them) and a jigsaw puzzle offers a welcome respite from the Christmas revelry. Pick one that has lots of color and activity and lay it out on a table in a quiet corner so that anyone passing can add a few pieces. Have a personalized one made up from a photograph of something familiar to your family.

THE CHOCOLATE BOX GAME

Find a tall chocolate box (or an empty cereal box) and stand it on a clear area of floor away from any furniture. Players take turns lifting the box using just their teeth, with only their feet touching the ground. Once everyone has had a go, tear an inch or so off the top of the box so that it stands a little lower than before and play another round. This time, it will be more difficult and it's possible that some people will lose their balance or use their hands. If they do, they are out. The box continues to get smaller and smaller until it is just a flat piece of card and only the most flexible and controlled players are left in the game.

PASS THE ORANGE

Players split into two teams and each team forms a line. The first person in each team tucks an orange under their chin. On "Go!" they pass the orange to the next person in line, neck to neck. Everyone must keep their hands firmly behind their backs. The oranges make their way down their respective lines but if at any point one is dropped, the player responsible for the fall must get onto their hands and knees and retrieve the orange using only their neck and chin. The sequence of passes is then resumed and the first team to get the orange to the final player in their line is declared victorious.

OTHER CHRISTMAS GAMES

- **After Eight:** *taking turns, balance an unwrapped After Eight mint on your forehead. Tilt your head back and try to shift it down to your mouth using only facial movements.*

- **Bouchon:** *you'll need corks and cards (page 61).*

- **Stop the Bus:** *great for all ages (page 61).*

- **The Hat Game:** *Divide into two teams. Each player writes the names of famous people on small pieces of paper, scrunches them up and throws them in a hat. Players take turns pulling out pieces of paper and describing as many of the famous people as possible in one minute without saying their names. The team who has guessed the most names correctly when the hat is empty wins.*

BOXING DAY

This is the day for some serious downtime—a welcome and wonderful contrast to the rigors of Christmas itself. The hype, hard work and deadlines are over and, even if you have guests, the atmosphere is likely to be lazy and laid back. Comforting, curative food is what's needed—a baked and glazed ham is inexpensive and perfect for a large gathering, along with leftovers from the Christmas feast. I like the idea of a Boxing Day plowman's: beautifully arranged platters of cold meats and cheese (Stilton blue cheese being essential), accompanied by a large green salad, apple slices, grapes, celery sticks, pâté, crunchy bread, chutney (page 388), and pickles. Some might be tempted to build their own individually tailored, seasonal tower sandwiches.

BOXING DAY HAM Serves 8–12

The ham is completely cooked in the liquid, so can be stored for up to 3 days before you add the glaze and roast it. Put one 4-pound skin-on boneless ham in a large pan with 2 quarts of apple juice, 2 to 3 quarts of apple cider and enough water to cover. Add 1 trimmed and coarsely chopped leek, 2 coarsely chopped celery stalks, 2 bay leaves, 1 peeled and chopped onion and 2 teaspoons of black peppercorns and bring to a boil. Skim off any scum that rises to the surface. Cover the pan with a lid and simmer for 2 hours until the ham is tender. Drain the ham and discard the vegetables and other flavorings. Set aside.

Preheat the oven to 400°F. Mix 4 tablespoons of orange marmalade and 3 tablespoons of soft brown sugar together to form a paste. Remove the skin from the ham and score the fat. Spread the marmalade mixture over the fat, then stud with 10 cloves and roast for 45 minutes, until golden and glistening.

Beaujolais, soft Côtes du Rhône or leftover wines from Christmas Day.

A WHOLE STILTON

Slice the top off a whole Stilton wheel and scoop out a little of the cheese. Pour in port, sherry, Madeira or old ale. Let the cheese absorb this for 2 to 3 weeks. Serve with an interesting selection of cheese crackers, such as Italian flatbreads, grissini sticks, thin herb crackers, oat cakes and water crackers. Add some fresh fruit, such as grapes and figs, and perhaps a little quince jelly.

TIP: *Use a Stilton scoop to dig out the soft insides of the cheese.*

MAKING USE OF LEFTOVERS

Turkey *works well as a fricassée, in a curry (page 142), stroganoff or pie (page 70) with other leftovers.*

Stilton *is delicious in soup with broccoli. Use it to add intense flavor to Cauliflower Cheese (page 55), served with baked ham.*

Brussels Sprouts *can be stir-fried with spices and soy sauce, or used with leftover potatoes and parsnips to make Bubble and Squeak (a traditional English dish usually made with cabbage).*

Ring out the old, ring in the new,
Ring, happy bells, across the snow:
The year is going, let him go;
Ring out the false, ring in the true.

"Ring Out, Wild Bells,"
Alfred, Lord Tennyson

NEW YEAR'S EVE

New Year's Eve looms large in the calendar due to its importance; it's one of the oldest festivals in the British Isles. It has its roots in Roman times, when people marked the occasion by feasting, dancing, singing and exchanging gifts—and is celebrated around the world. Although each country has its own traditional customs and superstitions, it's a universal experience as people wait for the first day of the new year to reach them. There is always an exhilarating feeling as the evening gathers pace—a wave of corks popping, glasses clinking and people cheering, which sweeps across the world and upon the thousands who gather to eat, drink and be merry.

As a result, a New Year's Eve celebration always comes with huge expectations, which explains why it can so often be a real anticlimax and a party many dread to host. Understandably, people often panic when it comes to organizing such an event, but in reality it's not so different from any other party over the course of the year. I know from past experience that it's important not to have preparations still looming over you the moment Christmas ends; otherwise you'll get in a flap and resent having volunteered to throw the celebration altogether. Fewer shops are open over this period and shelves are barer, so there's even more of an incentive to have it all organized before Christmas.

My favorite New Year's parties have not been the huge affairs but the more intimate ones with close friends and family, anything between eight and twenty-five people. Whatever the numbers, the pressure is on the host to magic up all the necessary ingredients for a fantastic atmosphere. A few good cocktails and canapés early on when guests arrive will get everyone in the mood. Have some great music and (perhaps not so great!) dancing to see in the New Year. Food isn't necessarily the focus, so a simple but colorful curry buffet is the perfect meal, especially as the food can be eaten with just a fork and seating doesn't need to be confined to the table. All the dishes in this chapter can be prepared in advance, or you can make it a more collaborative affair (and less of an expense) by asking your friends to contribute to the buffet. The curries make a welcome change from traditional Christmas fare; the aromas momentarily suggest the sensory pleasures of hot and exotic climes—a far cry from the cold winter outside.

SET THE SCENE

ROOM DECORATIONS

Because the house is dressed for Christmas, New Year's adornments should be quick and easy, adapted from your existing decorations. For an effervescent backdrop, hang shiny ornaments (or other sparkly tree decorations) at different heights from string tied across the room. Perhaps introduce a particular color scheme but keep silver as the dominant color throughout. Tissue-paper pompoms are quick and easy to make, and balls of varying sizes, hung with ribbon or glittery wire, will enhance the celebratory feel. Dot white Christmas lights about the room, wrapping them around silver-sprayed branches, mirrors and beams, or cluster them in tall cylindrical glass vases. If your ceiling is low, let a handful of helium balloons (tied with curling ribbon) hang freely and add a few silver-foil number balloons showing the year you are celebrating. Alternatively, you can tie them to balloon weights or to the backs of chairs to add height and drama to your table, or arrange them in empty corners of your room.

TISSUE-PAPER POMPOMS

These look beautiful hanging from the ceiling, or you can make smaller pompoms to tie around napkin rings.

1: Stack 12 sheets of tissue paper (approximately ten 15-inch sheets or double for larger ones) and accordion fold the paper, ½ inch wide, on the shorter side. 2: Fold in half to find the center and tie a long piece of ribbon or sparkly wire tightly in the center. Trim the edge of the paper in pointy or round shapes. 3: Open the fan back up and carefully separate the layers of tissue paper, pulling them away from the center one at a time.

CELEBRATORY TABLE

Let the food provide the color and keep your table palette relatively neutral, fresh and clean, with the focal point being beautiful flowers, twinkling candles and tea lights. Set candles in glass or etched antique silver holders (mirrored place mats and vases will double the light they give off). Other tablecenter ideas might include small globe vases lined with a large leaf and filled with white roses, Lisianthus (sometimes called a Texas Bluebell), hyacinths, freesias, ranunculus and eucalyptus. Add sparkle to empty spaces on the table using silver or gold confetti, glitter and glass nuggets with a few silvery party poppers stacked in the center—no need to go overboard, just go for delicate touches.

COCKTAILS FOR A CROWD

If there is ever a time to mix up cocktails, this is the occasion to do so. Set up a martini bar (page 69) for guests to make their own classic versions, or prepare the bases of the following cocktails in pitchers ahead of time for ease of entertaining, then just shake over ice and strain before serving. These are refreshing enough to sip all night long, and complement the curry theme of the evening (the pear martini on page 109 is also very seasonal). Don't forget to save some bubbly for midnight toasts.

PASSION FRUIT MARTINI Serves 4

One of my favorites. In a pitcher, mix together ½ cup of vodka and ¾ cup of passion fruit juice, together with 1½ ounces of pineapple juice and the juice of 1 lime. To serve, shake hard in a cocktail shaker filled with ice cubes, strain and pour into chilled martini glasses. Serve immediately to ensure a frothy top, and garnish with a few passion fruit seeds. If you want to use very fresh passion fruit juice, scoop the flesh out of 6 passion fruits and press the seeds to extract the juice through a fine sieve.

FRENCH MARTINI Serves 4

Quick and easy, the flavor is jammy and fruity. In a pitcher, mix together ⅓ cup of vodka, ⅓ cup of Chambord and ¾ cup of pineapple juice. To serve, shake hard in a cocktail shaker filled with ice cubes, strain and pour into chilled martini glasses. Garnish each with a raspberry. A friend serves these in his bar in teapots filled with ice.

MOSCOW MULE Serves 4

A drink you can enjoy all evening long, at any time of year. It's refreshing and goes particularly well with spicy food. In a pitcher, mix together ¾ cup of vodka and the juice of 1 lime, 2 tablespoons of turbinado sugar and 4 dashes of Angostura bitters. To serve, pour into 4 tall glasses with a wedge of fresh lime and some slices of fresh ginger. Stir together, add ice cubes and top with ginger ale. A Horse's Neck is a variation of this drink: just replace the vodka with 9 ounces of brandy.

COSMOPOLITAN Serves 4

In a pitcher, mix together ⅔ cup of lemon vodka, ¼ cup of Cointreau, 2 tablespoons of fresh lime juice, ¼ cup of cranberry juice and 2 teaspoons of sugar syrup (page 80). Pour the mixture in batches into a cocktail shaker, fill with ice cubes and shake. Pour through a strainer into chilled martini glasses and garnish with a slice of orange rind, pinched together to release the oils.

COLORFUL CURRY BANQUET

To kick off proceedings, especially if you are serving cocktails and planning to start dinner later, have a few canapés on hand—the evening is likely to be a long one. Spiced nuts (page 67) are perfect for all-night grazing and can be placed strategically for guests to munch on. Curries lend themselves to sharing and make for a bountiful and satisfying banquet to linger over. Everyone has a favorite, so a selection of main dishes served alongside fragrant rice, brightly colored chutneys, salsas and piles of poppadoms will look appetizing on the table. Label them using mini chalkboards with stands. Curries are also low maintenance (the word "curry" comes from the southern Indian word "kari," which simply means "sauce"), so each dish is self-contained and requires minimal last-minute prep, allowing you to enjoy the party with your guests.

The following make for colorful small bites along a subtle curry theme; they won't clash with the fuller flavors of the main meal to come. Serve these on plain white plates or silvery trays to bring out the colors. Allow two of each canapé per person.

NEW YEAR'S EVE MENU

Canapés
Coronation turkey boats
Curried blinis with raita
Stuffed eggs
Mini shrimp poppadoms
Spiced crab cakes

Main courses
Spicy red chicken curry
Thai green shrimp curry

Side dishes
Daal and Sag aloo
Basmati and jasmine rice
Mango, tomato and scallion salsa

Desserts
Winter fruit salad
Sparkling gold-leaf jellies
Meringue kisses

CORONATION TURKEY BOATS Makes 16

Mix together 2 tablespoons of mayonnaise, 1½ tablespoons of mango chutney, 1 teaspoon of curry powder and the juice of ½ a lime. Add 12 ounces of cooked, diced turkey breast (or chicken), season and toss until well coated. Separate the leaves of 2 baby gem lettuces or 1 head of butter lettuce and spoon a little turkey mixture into each lettuce leaf "boat." Cover and refrigerate. Garnish with chopped mango.

CURRIED BLINIS WITH RAITA Makes 16

Grate ¼ of a cucumber and squeeze the excess liquid from it. Mix with 7 ounces of plain yogurt in a bowl and refrigerate until needed. Preheat the oven to 350°F. Spread a little ready-made medium curry paste over 16 cocktail blinis, then place them on a baking sheet and warm in the oven for 4 to 5 minutes. Spoon a little raita onto each one and garnish with mint.

STUFFED EGGS Makes 16

Place 8 eggs in a saucepan, cover with water and bring to a boil. Lower the heat to a simmer and cook for 8 minutes. When cooked, cool under cold water and peel. Submerge in fresh cold water with 2 tablespoons of natural pink food dye for 5 minutes to absorb the color of the dye. Cut each egg in half lengthwise. Remove the yolks and mash in a bowl with 4 to 5 tablespoons of mayonnaise, a dash of Tabasco, a squeeze of lemon juice and season well. Place the yolk mixture in a piping bag and carefully pipe it into the egg whites. Garnish with a sprinkle of paprika.

MINI SHRIMP POPPADOMS Makes 16

Mix together 12 ounces of small peeled and cooked Atlantic shrimp with 2 tablespoons of Thai green curry paste, 1 seeded and finely diced cucumber, the juice of ½ a lime, 2 tablespoons of roughly chopped cilantro and ½ a seeded and finely chopped fresh red chili. Spoon the shrimp mixture onto 16 mini poppadoms, and garnish with finely sliced red chili.

SPICED CRAB CAKES Makes 16

Mix together 12 ounces of fresh-picked or canned white crabmeat, 1 seeded and finely chopped fresh red chili, a 2-inch piece of peeled and finely chopped fresh ginger, a small bunch of roughly chopped cilantro and the zest and juice of 1 lime with ¾ cup of bread crumbs and 1 beaten egg. Make walnut-sized balls of paste in your hands and pat them into small cakes. Refrigerate for at least 10 minutes. At this stage the cakes can be frozen for up to 3 weeks (defrost thoroughly before cooking). When ready to cook, dust the cakes in flour, dip into beaten egg and lightly coat in bread crumbs. Heat 3 tablespoons of vegetable oil in a frying pan. Gently place the cakes in the pan and fry for up to 3 minutes on each side until golden brown. Drain on paper towel, then serve warm with a sweet chili dipping sauce.

SPICY RED CHICKEN CURRY

The chicken thighs in this curry promise tender, tasty meat, but if you prefer to use breast, make the sauce in advance and add the chicken for the last 20 minutes of cooking to keep it from drying out. For more heat, add chopped chili peppers to the marinade. Lamb makes a lovely variation.

SERVES 8

For the marinade

8 tablespoons coconut cream

5 to 6 tablespoons ready-made curry paste, medium or hot

5 cloves garlic, peeled and minced

1-inch piece fresh ginger, peeled and grated

20 boneless, skinless chicken thighs, chopped into large chunks

For the curry

2 tablespoons vegetable oil

2 to 3 large onions, peeled and sliced

one 14-ounce can chopped tomatoes

½ cup chicken stock

1 tablespoon superfine sugar

one 14-ounce can coconut milk

sea salt and freshly ground black pepper

To make the marinade, mix together the coconut cream, curry paste, garlic and ginger in a bowl. Add the chicken, mix well to combine, then cover the bowl with plastic wrap and refrigerate for at least 20 minutes, or overnight if possible.

To make the sauce, heat the vegetable oil in a pan and fry the sliced onions for 5 minutes until lightly browned. Add the marinated chicken and continue to cook for another 4 minutes until aromatic. Sprinkle in some water if the paste begins to stick.

Add the tomatoes, stock and sugar and cook, uncovered, for 20 minutes. Cover with the lid and continue to cook for 10 minutes. Stir in the coconut milk and warm through, then check the seasoning and adjust if necessary. (At this stage, the curry can be frozen for up to 1 month.) Squeeze the juice of 1 lime over it and garnish with fresh cilantro. Serve with the aromatic rice below.

 *A fruity red like Australian Shiraz.*

AROMATIC BASMATI RICE *Serves 8*

To mold this colorful and fragrant rice into neat shapes, line ramekins with plastic wrap, press in the rice and turn out.

Place 2½ cups of basmati rice in a sieve and rinse with cold water until the water runs clear. In a large pot, bring 6 cups of vegetable stock to a boil with 2 teaspoons of turmeric. Add the rice and stir once. Add 3 whole cloves, 4 cardamom pods and 2 cinnamon sticks and simmer for 12 to 15 minutes. Taste the rice to test if it is done, then drain and fluff up with a fork. Remove the cloves, cardamom pods and cinnamon sticks before serving.

THAI GREEN SHRIMP CURRY

Fragrant, light and pale green in color, this sauce can be made and frozen up to a month ahead, and the raw shrimp (or scallops) added at the last minute to simply cook through.

SERVES 8

I tablespoon vegetable oil

2 to 3 leeks, trimmed and finely chopped

3 heaped tablespoons Thai green curry paste

I red chili, deseeded and finely chopped

I tablespoon palm sugar or 2 tablespoons soft light brown sugar

2 stalks lemongrass, smashed

two 14-ounce cans coconut milk

2 tablespoons fish sauce

4 dried kaffir lime leaves

I pound peeled and deveined raw jumbo shrimp

I¼ pounds sugar snap peas

juice of I lime

Heat the oil in a pan and gently sauté the leeks for a couple of minutes. Add the green curry paste, chili, sugar and lemongrass stalks and cook over fairly high heat for about I minute.

Add the coconut milk, fish sauce and lime leaves and simmer for 25 to 30 minutes. Add the shrimp and the sugar snap peas and cook for approximately 3 minutes, then taste for seasoning, adding more fish sauce if needed and lime juice to taste. Remove the lime leaves and lemongrass stalks. Garnish with cilantro.

 *An aromatic white like Riesling or Gewurztraminer.*

TIP: *Baby corn and thinly sliced red pepper make nice additions to this curry—stir them in with the shrimp. If using chicken, add it with the coconut milk and allow it to cook through.*

FLUFFY JASMINE RICE   Serves 8

My mum has a tried-and-tested way of cooking rice: whatever vessel you are using to measure out the rice always use one and a half the amount of cold water (a little more if using brown or wild rice, as these take longer to cook).

Place 2 mugs of jasmine rice and 3 mugs of salted cold water on high heat until the water starts to bubble. Turn the heat right down, add a lid and gently simmer for 10 minutes until all the water has been absorbed (you can test by tipping the pan on its side; you might also see small holes appearing throughout the rice). Don't touch or stir the rice until all the liquid has been absorbed. Leave to stand for 5 minutes, then fluff with a fork before serving.

SIMPLE SIDE DISHES

DAAL Serves 8

An Indian lentil dish and a classic, healthy vegetable side. If you are asking others to help you with the catering, this is a great one to delegate. For a Thai twist, substitute ¾ cup of the stock with coconut milk.

Pour 1 tablespoon of vegetable oil into a large saucepan, and add a peeled and grated 2-inch piece of fresh ginger, 1 diced green chili, 3 tablespoons of tomato purée, 1 teaspoon each of ground turmeric, cumin seeds and chili powder and 2 cloves of finely chopped garlic. Fry the spices over medium heat, stirring until they become fragrant.

Rinse 14 ounces of split yellow lentils (daal) under running water. Add them to the spices in the pan with 2½ cups of vegetable stock. Bring to a boil, then reduce the heat to medium and simmer for 15 to 20 minutes, adding more stock if necessary, to prevent the lentils from drying out. Finish with chopped cilantro, a squeeze of lime juice and season to taste.

SAG ALOO Serves 8

I prefer this dish when the spinach still has a bit of bite—it's a brilliant burst of green and really tasty.

In a large saucepan, parboil 14 ounces of cubed floury potatoes (use Yukon Gold) for 7 to 8 minutes, then drain and set aside. Put a large frying pan over medium heat and pour in 2 tablespoons of vegetable oil. When the oil is hot, add ½ teaspoon of cumin seeds and 1 large onion, peeled and finely chopped, and fry until the onion begins to brown.

Add the drained potatoes to the frying pan, with 1 teaspoon of peeled and grated ginger, ½ a clove of peeled and finely chopped garlic, and 1 teaspoon of garam masala. Fry until the potato softens. Add a splash of water to prevent the mixture from sticking to the pan. When the potato is cooked, add 14 ounces of washed leaf spinach and cook for 1 minute until it wilts. Stir in 3 tablespoons of unsalted butter, season to taste with salt and freshly ground black pepper and serve immediately.

MANGO, TOMATO AND SCALLION SALSA Serves 8

This salsa brings freshness and color to the table. It's also great for cooling a hot and spicy curry.

In a large bowl, mix together 1 large peeled and diced mango, 3 large peeled and diced tomatoes, 1 bunch of chopped scallions, 1 peeled, seeded and diced cucumber, a small bunch of freshly chopped cilantro, and 4 tablespoons of extra virgin olive oil. Squeeze the juice of 1 lime over the mixture, and season to taste with salt and freshly ground black pepper.

ELEGANT DESSERTS

WINTER FRUIT SALAD Serves 8

An array of citrus fruits will cut through any curry flavors that might linger and cleanse palates. This fruit salad is delicious with the sparkling gelatin. Serve with a sweet Muscat wine.

Slice 2 peeled oranges, 3 peeled blood oranges or 2 peeled pink grapefruit, and 2 star fruit into thin rounds. Arrange the slices on a platter, alternating for a pretty effect. Scatter the seeds of 1 pomegranate over the fruit and dot with the picked leaves from ½ a small bunch of mint. Refrigerate for at least 30 minutes to allow the juices and flavors to mingle. This will create its own citrussy dressing, but a drizzle of pomegranate molasses will also work well.

MERINGUE KISSES Serves 8

Glittering meringues in a large dish topped with fizzing sparklers give a celebratory feel to the table.

Allow 2 small meringues per person. These are easily available to buy ready made, around the holidays and at specialty food stores, or alternatively make your own meringue (page 326) and pipe or spoon the mixture onto a parchment-lined baking sheet and bake for 25 to 30 minutes at 300°F. When cool, dust with edible silver glitter, and serve with whipped cream or colorful scoops of ice cream.

SPARKLING GOLD-LEAF GELATIN Serves 8

This is an elegant and light finish to a New Year's Eve supper. The seeds of a pomegranate work well with pink Champagne and are particularly seasonal, but blueberries, raspberries, and blackberries all look pretty. The addition of gold leaf gives this a festive twinkle. Serve in stemmed glasses with the winter fruit salad.

Divide 9 ounces of blueberries or pomegranate seeds evenly among 8 glasses with 2 sheets of edible gold leaf (available online or at specialty food stores) torn into small pieces and chill. Put ½ cup of water into a small bowl and evenly sprinkle 2 teaspoons of powdered plain gelatin over the surface; let stand 10 minutes. Pour a scant ½ cup of elderflower or elderflower and pomegranate cordial diluted with a scant cup of water into a heatproof bowl and place over a pan of boiling water. Add 4 tablespoons of superfine sugar and allow to dissolve. Remove the bowl from the heat and add the bloomed gelatin. Keep stirring until the gelatin is dissolved. Pour this mixture into a large pitcher with 2½ cups of chilled pink Champagne or Prosecco and mix well. Divide between the chilled glasses and return them to the fridge for at least 2 hours to set.

TIP: *Keeping the fruit, sparkling wine and glasses chilled until you need them ensures fizz in the gelatin.*

Should auld acquaintance be forgot,
and never brought to mind?
Should auld acquaintance be forgot,
and auld lang syne?

For auld lang syne, my dear,
for auld lang syne,
we'll tak a cup o' kindness yet,
for auld lang syne.

WELCOMING THE NEW YEAR

As the clock strikes midnight, link arms with friends and family and sing in the new year to "Auld Lang Syne." Pop the corks and toast the year ahead. These games are great ice breakers for earlier on in the evening, but play them at any point or save them for New Year's Day. A session of karaoke might also add to the revelry!

TIP: *If any children are still up assemble them on the sofa and get them all to "jump" into the new year. (If they can't stay up until midnight, you could get them to do this in their pajamas earlier in the evening to your own countdown.)*

NOSTALGIA GAMES

Collect old school reports for all your guests and make photocopies of them. On these copies, obscure the identifying details of the pupil in question. Pass around the photocopies and have different guests read extracts aloud. Players should vote on who they think the report belongs to before the real recipient is revealed. For the second game, ask all your guests to bring a photograph of themselves as babies. Fix each photo to a pin board and number each one. On pieces of paper, against the numbers, guests should write down who they think is who.

GUESS MY RESOLUTION

Everyone writes down three of their New Year's resolutions on separate scraps of paper. The scraps are then folded up and thrown into a hat. One at a time, the resolutions are removed from the hat and read aloud. Players listen to each one and write down who they think it belongs to. At the end, everyone reveals their resolutions and then adds up how many of their own guesses were right. This is a fun way to share your hopes for the coming year.

NEW YEAR'S EVE AROUND THE WORLD

In China many traditional foods associated with luck or good fortune are served on New Year's Eve, such as a whole chicken, symbolizing family togetherness; noodles, representing long life; and spring rolls, which are supposed to indicate wealth as their shape is similar to gold bars.

There is an old folk tradition observed throughout Spain on New Year's Eve in which twelve grapes are eaten—one for each chime of the clock as it strikes midnight. This custom is thought to protect against witches and evil spirits and ensure twelve happy and prosperous months in the year ahead.

In Scotland and elsewhere in the UK, a widespread tradition called "first footing"—where the first friend or relative to cross the threshold after midnight brings symbolic gifts of coal, shortbread and whisky—is said to bring good fortune to the household for the coming year.

ROBERT BURNS

RARE PRINT COLLECTION

Some hae meat and canna eat,
An' some wad eat that want it,
We hae meat an' we can eat,
An' sae the Lord be thankit.

"Selkirk Grace", attributed to
Robert Burns

BURNS NIGHT

A Burns Night chapter may seem like an unusual addition to this book, but I have come to treasure Scotland, a land cloaked in nostalgia and history, as one of my favorite places. My love of the country stems from my days at Edinburgh University and is thanks to the hospitality of Scottish friends, who, in the spirit of their country's traditions, encouraged my enthusiasm for practices such as eating haggis, enjoying a Scottish reel or two and listening to nerve-tingling tunes on their bagpipes and fiddles. I read Scottish literature as part of my degree, and I grew to love Burns Night and its historical significance, as well as its warming, comforting components, from the rich colors of a clan tartan to a dram of amber whisky. There is also something about the Scottish countryside that feels wild and romantic: the moors and heather, lochs and burns, long windy walks and big open skies. Burns Night provides the opportunity to honor this epic and rugged landscape that has become like a second home to me.

Burns Night is the culmination of the Scottish winter festivals, which include St. Andrew's Day (celebrated on November 30) and Hogmanay (at New Year's), and also a great excuse to host a Scottish-themed evening. It celebrates the life and work of Robert Burns, widely regarded as Scotland's national poet. Burns was born in humble circumstances yet was highly skillful in his art, his work resonated with people at every level of society, and his desire to keep the Scottish language alive made him a symbol of his birthplace's national identity. The poet's friends first commemorated his contribution to Scottish culture soon after his death, and today Scots around the world mark the occasion on January 25th, mostly in the form of a supper.

My first experience of a Burns Night–inspired celebration was during my days at St. Andrew's prep school in Pangbourne. For lunch, meatloaf replaced the traditional haggis but we did have neeps and tatties (turnips and potatoes) with it, and one of the older pupils would deliver the seemingly age-old "Selkirk Grace," attributed to Burns. But it was in Edinburgh that I developed a real enthusiasm for this occasion. A few of us would arrange a Burns Night supper on an evening close to that date—it was our antidote to the winter blues and an opportunity to eat haggis to ward off the cold. Burns Night might be an institution of Scottish life, but, Scottish or not, you don't need a reason to toast the country's favorite poet and plan a Highland gathering. The format of the celebration largely depends on what you want to make of it: a black-tie affair that includes all the pomp of the night with bagpiping, toasts, speeches and dancing, or a simple supper (perhaps a Highland tea) at home with friends and family accompanied by a few poems from the Scottish bard's work.

BURNS NIGHT CRAFTS

A few homemade crafts will add personality to any Highland table. Make sure the palette of your yarns and materials is rich and warm, in keeping with the Scottish theme.

POMPOM THISTLES

Children will enjoy helping you make these. Stand single stems in a mismatch of small glass bottles and vases. Old blue, brown and clear drinks bottles that have had their labels dampened and peeled off are ideal.

I: For the pompoms, cut 2 identical disks from a piece of construction paper, 2 inches in diameter with a ¾-inch diameter hole in the center. Align the disks and wind yarn around them, through the hole, around the edge and back through the hole again, working continuously until they are completely covered and you can hardly wind any more through the center. 2: Snip the yarn along the outer edge of the disks. Pull the disks apart very slightly. 3: Cut two 8-inch lengths of leftover yarn. Wind them between the disks and knot tightly to secure the yarn. Remove the disks. 4: Take a twig and cover the top with craft glue, then push it into the pompom. Stick some dried leaves to the twig at the base of the pompom.

SCENTED TARTAN BAGS

These pretty fabric bags will add an instant touch of tartan to individual place settings. Fill them with your favorite potpourri or a few Scottish-inspired gifts, such as fudge, shortbread or a miniature bottle of whisky, for going-home gifts.

I: Cut a piece of tartan fabric into a 9-inch high x 6-inch wide rectangle. 2: Fold over ½ inch of fabric (on one of the longer sides) and sew a hem. Align the bottom edge of a 1-inch strip of lace with the stitching of the hem and sew onto the outside of the fabric. 3: Fold the fabric in half with the lace side facing inward, and, leaving the lace top open, sew the remaining two sides together. 4: Turn right side out and half fill with dried lavender or cedar balls (you can buy these in hardware and department stores). Tie a ribbon around the top.

RUSTIC NAME PLACES

These are quick and easy to make and the earthy materials add a touch of the country to the table. You can use different colored construction paper and replace the raffia string with thin tartan ribbon for variety.

I: Cut some construction paper into a 2¾-inch high x 4-inch wide rectangle. Fold in half lengthwise. Punch a hole through the top 2 corners just underneath the fold. 2: Tie the twig to the top of the construction paper using raffia, threading it through the holes, and making knots to secure it. 3: Write your guest's name on the front of the paper.

A HIGHLAND TEA

For a rustic Scottish tea, a tartan blanket laid over a table will add snugness and be fitting for a hearty spread for all ages: toast with marmalade, Scottish tablet (rather like fudge but with a grainier, more brittle texture), Millionaire's Shortbread and Drop Scones (page 205) dripping with butter and golden syrup or honey. Wash these down with a hot brew or, if it's really wet and windy outside, a hot toddy with heather honey will hit the spot (page 170). Chunky, earthy china is perfect for this occasion.

MILLIONAIRE'S SHORTBREAD Makes 24

This teatime morsel is a decadent three-layered treat that provides a perfect pick-me-up. For bite-size versions (great to serve as a sweet canapé), this recipe will make about 40.

Preheat the oven to 325°F. Lightly grease a 9 x 13-inch oblong jelly roll pan.

For the shortbread base, place 2 cups of all-purpose flour, ½ cup of superfine sugar and 2 sticks of unsalted butter in a food processor and blend together to form a smooth dough. Press the mixture into the base of the pan and prick with a fork. Chill for 15 minutes before baking in the oven for 25 to 30 minutes until golden and firm. Set aside to cool.

To make the topping, place 1¾ sticks of unsalted butter, 1 cup of superfine sugar, 3 tablespoons of golden syrup or honey and a 14-ounce can of condensed milk in a saucepan and stir over low heat until the butter melts. Turn the heat up to medium, bring to a boil and then cook the mixture gently for 5 to 8 minutes, stirring constantly to prevent scorching, until thick and golden brown. Pour evenly over the cold shortbread and leave to cool. Melt 7 ounces of chopped dark chocolate in a bowl over a pot of simmering water. Pour the chocolate over the cooled toffee and place in the fridge to set. Remove from the pan and carefully cut into squares. Store in an airtight jar for up to a week.

TIP: *To make Shortbread Hearts, use the above recipe for the shortbread base and roll out the dough thinly before cutting into hearts and baking for 20 to 25 minutes at 325°F. This makes about 24 cookies.*

A SCOTTISH TABLE

For a Burns Night supper, choose a warm and romantic place for your table: a fireside spot is welcoming and the amber glow will complement the earthy components of the feast. If you're having a more informal gathering in your kitchen, you'll still need plenty of flickering candlelight on this cold January night to make everyone feel as if you were all tucked up inside a croft in the depths of the Scottish hills. A plaid scarf or strips of tartan fabric work well as table runners. If you're after something more subtle, use a tartan ribbon tied around a white napkin, a set of tartan napkins or a tartan lavender bag (page 154) at each place. This will set the color scheme for the flowers and other table accessories. Thistles are emblematic of Scotland and ideal for a centerpiece, mixed with purple and white poppy anemones and green foliage. Arranged in a small vase, they will add a lovely feminine touch to this rather masculine affair. Use whisky-colored tumblers for water, warm colored candles, and old bone-handled knives in keeping with the Highland theme.

A CLASSIC BURNS NIGHT

The traditional supper celebration consists of several courses: soup; then haggis; perhaps a Steak Pie (page 70), which is great if you are serving the haggis as a starter or canapé; followed by a dessert or cheese. You can put your own contemporary twists on the food or just choose a menu that celebrates Scottish produce, as long as haggis features at some stage. The likelihood is that you'll want your Burns Night supper to be an intimate, cozy gathering after the more sociable Christmas celebrations of the previous month, so the recipes each serve four.

BURNS NIGHT MENU

Starter
Cullen Skink

Main course
Haggis and Clapshot

Dessert
Cranachan

BURNS NIGHT RUNNING ORDER

THE "SELKIRK GRACE" This short but important prayer is read to usher in the meal.

PIPING IN THE HAGGIS The haggis is ceremonially carried to the table by the cook, accompanied by a lone bagpiper. One guest will be responsible for reading the Robert Burns poem "Address to a Haggis."

TOAST TO THE HAGGIS During the reading the haggis will be cut, traditionally by making a St. Andrew's cross-shaped incision at its center. At the end of the recital, toasts are made to the haggis.

TOAST TO THE LASSIES Toasts are also made to the "lassies" to thank them for preparing the food (Burns was renowned to be fond of women). This is followed by a cheeky response from one of the lassies.

THE IMMORTAL MEMORY Often one of the central features of the evening, this is a lighthearted account of the life and works of Burns (like a best man's speech).

SONGS AND DANCING Burns songs and poems, and some traditional Scottish reeling music should come after the toasts.

"AULD LANG SYNE" The evening concludes with a rousing rendition of this song, which was written by Burns, during which all the guests join hands and sing together.

CULLEN SKINK

Usually Cock-A-Leekie (chicken and leek) soup is served on Burns Night, but Cullen Skink is a delicious alternative, as a starter or light main course. Originally from the fishing village of Cullen in northeast Scotland ("skink" is the Scots word for soup), it has a delicate flavor, and the smoked haddock provides a distinctive warming scent that is just perfect on a wintry night.

SERVES 4

14 ounces undyed smoked haddock, skin on, boned

2½ cups milk

1 tablespoon butter

1 medium onion, peeled and chopped

1 medium leek, chopped, green parts removed

14 ounces potatoes, peeled and diced

2 bay leaves

3½ ounces canned corn

sea salt and freshly ground black pepper

2 tablespoons chives or parsley, chopped

Cover the smoked haddock with the milk and butter in a saucepan, skin side down. Bring to a boil and simmer for 4 to 5 minutes, until cooked.

With a slotted spoon, remove the haddock from the pan and discard the skin and any bones you find. Break up the fish into flakes, then set aside. Add the onion, leek, potatoes and bay leaves to the reserved cooking liquid and simmer for 20 to 25 minutes.

When the potatoes are tender, remove the bay leaves and add the fish and corn to the pan. Simmer over low heat for 2 to 3 minutes until the fish is warmed through, then taste and season with salt and pepper. Serve immediately, garnished with chopped chives or parsley for a fresher taste.

 A delicate Manzanilla sherry complements this salty dish.

TIPS: *Finnan haddock is traditionally used in this soup—it has a light smoky taste. Smoked haddock is a great substitute and is more readily available. • You can use quartered new potatoes, and mash them into the broth to thicken the soup. • If using parsley leaves to garnish, use the stalk in the poaching milk first to freshen the taste of the dish. • Other hearty Scottish soups you could serve include Scotch broth, which consists of beef, barley and vegetables, or tattie (potato) soup.*

THE HAGGIS

Fair fa' your honest, sonsie face,
Great chieftain o' the pudding-race!
Aboon them a'ye tak your place,
Painch, tripe, or thairm:
Weel are ye wordy o' a grace
As lang's my arm.

"Address to a Haggis," Robert Burns

This Scottish delicacy is the focal point of a Burns Night supper, thanks to the poet's 1786 poem "Address to a Haggis." It consists of a mixture of the minced heart, lungs and liver of a sheep or calf mixed with beef fat, onions, oatmeal and seasonings, and is traditionally encased in a sheep's stomach, but is now more frequently produced using a synthetic skin, making it more appealing. Its nutty, wholesome taste is really unique, and steeping it in whisky or a rich whisky-based cream gives it that extra hearty flavor.

If haggis isn't your thing, you can find veggie alternatives or make your own vegetarian haggis using beans, nuts and oatmeal. The traditional accompaniments to haggis are neeps and tatties. Neeps (turnips) are known in England as swede, and tatties are potatoes. Alternatively, serve haggis in canapé form for a Scottish cocktail party.

OTHER WAYS WITH HAGGIS

- *Haggis doesn't have to be only for Burns Night; enjoy it year-round by storing it in the freezer.*

- *To save time, cook haggis by removing its casing, chopping roughly and microwaving for 6 minutes, stirring occasionally until piping hot.*

- *Fry a slice of haggis and serve it for breakfast with a poached egg on top.*

- *One of my great friends has a signature dish of chicken breast stuffed with haggis and wrapped in bacon. It keeps the chicken moist and bulks it up.*

- *Sprinkle haggis into the ground meat in a shepherd's pie or lasagna for a nutty taste.*

- *Mix haggis into sausage meat to make haggis Sausage Rolls (page 340), or use instead of mushrooms in a Beef Wellington (page 190).*

art your evening off with bite-size samples of haggis (allow 3 per person). I had some similar napés recently at a friend's wedding and everyone, Scottish or not, loved them.

AGGIS PARCELS Makes 12

ook 8 ounces of haggis and make 1 cup of whisky sauce (page 164). Cut 6 sheets of phyllo stry into quarters. Melt 3 tablespoons of unsalted butter. Take ¼ of the pastry and brush th melted butter, place another quarter on top and brush again with butter. Mix the oked haggis with 4 ounces of whisky sauce. Scoop a little of the prepared haggis mixture to the center of the pastry, brush the edges with melted butter and wrap the pastry up so at it gathers at the top, then twist gently to close. Transfer the prepared parcels to a baking eet lined with parchment paper and bake in a preheated oven at 350°F for 10 to 12 inutes, or until golden brown and crisp. Serve with the remaining whisky sauce alongside.

AGGIS CROUSTADES Makes 12

ook 8 ounces of haggis and make ½ cup of whisky sauce (page 164). Roll out 6 crustless ces of white bread as thinly as possible. Using a 2¼-inch round cutter, cut the bread to 12 circles. Brush a mini muffin tin with olive oil, then press the bread circles into the n and brush each with a little olive oil. Season with salt and pepper, and bake in a 350°F en for 8 to 10 minutes or until golden and crisp. Remove the baked croustades from the n and allow to cool, then spoon a teaspoonful of the cooked haggis mixture inside and rnish each with a little whisky sauce, red-onion marmalade (page 388) and chives to serve.

HAGGIS AND CLAPSHOT

2 pounds good-quality haggis

For the clapshot

10½ ounces neeps (turnips), quartered

1 pound tatties (potatoes), quartered

7 tablespoons unsalted butter

sea salt and freshly ground black pepper

¼ cup heavy cream

WHISKY SAUCE

Gently heat 3 tablespoons of whisky in a small pan until the alcohol evaporates. Add 1½ cups of heavy cream and stir to combine. Add 2 teaspoons of whole-grain mustard (optional), and then season to taste. Reduce over medium heat until the sauce has thickened. This makes enough for 4 with the haggis recipe on this page. Halve the amounts to make enough for the haggis phyllo parcel canapés (page 163) and quarter them to make ½ cup for the haggis croustades (page 163).

To cook the haggis, bring a large pot of water to a boil, add the haggis, then reduce the heat and allow it to simmer for 50 minutes, topping up with water if it runs low. Always check the packet instructions or with your butcher as cooking times may vary (you can also microwave it, see page 162).

Meanwhile, bring two saucepans of salted water to a boil. Put the neeps (turnips) in one pan and the tatties (potatoes) in the other. Reduce the heat and cook both for 20 to 25 minutes. When the neeps and tatties are tender, drain the water. Return the neeps to one pan, add half of the butter and mash until chunky. Season to taste and keep warm. In the other pan, mash the tatties with the cream until smooth. Season to taste and keep warm.

When the haggis is cooked, make the clapshot by mixing together the neeps and the tatties. Spoon the clapshot into four chef's rings on your warmed serving plates until three-quarters full, and press down. Cut open the cooked haggis, and fill each chef's ring to the brim. Remove the rings and drizzle whisky sauce (see box) around each plate. Serve with a shot of whisky on the side. Alternatively, simply spoon a portion of haggis onto each plate, put the neeps and tatties beside the haggis, pour over a little whisky sauce, and serve.

Hearty, southern French reds such as Côtes du Rhône.

TIP: *For an indulgent twist, cover the clapshot with grated cheese and bake in the oven for what is known as "Orkney Clapshot."*

CRANACHAN

A classic Scottish dessert, Cranachan was traditionally served as several separate bowls containing each ingredient so that each person could assemble their dessert according to their own taste. Served in layers in stemmed glasses, this is a visual treat.

SERVES 4

½ cup old-fashioned rolled oats

1¼ cups heavy cream

2 tablespoons Scottish whisky

3 tablespoons honey

8 ounces raspberries

Heat a frying pan over medium heat and lightly toast the oats for a few minutes, shaking the pan frequently, until they have turned golden brown. Remove the oats from the pan and set aside until completely cool.

In a bowl, lightly whip the heavy cream with the whisky and 2 tablespoons of the honey until it forms soft peaks and just holds its shape.

When you are ready to serve, assemble the cranachan. Don't make this too far in advance or the oats will lose their crunch. Divide half of the raspberries among 4 small serving glasses. Spoon half of the cream over them and then scatter some oats over each, reserving a few for the topping. Make another layer of raspberries and cream, and then sprinkle the remainder of the toasted oats on top and drizzle the remaining honey over each glass.

TIP: *"Tipsy Laird" is a Scottish trifle often served on Burns Night. To make this, follow the recipe on page 238, using soft ladyfingers for the base and replacing the sherry with 6 tablespoons of whisky.*

WHISKY COCKTAILS

With encouragement from whisky-loving friends, I have slowly come around to the taste of whisky, but for those less inclined to drink it straight, a few whisky-based cocktails wouldn't go amiss. When making these go for a blended whisky and save special single malts for unadulterated sipping, with just a splash or two of water, if anything. Rocking glasses with balloon bases are fun and different; as they roll around on a hard surface they will release the bouquet of the whisky.

ATHOLL BROSE
Makes 3 cups

Somewhere between a drink and a dessert, especially when cream is added on festive occasions. Put 1 cup of instant oatmeal and 1¼ cups of water in a bowl and stir until they form a thick paste. Allow the mixture to stand for 20 minutes, then strain to separate the liquid from the oatmeal. Discard the oatmeal. Mix the liquid with 5 ounces of honey, and stir until well blended. Pour this into a bottle, top off with 2 cups of whisky and seal the bottle. Shake vigorously, then leave to stand. Shake again before serving, adding a dash of cream to the glasses if you like.

TIP : *For those with a sweeter tooth, substitute Drambuie liqueur for the whisky.*

FLYING SCOTSMAN Serves I (make to order)

A fine, delicate cocktail served in a martini glass. Pour 2 ounces of whisky, I ounce of sweet vermouth, I tablespoon of sugar syrup (page 80) and a couple of dashes of Angostura bitters into a cocktail shaker with ice cubes and squeeze in the juice of ¼ of a lemon. Shake well, then strain into a chilled glass. Garnish with a lemon twist (page 80). Great for after dinner, this drink was inspired by the famous *Flying Scotsman* train, which carried passengers between Edinburgh and London.

ROB ROY Serves I (make to order)

This is drier than the Flying Scotsman. Stir 2½ ounces of whisky, I ounce of sweet vermouth and 2 dashes of Angostura bitters in a cocktail shaker filled with ice cubes. Shake well and strain into a chilled martini glass and garnish with a maraschino cherry in the bottom of the glass.

WHISKY SOUR Serves I (make to order)

Although this is an American cocktail made with bourbon and not typical for Burns Night, I have a soft spot for this one. Shake I½ ounces of bourbon, I½ ounces of lemon juice, I tablespoon of sugar syrup (page 80), a dash of Angostura bitters and I egg white in a shaker filled with ice cubes. Shake well. Serve in short glasses, garnish with a lemon peel and a maraschino cherry.

AFTER SUPPER

Burns Night is traditionally associated with Scottish dancing and bagpipes, but it's also known for toasts, reciting poetry and making speeches. The night is dedicated to Robert Burns after all, so a recital of his greatest poems is fitting. For the more energetic, try some Scottish reeling and, of course, a rendition of his most famous song "Auld Lang Syne" (see page 150 if you need a prompt!). For the less lively, a quiet game of cards with a whisky will round off the evening nicely.

POETRY RECITALS

Many of Burns's poems have a lovely story behind them. "Tam o' Shanter" tells the tale of a man who lingered too long at a public house, but "Scotch Drink" is also ideal for an after-supper recital if you've all been imbibing the water of life! Other great poems to read aloud include "A Red, Red Rose" or "To a Mouse," which Burns allegedly wrote after disturbing a mouse's nest in a field he was plowing and that inspired the title of Steinbeck's famous novel *Of Mice and Men* ("the best laid schemes o' mice an' men/gang aft agley").

Let other poets raise a fracas
'Bout vines, an' wines, an' drucken Bacchus,
An' crabbit names an' stories wrack us,
An' grate our lug:
I sing the juice Scotch bear can mak us,
In glass or jug.

O thou, my Muse! guid auld Scotch drink!
Whether thro' wimplin worms thou jink,
Or, richly brown, ream owre the brink,
In glorious faem,
Inspire me, till I lisp an' wink,
To sing thy name!
"Scotch Drink," Robert Burns

WHISKY: THE WATER OF LIFE

A whisky tasting can add another dimension to your Burns Night supper and is a great way to begin or end the evening. Scotch malt whiskies are classified by five regions: Highland, Speyside, Campbeltown, Lowland and Islay. They are so different and varied, even a sniff can be powerfully evocative. Alternatively, a hot toddy or Whisky Mac is the perfect nightcap.

For 1 hot toddy: Place 1½ ounces of whisky, 1½ tablespoons of honey and ½ cup of boiled water from a kettle in a saucepan. Add a slice of lemon, 1 cinnamon stick and 1 clove, and heat gently until the drink is warmed through, then remove the spices and serve immediately.

For 1 Whisky Mac: Mix equal quantities of Scotch whisky and ginger liqueur; serve hot or cold.

THE PARTY CUPBOARD

Closets, drawers or boxes should be packed full of useful odds and ends so you always have the basics at hand for spontaneous celebrations. You can find most of what you need at large supermarkets or online from party stores; buy discounted items just after a seasonal event such as Halloween, Easter or Christmas and save the items for the following year. Get in the habit of clearing out your supply areas once in a while. If you keep things organized, it's amazing how many items can be stored using the minimum amount of space.

THE PRESENT DRAWER

Create a go-to place for all your wrapping essentials and last-minute gifts. Keep an eye out throughout the year for things to add to it — you might spot the ideal present for someone, which you can save until the appropriate time. Support small stores in towns you might be visiting and use them as sources for homemade gifts, such as marmalades, olive oils, cookies and regional specialties, as well as odds and ends for the home.

TIP: *Tie a length of wide, colorful ribbon through rolls of different kinds of tape so you never lose them. All you have to do is remember to put the scissors and tape right back where you found them, for the next person.*

PRESENT DRAWER CHECKLIST

- **Wrapping paper:** *old and new, scraps of fabric, drawer liners and assorted colored tissue paper. Keep in gift-wrap storage bags and boxes.*

- **Scissors:** *sharp-bladed scissors to cut wrapping paper in one sweeping movement.*

- **Padded envelopes and bubble wrap:** *for sending and protecting fragile gifts.*

- **Sticky tape:** *use transparent tape and a desktop (or wrist) tape dispenser, which is ideal to wrap lots of presents at a time. Double-sided sticky tape is useful for tape-free presentation and patterned printed tape to jazz up plain paper.*

- **Ribbons:** *different widths and materials, e.g., wide satin, raffia and organza. Curling ribbon and string are inexpensive.*

- **Gift boxes and bags:** *a selection of sizes, including some for bottles, are useful for odd shapes that are tricky to wrap.*

- **Gift cards and envelopes:** *have a selection of birthday cards as well as blank cards that can be used for any occasion.*

- **Emergency gifts:** *scented candles and bath stuff; homemade jams and chutneys (pages 386–9) are lovely presents for supper parties.*

- **Gift tags:** *have a variety of themed tags as well as luggage-type brown-paper ones.*

WRAPPING IT UP

A well-wrapped gift helps express how much thought you've put into it. Don't forget to remove the price tag from the gift and if the packaging isn't attractive, put it in a box with loosely scrunched-up tissue paper or shredded tissue and a sprinkling of confetti. To achieve a perfect bow on the top, ideally the present should be a box shape or have hard edges. Gift bags are useful to disguise difficult or messy wrapping.

1 : Place the present on the paper to gauge how much you will need, then cut to length. 2 : Keep the seams and folds of the paper underneath the present, and stick down neatly with tape so the top is seamless. Fold the end flaps into a "V" shape and stick down neatly with tape. 3 : Wrap a long piece of ribbon around the top of the present lengthwise, then turn the present over and wrap the ribbon around it widthwise to form a cross. 4 : Turn it back over again so the seamless side is facing up and tie the ribbon in a neat bow (trim the ends, if necessary; for silk or luxury ribbons make a neat "V" and for curling ribbon pull between your thumb and scissors blade to curl). If you don't have enough ribbon for this, simply tie the ribbon widthwise. 5 : Attach your gift tag to the bow with your ribbon.

TIP : *Other decorative wrapping ideas include colored pompoms, feathers, charms, large buttons, bells, adhesive gift bows, fake flowers or any other items you can think of that are appropriate to the occasion or season.*

THRIFTY WRAPPING IDEAS

Sometimes you might want to get more creative with your wrapping (particularly if you've run out of gift wrap!).

- *For a personal touch, use the recipient's favorite magazine, old maps, calendar pictures, comics or newspaper as wrapping paper. For example, the pink pages of the Financial Times, tied with black ribbon, will look great.*

- *Brown parcel paper (craft paper) is cheap and chic in a minimalist way when coupled with colored or patterned ribbon or rickrack. You can also decorate it by potato printing, using an ink block and stamps or stickers. If you're feeling thrifty, recycle old wrapping paper (as long as it was opened carefully the first time), long pieces of ribbon, gift bags and boxes from past Christmases and birthdays, and save old jewelry boxes.*

- *Wrapping a present in a scrap of fabric using Japanese-style origami folds and tying with ribbon is both ecofriendly and pretty. Use pinking shears to cut the required size of material. Hold the fabric in place using double-sided tape and tie loose ends with ribbon. If you have a sewing machine, you can make pretty bags for presents (page 154) from fabric ends and cheap material, such as ticking.*

- *Try cutting out images, colored letters, numbers and illustrations from magazines and saving them in an envelope to make gift tags with, or to stick onto plain card. Buying a tag cutter will give a professional finish.*

PARTY CUPBOARD ESSENTIALS

These supplies are good to have on hand for celebrations as well as more general equipment for entertaining (page 78), be it an impromptu birthday party, farewell, reunion or baby shower.

- **Bunting and banners:** *homemade bunting (page 246) is charming; collect banners for all occasions: "Happy Birthday," "Welcome Home," etc.*

- **Cake accessories:** *candles, indoor sparklers, cupcake wrappers, flags, cake decorations, doilies, fold-away cake stand, cake boxes and boards.*

- **Balloons and balloon weights:** *in different colors and materials (clear, foil, numbers and themed). For helium balloons, check how many balloons your canister will fill when purchasing it.*

- **Curling ribbon and confetti:** *ribbon is good value and useful for balloons. Themed confetti and clear gems can be sprinkled along tables.*

- **Tablecloths, runners, napkins and place mats:** *in both paper and linen (napkins and place mats on a roll are very useful). Stock up on blank place cards and holders with clips to affix them.*

- **Bulk packs of tea lights and candles:** *battery-operated ones are good for outdoor parties, and ecofriendly sky lanterns are also fun.*

- **Games and accessories:** *board games, dice, playing cards and table trivia.*

- **Table favors:** *miniature bottles of bubbles, party poppers and streamers.*

THE CRAFT TOOLBOX

Craft materials needn't be expensive. Markets are useful for cheap fabrics and garage sales can be treasure troves. For reliability, craft stores or art shops have the best range, and sell useful all-in-one kits.

- **Pens and pencils:** *silver and gold, calligraphy and glass pens, fabric markers, crayons and colored pencils.*

- **Glue:** *glue stick works quickly on most papers and card stock; craft glue is better for tissue paper and large-scale projects.*

- **Paints and paintbrushes:** *acrylics, poster paints (mix with craft glue and water for découpage); at least three good-quality paintbrushes of various sizes.*

- **Colored paper, card stock and glitter:** *for homemade cards and paper hats.*

- **Sewing kit, yarn, buttons and safety pins.**

- **Pinking shears and X-acto knife:** *pinking shears will save you having to hem fabrics.*

- **Hammer and nails, straight pins, tape measure, string, fishing and gardening wire:** *for making and hanging decorations.*

TIPS: *Pick up wooden stirring sticks from coffee shops and keep jam jars or saucers for mixing paints. • A glue gun can be a good investment and a laminator can also be useful for signs and homemade place mats. • Store craft materials in clear containers to locate them at a glance; group similar items together.*

TIP: *For a costume party, get every guest to bring a costume and accessories in a black trash bag. Pile them all together, ask each guest to pick a bag before supper and put on the outfit they find inside. Alternatively, host a party where everyone has to come wearing some sort of hat.*

THE DRESS-UP BOX

Dressing up is all about small details — perhaps just a simple accessory you wear or carry — but humor and plenty of imagination are essential. You can find lots of inspiration and amazing all-in-one outfits online and in costume stores but these can be expensive. Old clothes in black, white or block colors can be a base for pretty much any costume (add variety with stripes, spots and animal prints). I have a substantial collection of dress-up items under my bed, which always comes in useful along the way. Save old clothes you no longer wear that have something authentic about them, such as uniforms or retro fashion items, and search charity stores for any bargains. Here are some ideas for a basic dress-up box suited to a variety of occasions.

- **Old pillowcases, fabric and sheets:** *cut up to form base layers. Use a stretchy belt and safety pins to give them structure.*

- **Colored tights, fishnets, leggings, old pajama bottoms and tartan kilts:** *these are all useful for a variety of costumes.*

- **Wire coat hangers:** *for wings, halos and antennae (if you're really creative!).*

- **Accessories:** *sunglasses, long gloves, scarves, faux fur, vests, suspenders, microphone, feather boa, grass skirts and lei, leg warmers, fake flowers, cape, bandannas, bow ties, fairy wings.*

- **Sparkle:** *tinsel, hair accessories, body glitter, glow-stick jewelry and clip-on jewelry.*

- **Disguises:** *masks, wigs, face paints and stencils, fake tattoos, eye-patches, mustaches and beards, animal ears, dry shampoo (for gray hair), colored hair spray and styling gel.*

- **Cotton wool or batting:** *for snow, white beards or hair, sheep's wool.*

- **Hats:** *bowler, beret, straw boater and panama, or pirate, cowboy and other themed hats.*

SPRING

VALENTINE'S DAY
SPECIAL BREAKFASTS
EASTER
AFTERNOON TEA

Freshness cuts through the gloom. March winds blow and unpredictable April showers bring renewal and growth. Bulbs break hard ground and drifts of snowdrops with pearly heads thrust up through heavy clods of earth. Buds appear on trees, birds sing joyfully and young lambs stay close to their mothers. Cherry blossoms hang in clouds and swaths of spring blooms scatter like colorful sweets.

Saint Valentine, who is so high aloft,
The little birds sing thus for your delight:
The winter weather you have put to flight,
And driven off the season of black night.

"The Parliament of Birds," Geoffrey Chaucer

VALENTINE'S DAY

The custom of choosing a valentine first came into existence in Europe in the fourteenth century and was inspired by the belief that birds started mating on this day, described most famously by Geoffrey Chaucer in his poem "The Parliament of Birds." It is referred to in parts of Sussex as the "Birds' Wedding Day." The romantic festival of Valentine's Day continued to grow in popularity in Victorian times. Even now, in the run-up to February 14th, every store window is awash with red and pink—a sea of cards, flowers, hearts and balloons, bringing color to this cold, dark month. However, Saint Valentine is a figure lost in the mists of time and very little is known about his life, let alone why he lends his name to this day associated with romance.

Valentine's Day should be a chance to prioritize time with your loved ones without everyday distractions. Treat your family to dainty heart-shaped foods: use a mold to fry an egg, cut shapes out of your toast for breakfast in bed, or make heart-shaped cookies (page 157). Traditionally, the custom on Valentine's Day was to exchange love notes called Valentines, which, by the mid-eighteenth century, were mostly in the form of handmade cards decorated with expensive materials, such as lace or satin. This is still the time of year when mailboxes are crammed with exciting crimson envelopes, and lovingly crafted cards (page 180) are better than any store-bought gift. Similarly, flowers are a traditional Valentine's token, and red roses are the classic symbol of romance, be it a dozen hand tied in a beautiful bouquet or simply a single stem. However, if you are willing to experiment, there are lots of lovely spring flowers and bulbs that make sweet and thoughtful gifts and which convey a variety of messages (page 264).

As evening falls, this is a time for grown-ups to slow down and enjoy time together, whiling away a wintry night with special food and conversation. An occasion like this could also be used to celebrate something in your lives together, to convey a heartfelt message, to say thank you—or to apologize. A supper for two at home is a cozy way to celebrate and gives scope for individuality and romance on a day that is no longer synonymous with spontaneity. If it's the two of you, you won't want to spend the whole evening in the kitchen slaving away—this is the time to prepare easy foods ahead of time, while keeping the ingredients luxurious and special. It might be things that you both love but don't get to eat that often. After all, the way to a lover's heart is through the stomach, so they say . . .

MADE WITH LOVE...

Candles, hearts and lovebirds are all traditionally associated with romance. These are lovely, simple crafts to make with children in the run-up to Valentine's Day.

HEART BUTTON CARDS

If you run out of buttons, collect other bits and pieces to decorate your cards: stickers, sequins, doilies, glitter, flowers or feathers. Find loving sentiments in poems and story books to put inside and finish with a ribbon bow.

I : Make a heart template. Place it on a piece of folded construction paper and draw around it in pencil. 2 : Using a needle and thread, stitch from the back of the card to the front, securing the thread with a small piece of tape. 3 : Sew the buttons to the card around the outline using a running stitch, with the buttons slightly overlapping. Fasten the end of your thread, as before. 4 : Using a glue stick, cover the thread inside the card with a plain piece of paper, cut to size.

LAVENDER HEARTS

Pretty fabric hearts nestled under pillows or hung on doorknobs outside bedrooms are charming.

I : With fabric (from old tablecloths or floral, romantic designs) facedown, draw 2 heart shapes, using a template. Cut both with pinking shears. 2 : Place front and back together (right sides out) and sew three quarters of the way around. (If you don't have pinking shears, sew with the right sides together and then turn right side out.) 3 : Add 8 teaspoons of dried lavender and continue sewing until completely sealed. Sew on a ribbon bow.

LACE-PAPER LANTERN JARS

Place these tea-light holders on side tables and in bedrooms for a pretty flickering light, or use as vases for delicate flowers.

I : Take a selection of different-sized glass jars and a packet of paper doilies. 2 : Cut out the prettiest part of the doily, wrap it around the jar and stick down with craft glue. 3 : Tie a ribbon around the neck of the jar and put a tea light inside.

PEANUT BIRD TREATS

According to folklore, it was thought that the first bird an unmarried woman saw on this day would provide an insight into her future husband's character. Hang these outside for the birds to nibble on.

I : Twist a length of thick gardening wire into a heart shape, with an inch left at each end. 2 : Pierce through the middle of each peanut shell with a skewer or thick needle. 3 : Thread the nuts onto the wire, reshape the heart and hook the ends together at the top. 4 : Tie a length of raffia around the top of the heart in a bow to hang the nuts from.

TABLE FOR TWO

Like many of the celebrations in this book, a Valentine's supper needn't be on the day itself; in fact, you could have your own romantic candlelit supper for two on any date throughout the year. To me, a candlelit supper at home beats jostling for elbow room in a couple-crammed restaurant over a romantic set menu hands down. The main dishes serve two but can easily be doubled or tripled for dinner with friends. Prepare as much of the menu as you can in advance so you can enjoy the evening without fussing too much in the kitchen.

VALENTINE'S MENU

Starters
Oysters *or*
Gravlax

Main course
Beef Wellington

Desserts
Raspberry Soufflé *or*
Chocolate Fondant
∞∞
Chocolate Truffles

If you often eat dinner at home, just the two of you, set the table somewhere you don't normally dine. A small table for two can be laid pretty much anywhere around your house. Fold away the extensions on your table, and take away extra chairs or use a smaller side table covered with a white cloth and have plenty of illumination in the form of tea lights, scented candles and firelight. Vary the color of the candles from rose pink to white and red, standing them in modern glass and antique-style holders. Finish with a delicate bunch of seasonal scented flowers. As well as sweet-smelling roses, other flowers renowned for their scent are freesias and stocks, paperwhite (narcissus) and hyacinth bulbs (plant with moss and twigs for a pretty centerpiece).

OYSTERS

I always associate eating oysters with special occasions, so what better time to have them than on Valentine's Day? Opening them can be quite a feat, so they are best served when there's only a couple of you to enjoy them. I like shucking them myself, but it helps if you have a good oyster knife to do this. To protect your hands and stop the knife slipping off the shell, use a mesh glove or a tea towel.

SERVES 2

6 live oysters

3 tablespoons red wine or sherry vinegar

1 shallot, finely chopped

To serve

lemon wedges

Tabasco

Irish soda bread and salted butter

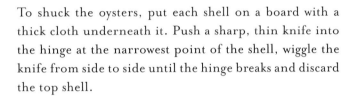

To shuck the oysters, put each shell on a board with a thick cloth underneath it. Push a sharp, thin knife into the hinge at the narrowest point of the shell, wiggle the knife from side to side until the hinge breaks and discard the top shell.

Run the knife around the oyster itself, and scrape the ligament free that joins the meat to the shell. Remove any grit or shell. Take care to retain the wonderful juice, known as liquor, inside the shell.

Put each prepared oyster on a platter on a bed of ice, cover with a damp cloth and refrigerate until needed. It's best to eat these as fresh as possible, so don't prepare too far in advance.

To serve, mix the vinegar and shallot together and serve in a small bowl alongside the oysters, with lemon wedges, Tabasco sauce, some Irish soda bread (page 189) and salty butter.

Crisp chilled whites like Chablis or a light Muscadet.

TIPS : *Make sure the shells are firmly shut or that they shut immediately when tapped. ● Save the oyster shells, wash them thoroughly and use them as salt and pepper dishes, place card settings or as serving dishes for canapés.*

GRAVLAX WITH DILL MUSTARD SAUCE

A good recipe to prepare ahead because it needs to cure for one to two days, this is delicious with cucumber pickle and dill mustard sauce, but set aside some other garnishes to sprinkle over, such as finely chopped shallots and capers. Serve with slices of homemade soda bread (page 189), or store-bought blinis warmed in the oven.

WHOLE CURED FISH SERVES 10–12

one 1½-pound skinless, boneless organic farmed salmon filet

4 teaspoons coarse sea salt

3 teaspoons superfine sugar

1 large handful finely chopped fresh chives, cilantro and dill

peel of 1 lemon and 1 orange

1 tablespoon crushed coriander seeds

1 tablespoon crushed mixed peppercorns

2 tablespoons gin

For the dill mustard sauce

2 tablespoons Dijon mustard

2 egg yolks

2 teaspoons sugar

pinch of salt

1 tablespoon white wine vinegar

⅓ cup sunflower oil

1 small bunch fresh dill, finely chopped

For the cucumber pickle

½ cucumber, seeded

1 tablespoon superfine sugar

splash of rice wine vinegar

sea salt and freshly ground black pepper

To cure the fish, put the salt, sugar, chives, cilantro and dill, lemon peel, orange peel, coriander seeds, peppercorns and gin in a food processor and pulse to combine. Spread the mixture over the salmon, using most on the top, but covering the sides and the underneath too. Tightly wrap in plastic wrap, place on a plate and apply a weight to the top of the fish. Refrigerate for 1 to 2 days.

To make the sauce, mix the mustard, egg yolks, sugar, salt and vinegar together. Slowly whisk in the oil until the sauce is smooth, then stir in the dill.

To make the cucumber pickle, peel and thinly slice the cucumber into strips, using a vegetable peeler or mandoline. Place the sugar and vinegar in a saucepan and heat until the sugar has dissolved. Remove from the heat. When cold, add the cucumber, season with salt and pepper and leave to marinate for at least 1 hour.

When you are ready to plate the fish, brush off most of the curing mixture from the fish and pat it dry. With a long, sharp knife, carefully carve thin diagonal slivers off the salmon. Serve the gravlax with slices of soda bread, capers and diced shallots, with a little cucumber pickle on top and the sauce drizzled over it.

Fino sherry, white Burgundy or rosé Champagne all go well with cured fish.

TIP: *There are likely to be leftovers, so enjoy gravlax for a special breakfast with scrambled eggs or as a light lunch with warm baby new potatoes dressed with the dill mustard sauce. It will keep in the fridge for a week.*

SODA BREAD WITH PARMESAN

This bread is delicious on its own as a snack or with any starter alongside a good quality olive oil for dunking and some flakes of sea salt.

MAKES ONE MEDIUM LOAF

2 cups whole-wheat bread flour, plus extra for dusting

½ teaspoon salt

1 teaspoon baking soda

1 teaspoon baking powder

large handful of fresh chopped herbs, such as thyme, rosemary and sage

2 ounces mixed pumpkin and sunflower seeds

2 ounces Parmesan, grated

10 ounces plain yogurt or buttermilk

For the topping

1 ounce Parmesan, grated

2 teaspoons mixed pumpkin and sunflower seeds

Preheat the oven to 400°F.

Place the flour, salt, baking soda and baking powder into a large bowl together with the chopped herbs, mixed seeds and Parmesan. Mix it all together then make a well in the center and pour in most of the buttermilk or yogurt, leaving about 2 oz in the measuring cup.

Using one hand, bring the flour and liquid together, adding more buttermilk if necessary. Do not knead the mixture or it will become heavy. The dough should be fairly soft, but not too wet and sticky. When it has just come together, turn the dough out on to a floured work surface and work it a little, then gently pat the dough into a round about 1½ inches deep. Cut a deep cross in the top and sprinkle over the Parmesan and mixed seeds.

Place the dough on to a baking sheet and bake in the preheated oven for 15 minutes, then turn down the heat to 300°F and cook for another 30 minutes. The loaf should sound slightly hollow when tapped on the base and be golden in color. Allow to cool on a wire rack for 5 minutes, then serve warm.

TIP: *Once baked and cooled, the loaf can be frozen, wrapped in plastic wrap, for up to 1 month. Defrost thoroughly before eating.*

BEEF WELLINGTON

A charming twist on a classic, this parcel for two is a real luxury—and it can be made in advance so your clothes won't smell of cooking and you can get yourself ready safe in the knowledge that dinner just needs a quick blast in the oven. Serve simply with roasted cherry tomatoes, store-bought French fries in the middle of the table to share, a dressed green salad and a quick Béarnaise—the steak is the star of the show here.

2 tablespoons unsalted butter

3½ ounces mixed mushrooms, finely chopped

sea salt and freshly ground black pepper

6 ounces coarse pâté

14-ounce piece of beef tenderloin filet

olive oil

9 ounces puff pastry

2 slices prosciutto

2 egg yolks, beaten

QUICK BÉARNAISE
Melt 1 stick of butter and leave to cool slightly. In a small saucepan, simmer 3 tablespoons each of white wine vinegar and dry white wine, 2 peeled and finely chopped shallots, a grinding of black pepper and 2 tarragon sprigs until reduced by half. Strain and add to a heatproof bowl with 2 large egg yolks. Put the bowl over a pan of simmering water, whisking for 2 minutes until thick and pale. Slowly add the melted butter, whisking constantly, until the sauce has thickened. Finish with 1 tablespoon of chopped tarragon and lemon juice and seasoning to taste.

In a saucepan, melt the butter over medium-high heat and stir in the mushrooms. Cook for 3 to 4 minutes until golden and any excess liquid has evaporated, then season. Once cool, add the pâté and mix well to combine.

Drizzle the beef with olive oil and season. Add to a hot frying pan and cook over high heat for 30 seconds on each side to give a golden-brown crust. Transfer the meat to a plate to cool. While the beef is cooling, roll out the pastry to a thin square large enough to completely encase the meat. From the remaining pastry, cut out two heart shapes.

Once the beef is cooled, wrap it with the prosciutto slices. Lightly brush the surface of the pastry with the beaten egg and place the meat in the center. Place the mushroom mixture on top of the beef, then bring the opposite corners of the pastry up to overlap in the center, tucking in the sides as if you were wrapping a box. Place the two pastry hearts in the center of the parcel and brush the surface with beaten egg.

Chill for at least 30 minutes, or until you're ready to cook the parcel. Preheat the oven to 425°F. Put the parcel on a high rack and cook for 20 to 25 minutes, which will give you medium-rare steak; add another 5 minutes if you would like your meat well done. To serve, cut between the pastry hearts.

Robust reds like an American Cabernet Sauvignon, Malbec, or Claret.

TIP: *In place of the prosciutto, a pancake can be used (page 205) to wrap the filet in before encasing in the pastry.*

RASPBERRY SOUFFLÉ

These are impressive from the moment they leave the oven, but they must be eaten right away. This recipe makes four soufflés as the mixture is easier to work with in a larger quantity. If making two and saving two for another day, use half the soufflé base and fold in half of the beaten egg whites. A fresh egg white mixture will need to be whisked up for making the second batch.

MAKES 4

For the raspberry coulis
10½ ounces raspberries
2 tablespoons confectioner's sugar
1 tablespoon lemon juice

For the soufflés
3 tablespoons melted butter, for greasing
6 rounded tablespoons superfine sugar, plus extra for the ramekins
4 tablespoons raspberry jam
⅓ cup heavy cream
1 tablespoon all-purpose flour
4 tablespoons cornstarch
¼ cup whole milk
2 egg yolks
4 egg whites

To make the coulis, purée the raspberries with the sugar and lemon juice in a food processor. Push it through a sieve to remove the raspberry seeds. Add more sugar to taste.

Brush the insides of 4 small ramekins with butter and coat with sugar, shaking out any excess. Place 1 tablespoon of jam in each, then chill in the fridge. Mix the cream, flour and cornstarch to a smooth paste. Warm the milk over medium heat until just boiling, then gradually stir into the paste. Whisk until smooth. Pour the mixture back into the saucepan over a gentle heat. Beat vigorously until thickened.

Place the egg yolks in a separate small bowl and add the superfine sugar. Mix to a thick paste, then add to the saucepan and mix well until smooth. Return to the stove to thicken, whisking until it begins to bubble. Take it off the heat—the mixture should look like pudding. Be very careful not to scramble the eggs. Put aside to cool completely. (At this point you can chill the mixture in the fridge for up to 2 days and finish the soufflés just before serving.)

Preheat the oven to 350°F. Put the egg whites in a large bowl and beat with an electric mixer until soft peaks begin to form. Add one large spoonful of the egg whites and 6 tablespoons of the raspberry coulis to the cooled soufflé base, then beat well. Gently fold in the remaining egg whites. Fill the ramekins to the brim and level off with a spatula. Place them on a baking sheet in the middle of the oven for about 14 minutes until risen and turning golden. Serve immediately, with the raspberry coulis and Shortbread Hearts (page 157).

A half bottle of Sauternes to share.

CHOCOLATE FONDANT

The fondant middle of this decadent dessert disappears on your tongue. Serve one to share and save the other for the following day; a drizzle of cream or dollop of crème fraîche will help to cut through the richness.

SERVES 2

5 tablespoons unsalted butter, softened

2 tablespoons cocoa powder

2 ounces good-quality dark chocolate (70% cocoa solids)

1 free range egg

⅓ cup superfine sugar

1 heaping teaspoon all-purpose flour

CHOCOLATE MOUSSE
You can adapt this recipe really easily to make chocolate mousse for two—instead of folding in flour and cocoa powder to the mixture add 3½ ounces heavy cream whipped to soft peaks. Fold the cream carefully into the sugar and egg, then mix in the melted chocolate, pour into glasses and leave to set in the fridge for an hour, or if it's a hot summer's day, churn in an ice cream maker before setting. Perfect for sharing, a spoonful of this is just like eating the best chocolate bar in the world.

Preheat the oven to 400°F.

Grease the insides of two small ramekins with about 1 tablespoon of the softened butter, making sure you have covered all the surfaces. Sprinkle 2 tablespoons of cocoa powder around the inside and turn the ramekin to thoroughly coat. Tip out any excess cocoa on to a saucer and set aside.

Melt the butter and chocolate in a bowl set over a pot of simmering water. Stir frequently, and do not overheat. Remove from the heat when completely melted. Set a clean bowl over the saucepan, then add the egg and the sugar—the heat will allow the sugar to dissolve and will lighten the mixture—and beat until light, fluffy and doubled in size.

Remove this bowl from the heat, and carefully fold in the flour and the remaining cocoa powder. Add in the melted chocolate and fold to combine. Pour the mixture into the prepared ramekins, and bake for 14 to 15 minutes. Serve in prepared ramekins with cream to pour over.

 Lightly chilled Tawny Port complements a chocolatey pudding.

TIP : *It's almost as good cold, but you could also reheat in the microwave for 60 seconds—it will still taste delicious. Uncooked, these can be frozen for up to a month; simply cook from frozen, adding 5 minutes to the cooking time.*

ENDING THE EVENING

This should be a night distinct from your typical routine. Switch off the television to play cards or a board game for two. Backgammon is a personal favorite, but I always forget how to set up pieces on a board, so use the photograph opposite to avoid any potential disagreements. Impress with homemade truffles or chocolate-dipped strawberries, served with a delicate rose-petal martini (a signature cocktail from Table Talk, where I used to work) or a more masculine Irish coffee.

CHOCOLATE TRUFFLES Makes 12–15

Break 5 ounces of good-quality dark (70 percent cocoa solids) or milk chocolate into small pieces and place in a heatproof bowl. Put ½ cup plus 2 tablespoons of heavy cream and ¼ cup of packed light brown sugar in a small saucepan. Bring to a boil, stirring to dissolve the sugar, and simmer for 1 minute, then cool for about 30 seconds. Pour the cream over the chocolate a little at a time and mix well, working quickly until smooth and glossy. Don't overmix. Allow the ganache to cool to room temperature, cover and refrigerate for at least 1 hour or until fully set. Remove from the fridge and allow to come up to room temperature—this will make it easier to handle. Sprinkle your hands with a little cocoa powder, then scoop out teaspoonfuls of the ganache and roll in your hands to make balls. Don't take too long over this as the ganache will begin to melt. Roll the truffles in cocoa powder, chopped almonds or dried coconut. Refrigerate until ready to serve.

TIP: *You can prepare the ganache up to 3 days in advance and keep it refrigerated, or you could freeze it for up to a month—just defrost thoroughly before coating and serving.*

ROSE-PETAL MARTINI Serves 1 (make to order)

Fill a cocktail shaker with ice cubes and pour over 1 ounce of vodka, ½ ounce of rose-petal liqueur, 1½ ounces of lychee juice and ½ ounce of fresh lime. Shake well and strain into a chilled martini glass. Garnish with a rose petal.

IRISH COFFEE Serves 1 (make to order)

Put 1 ounce of Irish whiskey in a mug or heatproof glass and top with freshly made coffee. Add 1 to 2 teaspoons of brown sugar and stir until dissolved. Top with lightly whipped heavy cream, poured carefully onto the surface of the coffee over the back of a teaspoon—this will ensure that the cream floats on top. Serve sprinkled with grated chocolate, nutmeg, or ground cinnamon.

"When you wake up in the morning, Pooh,"
said Piglet at last, "what's the first thing you
say to yourself?"

"What's for breakfast?" said Pooh.
"What do you say, Piglet?"

"I say, I wonder what's going to happen
exciting today?" said Piglet.

Pooh nodded thoughtfully.
"It's the same thing," he said.

Winnie-the-Pooh,
A. A. Milne

SPECIAL
BREAKFASTS

I like breakfast. A good morning meal brightens any day. Whether it's a core-warming bowl of oatmeal in winter, a golden-yolked egg with hot buttered toast on a bright and lazy summer morning or a lemony sugar pancake wolfed down in haste on Shrove Tuesday, breakfast is an important meal. It's the fuel for our engines, it boosts our concentration and sharpens our minds. Breakfast sets the tone and mood for the rest of the day, starting the morning off on the right foot with an added, often caffeinated, spring in the step.

Until the mid-fifteenth century, breakfast wasn't much to write home about. It was typically taken at first light and consisted of a small piece of bread and cheese and a mug of beer (a far less alcoholic drink then than it is now, and in those days safer than most drinking water). Instead, the main meal of the day was "dinner," served as early as 10 a.m., which marked the end of the morning's labor. Gradually, as the working day became longer and people began to work in offices, these two meals increased to three and an early breakfast became more of a necessity to see workers through to lunchtime. The invention of artificial lighting also allowed people the luxury of eating later. As new foodstuffs from all over the world became available, breakfast in the Victorian era gradually changed to become a meal full of culinary delights, many of which we still love, such as cold cuts of meat, grilled mackerel, sausages, bacon and eggs, as well as muffins, toast and jam.

The rhythm and pace of our lives continue to influence how we breakfast today; our busy weekday routines make leisurely breakfasts a bit more elusive, so weekends are the time to indulge in them. The beauty of this meal is that it's flexible, with endless variations and almost no rules—it might be a preciously quiet and private ritual, a family affair to be enjoyed early in the comfort of one's pajamas, or even a social breezy brunch at midday with friends grazing right through to the afternoon.

And then there are the really special breakfasts. Many families have particular breakfast menus for Christmas, but fewer do for birthdays, anniversaries or other festive occasions—perhaps it's time to start a new family tradition. I always look forward to a birthday breakfast at my parents', unfailingly prepared with a few celebratory touches to elevate it from the everyday. This type of breakfast doesn't need to be overly fancy; it just requires a little bit more effort to assemble, but it is always worth it because it puts you in a cheery, positive mood at the beginning of the day.

BREAKFAST IN BED

Breakfast in bed can be anything from a simple pot of tea with a few digestive biscuits or a piece of toast to a tray laden with early-morning goodies and flowers. Either way, nearly any breakfast becomes special when it's brought to you in bed. I have funny memories of creeping up the stairs with my brother and sister, carrying a breakfast tray for our parents as a surprise treat: desperately trying not to spill the tea and the orange juice or knock over the vase of flowers, stifling our giggles so that they couldn't hear us coming. Even if you've only got time to make an early-morning cup of coffee on a special day or birthday, it's the ideal way to surprise someone—an offering that marks a momentary pause before the rest of the day unfolds.

TIPS: *Instead of a vase of flowers, a spring bulb planted in a teacup makes a delightful change on the breakfast tray.* • *You can buy really comfortable "lap" trays, which have a beanbag base; some retailers will allow you to customize the surface with your own photographs. They're perfect for suppers in front of the television as well.*

FOR MOM ...

Moms rarely get an excuse to have breakfast in bed, and if there's ever a time when they should, it's on Mother's Day. This is something children can get involved in, picking a bunch of flowers (such as forget-me-nots) and arranging them in a vase, lining a tray with a napkin, making a handwritten card and helping set out a few delicious dishes. It's the thought that counts, so it should be a breakfast they can assemble such as a granola and fruit compote sundae (page 202) or cook easily like a boiled egg with toast. A special-occasion oatmeal can be decorated with small luxuries (fresh berries and cream, honey, toasted nuts or brown sugar). The only rule is to leave a clean kitchen afterward, so as not to create extra work for Mom and spoil what is meant to be her treat.

FOR DAD ...

Dad might not appreciate a bunch of flowers quite like Mom, but the morning newspaper or even just his favorite crossword or sudoku cut out and presented with a sharp pencil will do the trick. A pot of coffee and a crunchy piece of toast with marmalade will definitely win you brownie points, a fresh grapefruit sprinkled with brown sugar, a warm croissant straight from the oven or a bacon sandwich cooked to his liking. If you really want to spoil Dad (and his diet allows it) serve the bacon with maple syrup and pancakes (page 205).

GRANOLA AND FRUIT COMPOTE SUNDAE

Assemble homemade granola and fruit compotes in tall clear glasses with yogurt to make a sundae. As these components are sweet, stick to plain yogurt, and choose your compote flavors according to the season. Granola is easier to make in a larger quantity, so there should be plenty of leftovers for the rest of the week. Store the rest in a large glass jar for up to a month.

SERVES 4

Homemade granola: Preheat the oven to 325°F and grease a large roasting pan with sunflower oil. Gently warm 1 cup of honey and 1 teaspoon of vanilla extract in a small pan. Place 3 cups of old-fashioned rolled oats, ½ cup of raisins, ½ cup of chopped hazelnuts or almonds and ¼ cup of pumpkin seeds in a large bowl. Pour the warmed honey and vanilla over the oats and mix well to coat, then transfer it to the prepared pan and spread out evenly. Bake for 1 hour or until golden brown and crunchy, turning the mixture every 15 minutes to prevent it from burning. Remove from the oven and allow the granola to cool, then roughly break into chunks and add ¾ cup of mixed dried fruit, such as cherries, cranberries or chopped apricots.

Spring and summer berry compote: Put 2½ cups of mixed berries in a pan and add ¼ cup of light brown sugar, the zest and juice of ½ a lemon and the seeds from ½ a vanilla pod (or ½ a teaspoon of vanilla extract). Sauté the mixture for 10 to 15 minutes, stirring frequently, over medium to high heat, until the berries begin to soften and release their juices. Heat for another 2 minutes until slightly thickened.

Autumn apple and cinnamon compote: Put 4 peeled and roughly chopped apples into a pan with ½ cup of packed dark brown sugar and the seeds from 1 vanilla pod, 1 teaspoon of ground cinnamon and ¼ teaspoon of ground cloves. Add a small splash of water, then cook over medium heat for 10 to 15 minutes, stirring frequently, until the apples have softened but still have some texture.

Winter rhubarb and ginger compote: Put 14 ounces of trimmed rhubarb, cut into ¾-inch pieces, in a pan with the juice and zest of ½ an orange, a ¾-inch piece of fresh ginger, peeled and finely grated, and ⅓ cup of packed light brown sugar. Cook over medium heat for 10 to 12 minutes, or until the rhubarb has softened, but still retains some texture.

TIP: *The compotes will last for up to three days in the fridge and are delicious with ice cream.*

PANCAKE DAY

Pancakes work brilliantly at breakfast with lemon and sugar or with fruit compote (page 202). On Shrove Tuesday, get children together for an after-school session of pancake tossing and racing, or serve up Drop Scones as a high tea, fresh from the pan and laced with butter. These are smaller than pancakes and easier for younger children to flip in the pan. Both recipes make 10 to 12 pancakes or drop scones.

CLASSIC PANCAKES

2 cups all-purpose flour
2 large free-range eggs, beaten
1½ cups milk
sunflower oil, for frying
To serve: lemon, superfine sugar
(or Grand Marnier for grown-ups)

DROP SCONES

1¼ cups self-rising flour
2 tablespoons superfine sugar
1 large free-range egg, beaten
10 tablespoons milk
3 tablespoons unsalted butter, melted
sunflower oil, for frying

Sift the flour into a mixing bowl (add the superfine sugar for drop scones). Make a small well in the center of the mixture and pour in the eggs and a small splash of milk. Whisk until smooth, then very gradually pour in the remaining milk (and the melted butter if making drop scones) while continuing to mix, until you have a smooth batter.

Lightly grease a nonstick frying pan with the oil and warm over medium heat. To make classic pancakes, pour in roughly 3 tablespoons of the batter, or enough to thinly cover the bottom of the pan, and tilt it so that it is spread evenly. To make drop scones, add 1 generous tablespoon of batter per scone, in batches of 3 or 4 at a time. Cook until the pancakes are golden brown, then flip and cook the other side. Serve immediately.

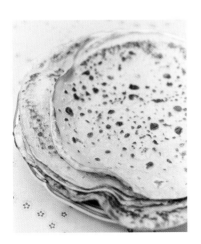

SHROVE TUESDAY AND PANCAKE RACES

Shrove Tuesday (Pancake Day) is the last opportunity for people to use up foods that were traditionally not allowed during Lent: meat and fish, fats, eggs and milk. Pancakes became associated with Shrove Tuesday as they used up most of the forbidden food in the house with just the addition of flour.

Pancake races happen all over the country these days and have a long history. To hold your own, get all the participants at the starting line—racers hold frying pans with pancakes in them—and let them race to the finish, flipping their pancakes as they run. Be sure that participants flip their pancakes a fixed number of times.

A BIRTHDAY BREAKFAST

As children grow up and family dynamics change, it can be hard to find a time to celebrate a birthday. A birthday breakfast is a great way to gather everyone together, particularly if it falls on a weekend. To maximize your time in bed, lay and decorate the table the night before with presents piled up at the birthday boy's or girl's place, cards stacked in a toast rack ready to be opened, bunting adorning a wall or two and perhaps a "Happy Birthday" banner placed somewhere prominent. The following morning, add little finishing touches, such as a few balloons tied to the backs of chairs, fresh flowers and the food presented in an attractive way. Pour the milk into a pitcher rather than bringing out the entire carton, and portion the butter and jam in the same way. Display fresh fruit playfully: you can make mango hedgehogs by crisscrossing one side of a cut mango with a knife and turning the skin inside out so that the flesh can be eaten in cubes.

Birthdays come only once a year, so the breakfast menu has to be thoughtful, with added indulgences, like freshly squeezed orange juice (topped with sparkling wine for a Buck's Fizz). Eggs can easily be made worthy of a breakfast celebration—cover boiled eggs with a homemade egg cozy (page 218) for an extra surprise, serve fried eggs in a shaped mold or try the ideas on page 209.

EXCELLENT EGGS

EGGS BENEDICT Serves 4

Halve 2 English muffins horizontally and toast until golden. Divide between the plates, spread lightly with butter and arrange a slice of ham on each. Warm a jar of store-bought Hollandaise sauce. To cook the eggs, bring a deep pan of water to a boil and add a generous splash of white wine vinegar. Crack 4 eggs into separate small cups or ramekins. Use a wooden spoon to create a whirlpool and carefully drop the eggs in. Let them cook for 2 to 3 minutes and remove using a slotted spoon. Drain briefly on a paper towel before placing the eggs on the prepared muffin halves. Spoon the warm Hollandaise sauce over the eggs and ham, and finish with a pinch of cayenne or ground black pepper.

TIP : *To poach lots of eggs at the same time, line a mug with a lightly oiled piece of plastic wrap so it overlaps the edges. Crack an egg inside and twist the plastic wrap to create a neat parcel, repeat with more eggs, then add to a pan of simmering water.*

SALMON AND SPINACH BAKED EGGS Serves 4

Preheat the oven to 400°F. Grease 4 small ramekins with butter. Over high heat, wilt 10 ounces of spinach in a pan for 2 to 3 minutes with a splash of water, then drain and squeeze out any excess liquid. Place the spinach in a bowl and season well. Add 4 tablespoons of heavy cream, a pinch of freshly grated nutmeg, a squeeze of lemon juice and 7 ounces of flaked smoked salmon. Mix together well, then divide equally among the ramekins. Crack an egg inside each and top with an extra drizzle of cream, a little more grated nutmeg and Parmesan. Bake for 10 to 15 minutes, until the whites are firm but the yolks are still soft and runny.

BOILED AND SCRAMBLED EGGS

There's a simple pleasure to be had from cracking the dome of a boiled egg with the back of a spoon as you wonder if it's been cooked perfectly, and from dunking that first bite of toast and the subsequent overflow of the golden yolk. To elevate them from the everyday, serve with a variety of toast: spread toast with smoked mackerel (page 343) or trout pâté (page 119), make Welsh rarebit (page 106) or Croque Monsieur fingers (page 213).

If I had to choose what to eat for my last breakfast, it would have to be perfectly cooked scrambled eggs and smoked salmon with toasted soda bread, but serving scrambled eggs in their shells (just wash well with hot water and dry upside down) is a fun idea—garnish with inexpensive caviar and truffle oil for a decadent treat. If the shells sit too far down, fill the egg cups with sea salt to rest them on. Serve sea salt and pepper in the other shell half.

A LAZY BRUNCH

A really late start warrants brunch, in lieu of lunch. This is a time for one-dish affairs that encompass both breakfast and lunch, such as a kedgeree or a full English frittata. Guests might come and go at different times, so prepare what you can in advance, and enjoy the benefits of a lazy brunch without spending all your time in the kitchen. Everyone is likely to arrive really hungry, having saved themselves for a feast, so arrange a platter of pastries for people to enjoy with their first cup of coffee—mini doughnuts and waffles nestled in cellophane or muffins wrapped in paper all look appetizing.

COFFEE

A large French press or two of freshly brewed coffee is the easiest solution for a crowd. A stove-top percolator (aka a moka pot) makes delicious espresso-style coffee and gives off a wonderful aroma, but also involves a rather lengthy process better suited to smaller numbers. Hot milk can make all the difference for those who like their coffee very milky, so pop it in the microwave or on the stove for a few minutes to heat up (be careful not to let it boil over). If you have a small frothing device, so much the better, but you can also put warm milk into a clean French press and pump the plunger vigorously to aerate it. Sprinkle drinks with chocolate powder, making playful shapes using stencils.

GRAND MIMOSA Serves 4

A Grand Mimosa is a variation on Buck's Fizz with the addition of Grand Marnier. Line up 4 chilled Champagne flutes and pour 1 tablespoon of Grand Marnier into the bottom of each one. Divide 1¼ cups of Champagne or Prosecco among them, and then use ½ cup of freshly squeezed orange juice to top up the glasses (approximately 2 tablespoons per glass). Serve decorated with half a squeezed kumquat.

A PITCHER OF BLOODY MARY Serves 8

In a pitcher, mix together 8 teaspoons of celery salt, 4 teaspoons of freshly ground black pepper, 2 tablespoons of horseradish sauce, just under a cup of vodka, 8 tablespoons of Worcestershire sauce, 4 tablespoons of Tabasco, 8 cups of tomato juice, 2 ounces of sherry and a squeeze of lemon juice. Stir with a celery stick, and adjust the seasonings to taste. Serve in tall glasses with ice cubes, celery and lemon wedges.

FULL ENGLISH FRITTATA

A full English breakfast is an institution and one of the best-known national meals in the world. For larger numbers it can be tricky to get all the components ready at the same time. A quick and easy solution is an all-in-one frittata. To prepare this ahead (no more than two hours in advance), complete all the steps before adding the eggs. Then, when you are ready to serve, simply reheat the base ingredients, add the beaten eggs and pop it under the broiler. Have favorite condiments on the side.

SERVES 8 (MAKES 2 FRITTATAS)

4 tablespoons olive oil

6 sausages, cut into chunks

12 slices bacon, cut into bite-sized pieces

7 ounces baby Portobello or small button mushrooms, halved

16 cherry tomatoes, halved

16 large free-range eggs

salt and freshly ground black pepper

5 ounces cheddar cheese, grated

Preheat the broiler to high. Divide the oil between two 10-inch ovenproof frying pans and heat, then divide the sausages between the pans. Sauté for a few minutes to brown them before adding half of the bacon to each pan. Continue cooking for another 2 to 3 minutes. Add the mushrooms to each pan, and fry for 5 to 6 minutes. Divide the cherry tomatoes between the pans and cook for another minute.

In a bowl, whisk the eggs and season generously. Pour half of the egg mixture into each pan and cook over low heat for 8 to 10 minutes to set the base. Scatter half of the cheese over one frittata, then transfer the pan to the broiler and cook for 4 to 5 minutes or until lightly golden and set. Do the same with the remaining cheese and the second frittata. When the frittatas have cooled slightly, cut each into wedges to serve.

CROQUE MONSIEUR *If a full English is too much for younger diners, this taste of France might hit the spot with kids. Spread a slice of white bread with Dijon mustard, layer ham and grated Gruyère cheese, season, and top with a slice of buttered white bread. Fry the sandwiches for a few minutes in butter on each side, until golden. Serve with a fried egg on top for a Croque Madame.*

CLASSIC KEDGEREE

This is perfect for larger parties, because it's easy to double the quantities—if there isn't room at the kitchen table, guests can eat this standing up with just a fork. A great friend served this at her wedding, adding quail eggs and locally caught mackerel to make it elegant and special. It goes well with a green bean salad, mango chutney and Tabasco on the side.

SERVES 8

1 pound undyed smoked haddock

1 cup whole milk

2 smoked salmon filets

1 tablespoon butter

2 medium onions, finely diced

¾ tablespoon medium curry powder

½ teaspoon turmeric

seeds from 2 cardamom pods

1 cinnamon stick

1¾ cups mixed basmati and wild rice

6 ounces frozen peas

6 large eggs

handful of chopped flat-leaf parsley

salt and freshly ground black pepper

lemon wedges, to serve

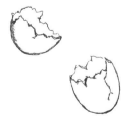

Put the haddock in a frying pan over medium heat. Pour the milk over, cover and simmer for 4 minutes. Take off the heat, add the salmon filets and let stand, covered, for 10 minutes to finish gently cooking the fish.

Meanwhile, heat the butter in a separate frying pan. Add the onion, curry powder, turmeric, cardamom seeds and cinnamon and fry until the onion is soft and golden, about 5 to 6 minutes. Cook the rice according to the instuctions on page 142.

Remove the fish from the milk and set it aside. Strain ¾ of the milk back into the pan. Add the cooked rice and peas and cover, cooking for 5 minutes over low heat until the liquid is absorbed.

Meanwhile, put the eggs in a pan, cover with cold water and bring to a boil, then boil for 6 minutes. Rinse the eggs under cold running water until they are cool enough to peel and quarter.

Break the fish into big flakes with a fork, removing any bones, and add to the rice. Throw in the parsley and stir gently to mix without breaking up the fish, adding the eggs at the end. Remove the cinnamon stick, season well with salt and pepper and serve with lemon wedges.

TIPS: *Use 6 slices of back bacon chopped into small pieces instead of the fish — add it when cooking the onions. • For a lighter version, heat the rice and peas in ¾ cup of hot vegetable stock in place of the poaching milk. • You can add cooked shrimp with the smoked salmon • For more heat, add 1 small finely chopped dried red chili.*

See the land, her Easter keeping,
 Rises as her Maker rose.
Seeds, so long in darkness sleeping,
 Burst at last from winter snows.
Earth with heaven above rejoices;
 Fields and gardens hail the spring;
Shaughs and woodlands ring with voices,
 While the wild birds build and sing.

"Easter Week," Charles Kingsley

EASTER

Easter brings feelings of excitement and renewal, like the sighting of the first yellow daffodils, which provide a sense of hope and a burst of brightness. It is the first significant festival of the year, when everything that has lain dormant over the winter months awakens and life feels busy again, both inside and out: churches fill with congregations, the spicy aroma of hot cross buns pervades kitchens and butterflies emerge from their cocoons. It is a celebration of the new season and the chance to be outside again: in woods for bluebell-carpeted walks, or for families with young children, visiting farms to see young lambs and parties of chicks.

Tradition, symbolism and religion lie at the heart of Easter. It is the most important festival in the Christian year, marking the death of Christ on Good Friday and celebrating his resurrection three days later on Easter Sunday. As a movable feast, Easter follows the lunar calendar—it falls on the first Sunday after the first full moon of the spring equinox. It is believed to derive from the Anglo-Saxon festival Eostre, which honored Eastre, the goddess of spring and dawn, but it is also linked to the Jewish festival of Passover, or Pascha. In many churches today there is still the ceremonial lighting of a special Easter candle, known as the Paschal candle.

Many rituals come together to form Easter; the foods that we enjoy today are centered on the luxuries that were prohibited during the preceding forty days of the Lenten fast. Eggs, symbols of hope and rebirth, were forbidden, which is why they were eaten on the day before Lent began, Shrove Tuesday (Pancake Day, page 205), and then again on the day it ended, Easter Sunday, as an emblem of resurrection. Eggs also became a popular part of the festival to be decorated and handed out as gifts, often in the form of wild birds' eggs rather than the hens' eggs we use today. They still form the basis of our celebrations and offer simple, inexpensive pleasure: boiled for breakfast, hidden in flowerbeds, rolled, thrown and tapped or even raced, carefully balanced on a spoon. Another popular symbol of Easter today is the Easter Bunny, who might leave his mark outside children's bedrooms with a trail of jelly beans, a single, beautifully wrapped egg or a wicker basket embellished with brightly colored ribbon and laden with a cluster of tiny sweets, shiny eggs and decorative chicks on a bed of straw or shredded tissue paper.

As children, the day before Easter we would make marbled eggs by hard-boiling them, cracking the shells and leaving them in water colored with food dye, which would seep through the cracks. It was always fun eating our creations for breakfast the next morning. We would look forward to a huge Easter egg hunt, which was (and still is) quite competitive in our household, and then have a family lunch, often with roast spring lamb, but always with plenty of chocolate before and after!

EASTER CRAFTS

Celebrations usually start a few days before Easter, so plan a craft day. It's good to give children something to do at Easter that doesn't focus on eating chocolate.

FELT EGG COZIES

These will look charming on your Easter breakfast table and can make a simple boiled egg look special.

I: Make a rectangular template (3 inches x 4 inches) with a curved top edge. Place this on a square of pastel-colored felt and use it to cut two identical shapes. Make a flower-shaped template (2-inch diameter) and cut flowers from two other pieces of colored felt. 2: Cut a circle (¾-inch diameter) of felt with pinking shears, then cut a second circle (½-inch diameter). Position the two flowers on top of each other so that both sets of petals are visible, then place the two circles on top and sew them all together through the center using yarn and a large needle. 3: Stitch these to the center of one of the egg-cozy shapes. Place the two shapes together, right side out, and blanket-stitch around the edge. Leave the bottom open, but stitch around the front edge for a pretty finish.

POMPOM CHICKS

Glue these into clean eggshells stuck on pieces of construction paper to make Easter chick place holders for the table.

I: Make pompoms as per the instructions for thistles on page 154, using yellow yarn. 2: Open up the pompom slightly. 3: Cover the back of a pair of plastic eyes and a felt beak with craft glue, and gently lodge them into the pompom so that they don't fall out.

EGG WATERCRESS MEN

Watercress provides children with a sense of anticipation as they wait for it to grow. Use empty shells from boiled eggs.

I: Fill an empty eggshell with damp cotton balls and sow some watercress seeds on it. 2: Draw a face on the shell and let the cress sprout on a windowsill; this will take 4 to 5 days if kept moist. 3: Give the cress head a "haircut" when it's time for a cress sandwich.

EASTER BONNETS

This is a wonderful way to revive an old hat and to inject some tradition into Easter Sunday.

I: Wrap a length of raffia around your fingers to form a disk. Feed the end of it into the center, then to the outside; repeat; and continue to weave it through to create a small nest shape. 2: Glue these nests to a hat, then stick toy chicks inside the nests with craft glue. 3: Tie a ribbon around the hat and finish with a bow, some feathers and more chicks.

MORE EASTER CRAFTS

SPRING HATS

1: Cut two circles (7-inch diameter) out of construction paper. Cut a disk (3-inch diameter) from the center of each to make two rings, which will form the brim of the hat. Keep one of the disks and the two larger rings. 2: Cut a rectangle (5½ inch x 12 inch) from construction paper and roll it into a cylinder (3-inch diameter) to fit through the rings. Stick it together with craft glue. Make vertical ½-inch snips around each end of the cylinder to make tabs. 3: Place one end of the cylinder through one of the rings, folding out the tabs underneath the ring to lock it in place and make a top-hat shape. Glue the tabs to the underside of the ring. 4: Attach two 20-inch lengths of ribbon to the underside of the ring with craft glue. 5: Stick the second ring to the underside of the first, sandwiching the tabs and the ends of the ribbon to hide them. 6: Fold in the tabs at the other end of the cylinder and glue the disk on top. 7: Cut a strip (2 inch x 12 inch) from green construction paper, snip vertically along it to create a grass-effect trim and stick to the hat. 8: Decorate with a chick-filled raffia nest (page 218), more ribbon and egg shapes made of construction paper.

PAPER BAGS

1: Decorate white or colored paper bags with any pattern you like, using potato prints or acrylic paints and brushes, and use them for Easter egg hunts (page 241).

EGG DECORATING

To prepare your eggs, first add a splash of vinegar to boiling water to make sure the eggs don't crack, then hard-boil them for 7 minutes.

Set up a large table covered with newspaper or a plastic cloth and lay out a range of acrylic paints, glitter, sequins and other bits and pieces that can be used for decorating. Also make sure you have plenty of craft glue. Give every child a hard-boiled egg to decorate as brightly and attractively as possible. You might want to suggest a theme for the decoration. Animal eggs are fun, or silly faces (cotton balls and string make good hair). If you want to turn it into more of a game, you can give players two minutes for decorating and then tell them to pass their eggs to the player next to them—a bit like pass the parcel. That way, everyone gets to work on each egg and the finished products are the combined result of everyone's talents.

TIP: *To make marble eggs, hard-boil eggs, then gently crack the shells. Prepare a range of deep mixing bowls, each filled with diluted food coloring (enough to submerge the eggs). Add quite a bit of food coloring to get a dark, rich color. Submerge the eggs and leave them for 10 minutes to 1 hour. Peel to reveal the marbled effect.*

PASTE EGGS *Exquisite, beautifully decorated paste (pace) eggs were popular in medieval Europe—the shells were pressed with flowers, foliage and scraps of material held together with a piece of linen tied to form a bundle, then boiled in water for a few hours so the colors of the material would stain the eggshells in the patterns of the petals and foliage. Often these were strung in garlands on a mantelpiece, as many as twenty at a time. Today such decorative eggs are a rarity and have been almost entirely replaced by chocolate confections.*

EGG BLOWING

To get light, hollow eggshells that you can decorate and hang up with ribbons on branches, you will need to blow out the contents of the eggs. Get a small clean bowl or ramekin and place it on the table in front of you. With a pin or needle, make a hole at each end of the egg. Carefully try to enlarge the hole at the rounded end of the egg so that it's bigger than the hole at the pointy end. With the needle, try to pierce the yolk inside so that it's easier to blow out of the shell. Holding the egg carefully over the bowl, put your lips over the larger hole at the rounded end and blow steadily so that the contents come out into the bowl (it's quite hard work, so an adult might need to help with this). Once the shells are empty, rinse carefully under cold water and decorate when dry.

To hang, use approximately 24 inches of thin ribbon and wrap the egg like a present. Place the egg at the mid-point of the ribbon and curve the ribbon lengthways around the egg, then cross the ends over and back down the opposite side, dividing the egg into four sections. At the top, tie your ribbon securely in a double knot and use the excess to tie your egg around the Easter tree.

GOOD FRIDAY SWEET TREATS

Have a few edible activities for children to make and enjoy. These are perfect for a spring tea along with hot cross buns. Serve Simnel Cake (page 226) for the grown-ups.

SQUASHED-FLY BUNNIES Makes 24

My granny convinced me that the currants in these cookies were squashed flies and the name has stuck. Use cutters to shape them into bunnies and tie their necks with ribbon if you're handing them out as gifts.

Place 1½ cups of all-purpose flour and 4 tablespoons of unsalted diced butter in a food processor and pulse together until the mixture resembles fine bread crumbs. Add 6 tablespoons of superfine sugar, 3 tablespoons of milk, 1 teaspoon of pumpkin pie spice and the zest of ½ an orange. Pulse briefly until the mixture comes together and turn out onto a floured surface. Knead into a smooth dough, then wrap in plastic wrap and chill for 30 minutes.

Preheat the oven to 375°F and grease two baking sheets. Roll the dough out on a lightly floured surface into a large square approximately ¼-inch thick, then cut it in half. Scatter one half with ⅓ cup of golden raisins and ⅓ cup of currants and put the other half directly on top. Roll out again to ¼-inch thick so the two pieces are sandwiched together and the currants and golden raisins are showing through. Cut out the dough using a bunny cutter and transfer the cookies to the baking sheets. Push a few extra currants onto the bunnies' faces for eyes, then brush the cookies with 2 beaten egg yolks mixed with a little water. Sprinkle with a little superfine sugar. Bake for 15 to 20 minutes, or until crisp and a light golden color. Transfer to a wire rack to cool.

CHOCOLATE NESTS Makes 24

Kids can help to make these and spoon them into colorful cupcake wrappers. Decorate them with chocolate eggs.

Lay out 24 paper cupcake wrappers on a tray that will fit in the fridge. Place 5 ounces of shredded wheat cereal and 5 ounces of cornflakes in a large bowl and crush them using your hands or a rolling pin. Break 8 ounces of milk chocolate and 3½ ounces of dark chocolate into pieces and melt with 3 tablespoons of butter in a bowl over a pot of simmering water. Add 4 tablespoons of corn syrup and stir. Carefully pour the chocolate mixture over the crushed cereal and mix together well. Divide between the cupcake wrappers and make a small dip in the middle of each one to create a "nest." Arrange three mini eggs in each nest and chill until set.

TIP: *Use the same mixture to make "Birdseed," a dessert I loved to eat at school. It was always served with warm custard that would slowly turn chocolatey as it mixed with the Birdseed. Make the same mixture as above but scatter it in a large rectangular baking dish and leave in the fridge to harden.*

SIMNEL CAKE

This fruit cake, similar to Christmas cake, has been eaten at Easter since medieval times. If, like me, you are not a huge fan of marzipan, try covering it with rolled fondant icing and using edible sugar flowers, mini eggs or sugared almonds instead of the traditional decorations. Tie a ribbon around the cake.

SERVES 8–10

2 sticks unsalted butter, softened

1 cup packed light brown sugar

zest of 1 lemon and 1 orange

5 medium eggs

2 cups all-purpose flour

1 teaspoon pumpkin pie spice

1 teaspoon ground cinnamon

1 teaspoon almond extract

5 ounces candied cherries, chopped

4 ounces currants

5 ounces golden raisins

3½ ounces diced candied citrus peel

3 ounces packaged marzipan

2 tablespoons apricot jam

3½ ounces packaged white fondant icing (available online or at baking supply stores)

Preheat the oven to 325°F. Grease and line an 8-inch round cake pan with parchment paper. Beat the softened butter and sugar together in a large bowl using an electric mixer until pale and fluffy. Stir in the lemon and orange zest and then gradually beat in the eggs. Add the flour, pumpkin pie spice, cinnamon, almond extract, cherries, currants, golden raisins and citrus peel, and fold together until well combined. Spoon half of the mixture into the prepared pan, smoothing down the surface evenly.

Cut half the marzipan into a neat circle (approximately ¼ inch thick), the same size as the cake pan. Place the circle on top of the cake mixture, then spoon the remaining mixture on top. Bake for between 1½ hours and 1 hour and 45 minutes, until golden brown. Check after 1 hour, and cover the cake with foil if it browns too fast. Once done, remove from the oven and let it cool slightly before removing it from the pan and transferring it to a wire rack.

Once the cake is cool, brush the top with the apricot jam. Cover this with a circle of the white fondant icing and use the trimmings to decorate. Dab a touch of apricot jam on to the bottom of the shapes to stick them around the top edge of the cake. Or see page 265 for how to make edible sugar-frosted flowers.

TIP: *Use the same recipe to make your Christmas cake, adding green holly and red berry decorations made of fondant icing.*

MARZIPAN DECORATIONS *Simnel Cake traditionally contains ingredients forbidden during Lent and was distinguished by its decorative topping of marzipan balls to represent Christ's twelve apostles. There is some debate as to how many should be used, though, ranging from eleven (excluding Judas) to thirteen (to include Christ).*

CAKES FOR MOMS

Originally Simnel Cakes were made for Mothering Sunday (the fourth Sunday in Lent) as people would make pilgrimages to the mother church of their parishes. Working children were given leave to visit their mothers, bringing the cake as a gift. It's a lovely tradition that could be revived on Mother's Day.

THE EASTER TABLE

Decorations should be a fusion of Easter symbols, fresh blooms and the scents of spring. Colorful bunches of tulips and daffodils are easy to come by, or choose fragrant hyacinth bulbs in a variety of pretty pastel hues. Use clusters of shiny wrapped eggs, jelly beans and sugared almonds to dot among potted plants or place in small baskets and egg cups. Easter bunnies, straw, or china Beatrix Potter figurines add extra amusement to spring table displays.

PLACE SETTINGS

Tie a packet of seeds around a napkin with raffia at each place setting as a gift or perch pompom chicks cheekily inside eggshells as place names for a more playful touch (page 218).

TIP: *Bulbs planted in teacups bedded with moss will sit nicely alongside vases of cut spring flowers, and they also make great Easter presents.*

EASTER TREE

Have an Easter tree in a pot, which is not only fun for the whole family to decorate but also provides a cheery focal point on a table or mantelpiece. Luscious branches of blossoms are beautiful and long stems of pussy willow will last for weeks—both can be arranged in tall vases or ceramic or enamel pitchers. Decorate the branches with hanging blown eggs, painted and glittered and tied with colorful ribbon (page 222). Even a simple bunch of green foliage set above a mantelpiece can be hung with eggs (weight the vase down inside to prevent the display from toppling over).

EASTER LUNCH MENU

Canapés
Quail eggs
Mini baked potatoes

Main courses
Salmon and shrimp pillow *or*
Stuffed roast lamb

Side dishes
Potato dauphinoise
Asparagus and spring greens *or*
Peter Rabbit lettuce and peas

Dessert
Easter trifle

EASTER DRINKS AND CANAPÉS

Depending on what you're serving for your main course, offer a few of these at your Easter gathering. Serve sparkling soft drinks with primrose ice cubes (page 265).

QUAIL EGGS WITH CELERY SALT Makes 16

Boil 16 quail eggs (allow 2 per person) for 4 minutes, then rinse under cold water and leave to cool. Remove half of each shell and serve with a sprinkling of cayenne pepper and celery salt for dipping. These are also great served with a Bloody Mary (page 210).

MINI BAKED POTATOES WITH CRÈME FRAÎCHE AND CAVIAR Makes 24

Preheat the oven to 375°F. Place 24 baby new potatoes (allow 3 per person) on a baking tray and drizzle with a little olive oil. Season with salt and white pepper and roast for 20 to 25 minutes. Remove from the oven, and once cool enough to handle, cut a small cross in the top of each potato and press the sides together to reveal the flesh.

Mix 3½ ounces of crème fraîche, 2 tablespoons of horseradish, 1 tablespoon of finely chopped flat-leaf parsley, 2 finely chopped scallions and the zest of ½ a lemon in a bowl and season to taste. Top the potatoes with a teaspoonful of the crème fraîche mixture and some Sevruga caviar (or smoked salmon), and garnish with chopped chives. Serve on a bed of straw.

RHUBARB COCKTAIL Serves 1 (make to order)

An Easter martini, using seasonal rhubarb. Fill a cocktail shaker with ice cubes and add 1½ ounces of vodka, ½ ounce of pomegranate (or cranberry) juice and about 2 ounces of rhubarb purée (see below). Shake well and pour into a chilled martini glass. Garnish with a thin strip of rhubarb tied in a knot.

TIP: *To make rhubarb purée, cut 1 pound of rhubarb into chunks and place in a saucepan with 1 cup of water and 1 cup of sugar. Bring to a boil, then reduce the heat and simmer gently for approximately 15 to 20 minutes until the fruit is soft and the liquid has thickened. Purée until smooth. Makes approximately 14 ounces.*

WHITE LADY Serves 1 (make to order)

Fill a cocktail shaker with ice cubes and add 1½ ounces of dry gin, ¾ ounce of Cointreau, a splash of sugar syrup (page 80) and the juice of ½ a lemon and 1 egg white. Shake well and pour into a chilled martini glass or Champagne coupe. Garnish with lemon peel (page 80).

SALMON AND SHRIMP PILLOW

The practice of eating fish on Good Friday stems from the early Christians, who believed that meat should be forbidden on the day that Christ was crucified. This is a welcome Easter bundle—serve with Peter Rabbit Lettuce and Peas (page 237) and a warm, store-bought Hollandaise sauce. The uncooked pillow can be frozen for up to a month. If baked from frozen, add another 15 minutes to the cooking time.

SERVES 8

2 tablespoons unsalted butter

1 small onion, peeled and finely chopped

1 leek, cleaned and finely sliced

4 tablespoons all-purpose flour, plus extra for dusting

2 teaspoons mustard powder

½ cup fish stock

1½ cups heavy cream

salt and freshly ground black pepper

7 ounces baby spinach

zest and juice of 1 lemon

4 tablespoons chopped dill

28 ounces frozen puff pastry, thawed

four 4 ounce skinless salmon (or other fish) filets

8 ounces raw tiger or large shrimp, peeled

2 egg yolks, beaten

Preheat the oven to 375°F. Melt the butter in a large pan and sauté the onion for 4 to 5 minutes to soften. Add the leek and cook for 2 minutes. Stir in the flour and mustard powder and cook for 1 minute, stirring all the time. Add the stock and simmer until reduced by half. Add the cream, reduce the heat and cook for 6 to 8 minutes until the sauce has thickened. Season well, stir in the spinach and cook until the sauce becomes thick and creamy. Remove from the heat and cool, then stir in the lemon zest and juice and chopped dill.

Cut the pastry in half and roll each half out on a floured surface to a rectangle, one approximately 8 x 12 inches and ¼ inch thick and the other slightly larger and thinner. Cut the salmon into ¾-inch chunks, season well and add to the sauce with the shrimp. Mix well to coat. Lay the thicker pastry rectangle on a nonstick baking sheet, then spoon the mixture down the center, piling it up high. Mix the beaten egg yolks with a little water to make an egg wash and brush the edges of the pastry with it. Place the other piece of pastry on top, trimming any excess and crimping the edges together to make a "pillow." Use leftover pastry to cut out Easter-themed decorations for the top. Brush all over with the rest of the egg wash and bake in the preheated oven for 25 to 30 minutes. Remove from the oven and allow to stand for a few minutes before slicing.

 White Burgundy or good-quality New World Chardonnay.

STUFFED ROAST LAMB

Throughout Europe there is a tradition of eating the new season's lamb at Easter. The stuffing is really tasty, but give yourself time to carefully tie up the lamb to create a neat parcel. If you are roasting lamb on the bone (see timings opposite), roll the stuffing into small balls and bake on a greased baking sheet for 30 to 35 minutes until crisp and golden.

SERVES 8–12

For the stuffing

5 ounces dried apricots, finely chopped

5 ounces prunes, finely chopped

1¼ cups white bread crumbs

zest and juice of 2 oranges

4 garlic cloves, peeled and finely chopped

½ cup chopped flat-leaf parsley

1 egg, beaten

salt and freshly ground black pepper

For the lamb

two 3-pound boneless legs spring lamb

4 tablespoons olive oil

2 garlic bulbs, cut in half horizontally

8 sprigs rosemary

For the gravy

4 tablespoons all-purpose flour

1 quart beef stock

1¾ cups red wine

4 tablespoons red currant jelly

salt and freshly ground black pepper

Preheat the oven to 375°F. To make the stuffing, mix the apricots, prunes, bread crumbs, orange zest and juice, garlic and parsley together in a large bowl with the beaten egg to combine. Season well with salt and pepper.

Lay the lamb legs out on a chopping board, skin side down; season, and place the stuffing down the middle of each. Roll up the lamb, tying in four to six places on each leg using butcher's string. Heat the oil in a large roasting pan and, once hot, add both legs and brown all over until nicely golden. Roast in the oven for approximately 1 hour 20 minutes until pink. After 15 minutes of cooking, add the halved garlic bulbs and the rosemary sprigs to the pan. Continue to roast for the remaining cooking time. Remove from the oven, transfer the lamb to plates and cover with foil. Let it rest for at least 20 minutes.

For the gravy, heat the meat juices in the roasting pan in which the lamb was cooked over high heat. Whisk in the flour to combine, and cook for 1 minute, then gradually pour in the stock and wine, whisking constantly. Bring to a boil, then reduce the heat and allow to simmer and reduce for 8 to 10 minutes, or until thickened. Stir in the red currant jelly and season to taste. Strain the gravy into a small pan and warm it to serve.

Carve the lamb and serve with asparagus and spring greens and potato dauphinoise (page 237).

 A velvety rich red wine, such as Ribero del Duero or Claret.

ROAST LAMB ON THE BONE *Calculate the roasting time for lamb on the bone at 30 minutes per pound. For pink lamb, reduce the overall cooking time by 30 minutes. Make sure to check and baste the meat frequently and adjust the timings for your particular oven.*

POTATO DAUPHINOISE Serves 8

A rich and indulgent potato dish that can be made up to a day in advance and goes well with any roast, particularly lamb. Peel and slice the potatoes ahead of time and keep fresh in cold water to prevent them going brown—just pat dry before using them.

Preheat the oven to 350°F. Grease an 8 x 12-inch baking dish with a little butter. Heat 2 tablespoons of unsalted butter in a large nonstick frying pan over medium heat. Place 2 medium peeled and finely sliced onions in the pan and cook for 6 to 8 minutes until soft but not colored. Add 3 cloves of peeled and finely chopped garlic and cook for another 1 to 2 minutes. Season with salt and freshly ground black pepper and turn off the heat.

Peel and finely slice 2 pounds of Yukon Gold potatoes, preferably using a mandoline or a slicer attachment in a food processor. Layer the potatoes in the dish, overlapping slightly. Scatter a small amount of the cooked onion mixture between each layer and season well. Repeat until all the potato slices have been used. Place the dish on a baking sheet.

Place 1 cup of milk and 1½ cups of heavy cream or crème fraîche in a pan over low heat and bring to a simmer. Pour the liquid over the potatoes—it should come just to the base of the top layer of potato. Bake for 1 hour, sprinkling ⅓ cup of grated Gruyère, Parmesan or cheddar cheese over the top for the final 15 minutes. Remove from the oven and let it stand for a few minutes before serving straight from the dish, or use a round chef's ring mold to stamp out elegant individual portions.

ASPARAGUS AND SPRING GREENS Serves 8

You can serve these together or separately, adding Parmesan shavings and a drizzle of good-quality olive oil to the asparagus (a platter of these work well as spring canapés with Hollandaise sauce as a dip).

Steam 2 pounds of spring greens and 1½ pounds of asparagus for 2 to 3 minutes until soft, or alternatively fry in a pan with 1 tablespoon of oil for a few minutes. Add 2 tablespoons of water and a pat of butter and simmer gently with the lid on for 2 to 3 minutes. Season well.

PETER RABBIT LETTUCE AND PEAS Serves 8

These are delicious with the salmon on page 233 and can be made with both fresh and frozen peas.

Melt 2 tablespoons of unsalted butter in a pan and add 1 peeled and finely chopped small onion. Soften over low heat for 4 to 5 minutes. Increase the heat, then stir in 14 ounces of garden peas or frozen baby sweet peas and the finely shredded leaves of 2 little gem lettuces or 1 head of butter lettuce, and sauté for 2 minutes. Add ⅓ cup of chicken stock and allow to reduce by half. Pour in ¼ cup of heavy cream, season well.

EASTER TRIFLE

This is an Easter twist on the classic version. Using toasted hot cross buns as a base gives this trifle a beautifully intense flavor, but to guard against their becoming soggy, the trifle should be assembled no more than one hour before serving. If you need to make this in advance, use pound cake or soft ladyfingers. You could also use a small toasted panettone as the base for a Christmas trifle.

SERVES 8

4 hot cross buns or brioche rolls, toasted and cut into bite-sized cubes

9 tablespoons dry sherry

two 10½-ounce cans mandarin segments, drained

one 3-ounce packet orange gelatin, made and set in advance, according to packet instructions

2 cups premade thick vanilla pudding

2½ cups heavy cream

⅓ cup confectioner's sugar, sifted

4 tablespoons sliced almonds, toasted

2 tablespoons Cadbury mini chocolate eggs

Arrange the bun pieces in the base of a large trifle dish and drizzle 3 tablespoons of the sherry over them. Scatter the mandarin segments on top. Cut the orange gelatin into thin slices or cubes and arrange on top of the fruit. Pour the pudding over and place in the refrigerator for 1 hour.

Whip the cream, confectioner's sugar and the rest of the sherry (to taste) in a large bowl until you have soft peaks and the cream just about holds its shape. Spoon the cream on top of the pudding, making sure it reaches the edges of the bowl, and finish it with attractive peaks on the top using the back of the spoon. Scatter the almonds over the top and garnish with mini eggs.

An Italian slightly sparkling dessert wine, such as Moscato d'Asti.

HOT CROSS BUNS

Hot cross buns!　　　*If you have no daughters*
Hot cross buns!　　　*Give them to your sons*
One a penny, two a penny,　*One a penny, two a penny,*
Hot cross buns!　　　*Hot cross buns!*

English nursery rhyme, c. 1798

Hot cross buns are typically eaten on Good Friday and are marked on top with a cross, either cut in the dough or composed of strips of pastry. They can be toasted over an open fire with a long fork (or these days, under the broiler). Many cultures have a similar tradition of preparing Easter bread or sweet cakes studded with raisins, honey and other dried fruits—these are often beautifully shaped into rings or even braided.

ACTIVITIES AND GAMES

With Easter so often a family affair, play these games with both grown-ups and children. As well as the ceremonial and all-important egg hunt, there are plenty of other egg-inspired games to get everyone involved, or you could play a seasonal twist on Pin the Tail on the Donkey (page 295) and pin the tail on the Easter Bunny instead. Mix up the teams, putting enthusiastic younger players with their more measured elders; the different age groups will bring their own skills and dynamics. For prizes, award bags of bunny biscuits (page 225) or cheaper candy eggs. They can be made to look more appealing by wrapping them in pastel tissue paper and tied with a spring-colored ribbon.

EASTER EGG HUNT

The traditional Easter egg hunt is one of the simplest but most enjoyable Easter games. This is one of those precious activities that is part game, part ritual. It's hugely enjoyable for a large gathering and can be played almost anywhere. For young children, keep it fairly simple. An adult hides a selection of eggs (they should be low down within easy reach of the children). I recommend using small eggs or painted hard-boiled ones that can be exchanged for chocolate ones at the end of the game. That way, your young players won't be too distracted by eating their eggs during the hunt, and you can make sure that everyone gets a fair share of the goodies once the game has finished. For older children, you can make the eggs harder to find and give clues to help them track them down—picture clues are good. For instance: take a photo on your phone of the kind of flower or shrub that the eggs are near. Show the picture to the children and then send them off to find the eggs. Written clues for older players can be as complicated or as subtle as you like. I know some families who devise clues that form part of a crossword and others who compose poems. Most people, though, are happy to make up something more straightforward, such as "What rhymes with bath?" for looking on a path. It is almost as much fun composing the clues as it is going on the hunt.

EGG TAPPING OR EGG JARPING

This is a simple and traditional Easter game along the lines of a conker tournament (a traditional British children's game played with chestnuts). Players split into pairs. Each player holds a hard-boiled egg and attempts to tap and break their opponent's egg without their own breaking. The winner then moves on to play the winner from another pair. The overall winner is the player who succeeds in cracking the greatest number of eggs while keeping their own egg untarnished.

EGG AND SPOON RACE

This is an old Easter favorite—and if there's a crowd of you, introduce some team spirit and organize a relay race. Everyone is given a spoon, and players are split into teams, arranging themselves in single file behind a starting line. Opposite each team is a flag (a stick with a handkerchief tied to it will do fine) stuck into the ground. The first person in each line places an egg on their spoon. On "Go!" they must move as quickly as they can around their flag and back again, without letting their egg fall. Once they have made it back to the starting line, they must transfer their egg to the next player's spoon. If at any point an egg is dropped or anyone is caught holding the egg in place with their hands, the player responsible must head back to the beginning and start their leg of the race again. The first team to have all their players back home wins. It's fun to play this with raw eggs but it depends on how much mess you are willing to put up with—hard-boiled eggs work just as well. Or try making it harder—ask everyone to hold the spoons in their mouths instead of their hands.

EGG TOSS

Players split into pairs. Each pair receives a fresh egg. To start, partners stand 6 feet away from each other (but reduce the distance for children as appropriate). Across this distance, one player throws their egg gently, to be caught by the other. If it breaks or touches the ground, the pair is out. Pairs who manage to throw and catch their egg successfully then take a few steps farther away from each other. The person who caught the egg last becomes the thrower for this round, and so on. The game continues, with partners moving farther and farther apart after each throw and catch. The team that manages to keep their egg intact for the longest, successfully tossing it across the greatest distance, wins the game.

There are few hours in life more agreeable than the hour dedicated to the ceremony known as afternoon tea.

The Portrait of a Lady, *Henry James*

AFTERNOON TEA

There is something very British about tea. This ritual has prevailed for centuries, and even today there is still great enthusiasm for indulging in all the ceremony and pomp that goes with it. Afternoon tea is wonderfully versatile: it might be enjoyed early or late, as a quick cup, with a cookie or two, as a hearty, warming high tea, or as a more formal cream tea with a batch of scones and thick yellow clotted cream. It can be shared with grandparents and favorite great-aunts in the garden at home or wolfed down alone in the kitchen after a wet and muddy day outside, with a thick doorstop of bread and hot crumpets dripping with butter. Tea can also be a celebratory event; it's an increasingly popular way to commemorate birthdays, baby showers and even bachelorette parties. Whichever way you have it, it always feels like a treat, and a nostalgic, British one at that.

Teatime is an experience most of us remember fondly from our childhoods. One of my most treasured associations with it is in the form of our school match teas. Eaten at halftime or after a sports game, it was welcome refreshment for players and spectators alike. It always tasted much better after a sporting success! Tea and cake seem sweeter when you've done the exercise to earn them.

Afternoon tea developed in the late 1800s as a small extra meal to fill the gap between lunch and dinner, one that continued to widen as people took their evening meal ever later in the day. These days, changes in our social customs and working hours mean that most of us rarely take a proper, ceremonial afternoon tea, which makes it all the more special if you decide to make an occasion of it. A lazy summer day is the perfect time for this celebration: as the afternoon stretches before you, there is nothing more glorious than sharing a full teatime spread complete with pots of tea and dainty confections arranged next to a variety of finger sandwiches made with cotton-soft bread.

Afternoon tea certainly makes for a less stressful form of entertaining than lunch or dinner—you can easily set up a spread at home or in the garden, and everything can be baked ahead, and stored well or frozen undecorated days before. Then you can sit back and enjoy the company, letting the late afternoon drift by in a leisurely fashion, and relax to the sound of spoons tinkling against china cups and saucers. How civilized!

AFTERNOON TEA CRAFTS

A few homemade and inexpensive crafts can make all the difference to your teatime spread and will bring a personal touch. Make quick invitations and pretty envelopes, get a creative friend to help design some labels and make vintage-looking cake stands and bunting which can be reused throughout the year.

BROWN-PAPER TAGS

For a "bring your own bake" tea party, send guests a couple of plain tags in decorative envelopes and ask them to personalize their offerings. These are also useful for labeling foods on a buffet table or as gift tags.

I: Buy a selection of plain paper tags. 2: Using pens, watercolor paints and ink stamps, illustrate them with your own designs. 3: Thread some string through the hole and secure with a knot.

DECORATIVE ENVELOPES AND INVITATIONS

A creative way to decorate plain envelopes and cards. Use a calligraphy pen or fine paintbrush to write details.

I: To make your own lined envelopes, unfold a standard envelope. 2: Use it as a template to cut out your chosen paper, such as pretty drawer liner or wrapping paper. 3: Line the insides and reseal with a glue stick. 4: For decorative invitations use a selection of watercolors on cards and illustrate with tea-themed symbols. Use a craft punch to cut pretty shapes.

HOMEMADE BUNTING

Make vintage-looking bunting using leftover fabric scraps. It's useful decoration for all celebratory occasions.

I: Make a triangle template out of cardboard. 2: Place the template on cotton fabric and cut around it with pinking shears. Repeat as required. 3: Sew the triangles onto the back of a ribbon, pattern side out. Leave 10 inches at both ends to tie around a pole or branch.

CAKE STANDS

This is a fun way to make your own mismatched cake stands. Handle carefully as these are very fragile.

I: Using a large plate as the base of the stand, stick down a glass or teacup in the center using epoxy glue (available in hardware stores). 2: Continue the sequence for as many layers as desired, using smaller plates as you go along and finishing with either a plate or a cup. 3: Leave to dry in a safe place for 24 hours before use. Clean with care, using a damp cloth.

SETTING THE TEA TABLE

Decide whether you are going to have a buffet-style spread laid out on a table so that your guests will be standing and helping themselves, or whether you're after a smaller, more intimate affair with beautifully set places at a table. Cover tables with delicate

floral or pastel-colored tablecloths. Use small side plates and little napkins (pretty paper cocktail ones are quick and easy) with mismatched china—you can seek out interesting crockery at antique or charity shops to create a tea set. Add comfort to wrought-iron chairs with pretty cushions and drape sweeping bunting as a backdrop to bring a celebratory feel to the scene. Old-fashioned birdcages can be found at garden centers or antique shops and work well as features on a central table. Weave ivy through the bars of the cage, or fill it with a bunch of mixed flowers, such as roses, stocks, peonies and sweet peas. Old tea caddies look authentic as "aged" vases to hold extra flowers, and stack teaspoons, which can easily be overlooked, in jam jars decorated with ribbons.

AFTERNOON TEA MENU

Teas and Infusions
One or two pots of classic teas (page 250)
A selection of herbal or fruit teas
Lemon and Mint Iced Tea (page 251)

Finger Sandwiches
Allow one round per person, with two
or three different fillings (page 253)

Bite-sized Fancies
Allow a couple per person:
Nutella Madeleines (page 261),
Mini Fruit Tarts (page 254) or Macarons

Traditional Scones
Allow one per person (page 254) –
serve with jam and clotted cream

Whole Cakes
Offer two varieties:
Carrot and Walnut Cake (page 257),
Coffee Cake (page 258), Victoria Sponge
(page 253); Lemon Drizzle Cake
(page 254)

Fresh fruit
Bowls of cherries or berries, or glasses
of Sparkling Fruit Jellies (page 149)

A TIME FOR TEA

Tea is the second most popular drink in the world after water. In the eighteenth century it was so popular that supply couldn't meet demand and it also carried a heavy import duty, which many people couldn't afford. As a result it was bulked out with substitutions, such as leaves from various native trees, as well as other things, like used tea leaves. It's easy to see why tea was so admired: it's endlessly varied, with a remarkable array of subtly different flavors. Earl Grey, with its delicate and fragrant aroma, is a favorite afternoon tea in the Western world—its sales far surpass any other tea variety. It makes for a refreshing, light summer tea, although in the winter I enjoy a good English Breakfast tea.

At a proper tea party, the tea bags should go in a teapot, rather than individually in mugs. That said, it can be fun for guests to choose their own flavored tea bag from a range of several types set out in baskets or tea chests. Loose-leaf tea in pots makes for excellent, fuller and fresher flavored tea, and it can be fun to experiment with different varieties, but on a larger scale it might be less practical and not everyone (except for connoisseurs, like my tea-loving brother) will appreciate the difference.

Fresh herbal and flower-based teas are cleansing, elegant and look great in clear glass teapots (jasmine tea with dried flowers looks pretty as the flowers unfurl). Serve a refreshing, chilled iced tea in the warm summer months from teapots filled with ice (great for children). Cocktails poured into teacups and served with saucers are a fun idea for a bachelorette party or baby shower.

TEAS TO TRY

- *Fragrant tea (such as Earl Grey or Lady Grey).*

- *Lapsang Souchong (its smoky and refreshing flavor is an acquired taste— a favorite of my father); mix with English Breakfast for a more subtle flavor.*

- *Black tea with or without milk (try Darjeeling, Assam or Ceylon); offer slices of lemon, or sugar or honey to sweeten.*

- *Fruit or flower-based tea (such as lemon and ginger, berries, jasmine or rose); try adding slices of lemon studded with cloves.*

- *Herbal tea (both dried teas and infusions of fresh mint, ginger slices or rooibos/ redbush tea are popular).*

- *Green tea (plain or a flavored variety).*

LEMON AND MINT ICED TEA Serves 4

Place 1 quart of water, the juice of 2 lemons, 4 tablespoons of superfine sugar and a handful of mint leaves in a large pan and bring to a boil. Turn off the heat and add 3 lemons and ginger tea bags to the liquid. Let the tea bags infuse for 10 minutes. Strain the liquid into a large pitcher and allow to cool completely. Divide crushed or cubed ice between 4 serving glasses, and pour the cold tea mixture over the ice. Garnish each glass with a sprig of mint and half a slice of lemon.

TEATIME CLASSICS

A celebratory afternoon tea calls for plump rounds of springy cakes iced high and fanciful tarts filled to the brim. Choose a variety of sweet treats of differing shapes, textures and flavors, both home baked and store-bought. Display finger sandwiches, scones and delicate individual bites, such as madeleines, fruit tarts, or fondant fancies on tiered stands, and plate cakes to complement their icing and decorations on simple-stemmed pastel, white and glass stands. Colorful paper doilies will elevate plain white plates. If setting up a buffet table, arrange one end for food, with the tea service, crockery and cutlery at the other end. Have plenty of cake knives to cut slices, small plates with forks for stickier cakes, sugar bowls filled with cubed or shaped sugar and milk pitchers. And don't underestimate the number of pots of tea required. You can buy giant teapots that serve 8 to 12 people, or just make sure that you have extra pots of boiling water to top off as required.

FINGER SANDWICHES

An essential addition to a teatime spread. Remove the crusts using a large chef's knife and cut them into fingers or triangles with a single cutting motion to create plump-looking sandwiches. Thinly sliced cucumber is a classic filling, or try the fillings in the box. Cover them with a damp tea towel or kitchen towel to keep them from drying out, or wrap them tightly in plastic wrap.

TIP: *Make sandwich flags so that guests can see fillings at a glance. Cut pretty paper and construction paper into 6 x ¾ -inch strips. Cover the construction paper strip with a glue stick and attach a toothpick to one end, then stick the paper strip over the top to cover it. When dry, cut out a "V" shape to make a flag, and write on the sandwich filling.*

FILLINGS

- *Homemade egg mayonnaise with watercress.*
- *Mature cheddar with homemade chutney (page 388).*
- *Chicken, avocado and watercress.*
- *Baked ham (page 130) with mustard and salad.*
- *Brie, ripe tomato and basil.*
- *Smoked salmon, cream cheese and arugula.*
- *Shrimp mayonnaise.*
- *Smoked trout pâté (page 119), cucumber and mache.*

VICTORIA SPONGE Serves 8–10

An all-time classic sponge cake, and quintessentially British. Preheat the oven to 350°F. Grease and line two round 8-inch pans with parchment paper. Evenly divide the basic sponge mixture on page 291 between them. Bake in the oven for 35 minutes, then cool on a wire rack. Fill with jam (page 387) and cream, buttercream (page 291) and fresh berries, or whatever takes your fancy. Decorate the top with confectioner's sugar.

MINI FRUIT TARTS Makes 24

Fill 24 store-bought pastry tart shells with simple fruit jams (page 387) or lemon curd, and bake on a lined tray at 350°F for 6 to 8 minutes until the filling melts. Leave to cool. Alternatively, fill with store-bought vanilla pudding or sweetened cream topped with ripe fresh fruit and glazed with warmed apricot jam.

TIP: *To make sweetened cream, whisk ¾ cup of heavy cream with 1 tablespoon of sifted confectioner's sugar and ½ teaspoon of vanilla extract to soft peaks. Add more sugar to taste. Makes enough for 24 individual tart shells.*

LEMON DRIZZLE CAKE Serves 8–10

Grease and line an 8½ x 4½-inch loaf pan. Preheat the oven to 325°F. In a bowl, cream 1½ sticks of softened unsalted butter and 1 cup of superfine sugar until light and fluffy. Gradually beat 3 medium eggs into the mixture one at a time. Fold in ¾ cup of self-rising flour, 1 cup of ground almonds, 3 tablespoons of milk, the zest of 2 lemons and 1 teaspoon of vanilla extract. Pour the batter into the pan and level the surface. Bake in the center of the oven for 45 to 50 minutes until firm. Let the cake stand in the pan for 5 minutes before turning out onto a wire rack. In a bowl, mix the juice of 2 lemons and ¼ cup of superfine sugar until combined. Prick the warm cake all over with a fork and brush the mixture over it. For a thick lemon icing, beat 1½ cups of confectioner's sugar with the juice of ½ a lemon and 1 tablespoon of water. Spread over the cake. Garnish with candied lemon peel.

TIP: *For candied lemon peel, add the zest from 2 lemons to a saucepan with ½ cup of water and ½ cup of superfine sugar. Bring to a boil and simmer for 10 minutes until the peel is translucent and crinkles at the edges, and drain.*

TRADITIONAL SCONES Makes 12

Preheat the oven to 400°F. In a bowl, mix together 2 cups of self-rising flour and a pinch of salt, and rub in 3 tablespoons of unsalted butter, cut into cubes. Stir in 2 tablespoons of superfine sugar, then slowly add 3 tablespoons of milk and ¼ cup of water until you have a soft dough. Turn the dough out onto a floured work surface and bring together gently with your hands; to ensure a light scone, do not overwork. Pat out the dough to ¾-inch thickness and, using a 2-inch cutter, stamp out rounds and place them on a baking sheet. Repeat until you have used up all the dough. Brush the tops with beaten egg yolk, sprinkle turbinado sugar over them and bake for 15 minutes until well risen and golden. Serve with jam (page 387) and clotted cream.

MACARONS *Add a touch of Parisian chic to the table and offer macarons in an assortment of sizes and gemlike colors. They are quite tricky to make, so I'd recommend buying them from a good bakery. Experiment with different flavors; their vivid shades will really vamp up the tea spread.*

CARROT AND WALNUT CAKE

Decadent and moist, this cake is best eaten from a plate with a fork as it can get quite gooey using your fingers. A glass or net food cover can be useful to protect sticky cakes like this from flies.

SERVES 8–10

1 cup vegetable oil

¾ cup packed light brown sugar

3 medium eggs

1½ cups self-rising flour

1 teaspoon baking powder

a good pinch of nutmeg

a good pinch of cinnamon

a good pinch of ground ginger

a small pinch of salt

1 cup walnuts, roughly chopped

½ cup raisins, soaked in water and drained

8 ounces carrots, grated

For the cream-cheese icing

2 tablespoons unsalted butter, softened

1¼ cups confectioner's sugar

11 ounces cream cheese

¾ cup whole walnuts

Grease and line two 8-inch round cake pans with parchment paper. Preheat the oven to 325°F.

Beat the oil and sugar together until combined, then add the eggs and mix well. Sift in the flour, baking powder, spices and salt, then add the walnuts, raisins and carrots and beat well.

Divide the batter between the pans. Bake for 25 to 30 minutes until the cakes are well risen and spring back when lightly touched. Transfer to a wire rack to cool completely.

To make the icing, beat the butter and confectioner's sugar together until light and fluffy, then mix in the cream cheese. Thickly spread half the icing on one of the cake layers, sandwich the two together and spread the remaining icing on top. Place the whole walnuts on top of the cake before serving.

TIPS: *There is always cake left over at tea parties. Cakes and cookies do store well for up to five days (if kept in a cool, dry place), so you can keep any untouched slices in airtight cake tins or plastic containers. Alternatively, buy a selection of cake boxes and send guests home with the leftovers. • You can freeze the cooled cakes before the icing stage for up to 1 month. Defrost fully and ice as directed above.*

 CUPCAKES *To make cupcake versions, grease and line 2 muffin pans with 16 paper liners and divide the mixture among each. Bake for 18 to 20 minutes.*

COFFEE CAKE

One of my favorite flavored cakes; the rich, deep flavor of the coffee sponge makes a slice perfectly satisfying. This cake is a lovely contrast to lighter-colored sponge cakes on a tea table.

¾ cup superfine sugar

1 cup golden syrup (or honey)

1½ sticks unsalted butter

2 tablespoons instant coffee powder or granules

2 large eggs

2 tablespoons milk

2 cups self-rising flour, sifted

1 teaspoon baking powder

For the buttercream icing

7 tablespoons unsalted butter, softened

1 cup confectioner's sugar

3 teaspoons coffee flavoring or extract

cocoa powder

Preheat the oven to 350°F. Grease and line an 8-inch round cake pan with baking parchment.

Melt the sugar and syrup in a saucepan, together with the butter, over gentle heat. Stir in the instant coffee until dissolved.

Allow to cool completely (you could put the pan in a large bowl of ice cold water to speed up this process), then gradually stir in the eggs and milk.

Pour this mixture with the sifted flour and baking powder into a large bowl. Beat until smooth, then pour into the cake pan and bake for 20 to 25 minutes, until well risen and the cake springs back when lightly touched. Transfer to a wire rack to cool completely.

For the buttercream icing, mix together the butter and confectioner's sugar in a bowl, then stir in the coffee essence. Spread the icing over the cooled cake, dust with sifted cocoa powder and decorate with chocolate-coated coffee beans.

> CHOCOLATE-COATED COFFEE BEANS *Line a tray with baking parchment. Melt 3½ ounces of chopped dark or milk chocolate in a bowl set over a pan of simmering water. Add 2 ounces of roasted coffee beans and stir to coat. Turn out onto the tray, separate them with a fork, and leave to cool, dusting with cocoa powder, if desired, just before the chocolate has set.*

NUTELLA MADELEINES

These are irresistible to both adults and children and so easy to make. Nutella isn't just for spreading on toast! You can also try using white or plain chocolate spread instead.

MAKES 24

5 tablespoons unsalted butter, melted and cooled slightly, plus extra for greasing

2 tablespoons all-purpose flour, for dusting

6 tablespoons superfine sugar

3 medium eggs

1 teaspoon vanilla extract

½ cup self-rising flour

2 tablespoons good-quality cocoa powder

For the topping

½ cup Nutella

½ cup confectioner's sugar

¼ cup hazelnuts, toasted and chopped

Preheat the oven to 350°F. Brush two madeleine pans with melted butter. Dust with flour, invert the pans and tap out the excess.

Place the sugar, eggs and vanilla extract in a large bowl and whisk together for at least 5 minutes or until pale, thick and able to hold a trail on the surface. Carefully sift the self-rising flour and cocoa powder over the mixture, then fold in with a large metal spoon. Pour the melted butter down the edge of the bowl and fold it in quickly and gently.

Spoon 1 tablespoon of the mix into each of the madeleine molds. Bake for 10 minutes. Remove from the oven, transfer to a wire rack and leave to cool completely.

To make the topping, mix together the Nutella, confectioner's sugar and a touch of hot water to loosen the mixture slightly. Spread over the tops of the madeleines, and sprinkle the chopped hazelnuts over the top to serve.

TIPS: *If you are worried about those with nut allergies, most supermarkets stock nut-free chocolate spreads. Check the label for nut content. • To make plain madeleines, leave out the cocoa powder from the recipe above and increase the flour to ¾ cup. Add the finely grated zest of ½ a lemon, and bake as directed. Dust with a little confectioner's sugar before serving. • The sponges will freeze uniced for up to 1 month.*

FABULOUS FLOWERS

Flowers add the finishing touch to any celebration. You don't need to spend a lot on elaborate arrangements—even a bunch of fresh herbs or a few stems picked from the garden in a small glass jar, pottery pitcher or vintage tin can look good.

SIMPLE FLOWER ARRANGEMENTS

There's no right way to arrange flowers, but the following steps give a few basic tips for displaying flowers in a vase or as a more formal arrangement; adapt to suit the occasion and your personal taste.

VASE ARRANGEMENTS:

1: Choose your vase according to the flowers you are working with—tall fluted or convex vases for long stems, square or globe vases for shorter arrangements. Fill with clean water and flower food. 2: Begin by adding a mix of greenery. The foliage will act as a base to support your blooms. Place your flowers in between. 3: For a large vase arrangement with tall flowers, place crumpled chicken wire in the bottom of the vase and use it as a support, placing the stems in the holes in the wire to stop them from moving.

FORMAL ARRANGEMENTS OR TABLE CENTERPIECES:

1: Cut floral foam to fit your container and soak it in water. 2: Secure the foam to the container with floral tape and begin to create the shape of your arrangement using foliage or aromatic herbs. Start with the largest and longest pieces of foliage in the center and work outward. 3: Intersperse the foliage with flowers, starting with the largest and finishing with the more delicate flowers for texture.

TIP: *If arranging long stems, such as amaryllis, use a garden cane (and ties) to support the weight of the flowers.*

TABLE ARRANGEMENT DOS AND DON'TS

- Do use ordinary jars or pitchers for flowers if you've run out of vases.

- Do choose round globe vases, which are low and can be filled with a few flower heads, such as hydrangeas, or decorated by wrapping calla lilies and grass around the insides.

- Do form clusters or rows of potted flowers or small bud vases to suit the size of your table.

- Don't use strongly scented flowers on a dining table.

- Don't clutter the eye line—ensure tall arrangements sit above eye level, or move them aside when guests are seated.

- Don't leave the stamens on lilies as they will stain furniture, tablecloths and clothes; pull them off with your fingers.

CUT-FLOWER CARE

Make your flowers last longer with these simple tips:

- Cut flowers or herbs in the morning or evening, when they are holding water, rather than in the heat of the day.

- When buying flowers, choose ones that are not yet in full bloom. If using flowers from the garden, to keep them from wilting, condition them prior to use by stripping the stems of leaves, cutting the stems at an angle and giving them a good drink. This is especially important if putting them into an arrangement with floral foam.

- If you receive a hand-tied bouquet as a gift, it will stay fresh until you're ready to put it into a vase. Carefully remove the packaging and recut the stems about 1 inch up at an angle before putting into a vase filled with fresh lukewarm water. You don't need to untie the bouquet unless you want to rearrange the flowers or split them up. Do snip off any leaves and foliage below the water line.

- Flowers will last much longer if you use flower-food packets (usually supplied with bouquets). Make sure the vase is clean and change the water every couple of days. Recut the stems every few days and remove any dying flowers.

- Keep vases of flowers out of direct sunlight and away from ripening fruit, in a cool, well-ventilated place.

- If flowers, such as hydrangeas or roses, wilt: recut the stems and submerge them in deep water up to the base of the flowerheads to revive them.

- For flowers arranged in floral foam, water the foam every couple of days.

WORKING WITH THE SEASONS

All kinds of imported flowers are available year-round, but the cheapest and greenest option is to go for seasonal, locally grown flowers and plants:

- All year: alstroemeria, carnation, freesia, gerbera, gypsophila, lily, rose.
- Spring: poppy anemone, blossom (such as cherry blossom), bluebells, daffodils, forget-me-nots, hyacinth, primrose, pussy willow, tulips.
- Summer: alchemilla mollis (lady's mantle), cornflower, daisy, delphinium, elderflower, herbs, hydrangea, lavender, lilac, peony, stock, sunflower, sweet pea.
- Autumn: calla lily, dahlia, gladiola, hydrangea, phlox.
- Winter: amaryllis, bulbs, cyclamen, evergreens, holly, ivy, mistletoe, poinsettia.

DRYING AND PRESSING FLOWERS

Dried flowers, particularly lavender, are lovely for making scented bags as gifts (page 154) or as "confetti" for scattering along tables (but you can buy biodegradable dried-flower confetti packs if you don't have the time or patience to make your own). Pressed flowers look lovely stuck on cards or on the outside of pillar candles. For enthusiasts, a flower press makes a lovely present.

To dry flowers, pick them in the heat of a dry day, strip the stems of their leaves and hang them upside down in small bunches secured with a rubber band in an airy, dark place. Leave them for about two weeks. Some flowers, like hydrangeas, need to be dried upright in about ¾ inch of water.

To press flowers, place them between sheets of absorbent paper inside a heavy book, and weight it down with a stack of other books. Leave for a few weeks.

MEANINGFUL BLOOMS

- Freesia: lasting friendship.
- Pansy: "think of me."
- Gypsophila Baby's Breath: everlasting love.
- Lily: majesty and great beauty.
- Ranunculus: radiant with charms.
- Snowdrops: lift the spirits, bringing hope and consolation.
- Orchid: refined beauty, elegance and grace.
- Rose: the stronger the affection, the deeper the color; white roses for a heart unacquainted with love, pink for grace and red for a full emblem of love.
- Carnation: a pink carnation for pure love, a red carnation for an avowal of love and a white carnation as an affectionate gesture.
- Myrtle: this fragrant shrub with delicate white flowers symbolizes love.

FLORIST'S TOOL KIT

- *Floral shears.*
- *Assortment of vases, both tall and short (tank, fluted, convex, column, globe and bud vases) in glass and china.*
- *Enamel jugs, terra-cotta pots, metal buckets, old decanters and jam jars.*
- *Floral foam and florist wire.*
- *Fine gravel to weigh down pots and vases.*

EDIBLE FLOWERS

Here are a few decorative ways to use flowers in food. It's important to identify them correctly, and use only unsprayed flowers.

- **Salads and garnishes:** nasturtium or dandelion add a splash of fresh color.

- **Ice cubes:** when starflower, also called borage, is in bloom, freeze the pretty blue blossoms in ice cubes. These are amazing with Pimm's. Primrose is wonderful in springtime cocktails (page 231).

- **Cake decorations:** crystallized flowers and leaves, such as violets, primrose, cowslip and mint, are easy to make and are fabulous for decorating cakes or garnishing drinks. If using rose petals, remove the white part as it is bitter.

MAKING CRYSTALLIZED FLOWERS OR LEAVES

Brush each petal or leaf carefully with lightly whisked egg white and dip gently in a dish of superfine sugar. Shake off the excess sugar and dry on a wire rack in a warm place for a few hours or overnight, until the petal or leaf has hardened.

GARDEN SHED MUST-HAVES

Keep these items handy when you're entertaining outdoors:

- *Plastic sheeting for a slip and slide, water guns and sprinklers.*

- *Wheelbarrow (to chill drinks in).*

- *Gazebo, tent and hammock.*

- *Fold-away chairs and collapsible tables.*

- *Fire pits, braziers and firelighters.*

- *Garden torches, storm lanterns, citronella candles.*

- *Kite, frisbee, sun canopy and beach kit.*

- *Burlap cloth and table clips for outdoor tables.*

- *Wooden crates, buckets and bamboo sticks.*

- *Croquet, badminton and boules sets.*

- *Wiffle ball and baseball bats.*

- *Balls: football, soccer, baseball, wiffle ball and tennis.*

- *Giant games: Jenga, Pick Up Sticks and Connect Four.*

SUMMER

CHILDREN'S PARTIES
BARBECUES
PICNICS
CAMPING

Days stretch long into violet dusks where swallows dip and swoop. Borders of sweet-scented flowers buzz with industrious bees and butterflies. This is a time to be outside with the hum of lawnmowers and sizzle of barbecues, playing barefoot, soaking up the sun or cooling off in dappled shade. A distant roll of thunder echoes through the heat-charged afternoon—a close promise of rain. It clears and turns into a balmy, pink-skied evening.

"*We do not stop playing because we grow old,*
we grow old because we stop playing."

Benjamin Franklin

CHILDREN'S PARTIES

This chapter is all about creating a colorful children's party that is fun, achievable and traditional. The key to any successful children's party is not how much you spend on it, but that you approach it creatively and thoughtfully—making it special and magical for your children and their friends. Some of my fondest childhood memories are of birthday parties at home or at friends' houses, playing all our favorite games (many of which are included here, and all of them are very easy), enjoying party treats . . . and, of course, judging the greatness of the event by the size of the birthday cake and the contents of the party favor bags. I used to love helping Mum prepare for my birthdays at home: writing the invitations, filling the party favor bags the day before and blowing up balloons to decorate the house. Choosing a favorite dress to wear and being involved in the decisions and the preparations was all part of the excitement—rather like the anticipation I felt in the build-up to Christmas.

What should always be at the forefront of your mind while you're planning a celebration like this is that children's birthday parties should be happy occasions, full of fun and enjoyment, with the children at the center of it—and that you're not doing this, as can often be the case, to impress other moms or dads. Birthdays are really important to little ones; I recall being so excited about being a whole year older and having a day to revel in things I wouldn't normally be allowed to do or eat. This is not to say that every birthday party should be an expensive extravaganza. You can still organize a successful party at home or in a nearby venue affordably and simply, even if it means getting a friend to help you. Doing things within your means and sticking to a budget can bring an immense sense of satisfaction. You may even decide that you want to dedicate the majority of your budget to an entertainer who can generate a few seamless hours of amusement and games to keep the children happily occupied.

The amount of time you dedicate to planning the party all depends on what you can manage, but it's worth remembering that these occasions do not need to be very different year after year—the main components can remain the same. Subtle changes can be brought about with a topical theme, and food and drink labeled accordingly or a novelty cake, for instance—small details that help make these parties so special and memorable.

PLANNING AND PREPARING

PARTY TIME LINE

The following guide will help you start planning your party, keep things on track and avoid any last-minute panic. Keep a party diary or journal and make notes of useful tips, games, and ideas you used. Jot down reminders of what worked and what didn't to refer to next year.

8 WEEKS AHEAD Set a date and time. Decide on the number of children, the location and theme. Book a venue and entertainer, if necessary.

3 WEEKS AHEAD Send out invitations with an RSVP date and arrange helpers.

1—2 WEEKS AHEAD Shop for any party supplies when you know how many children are coming. Prepare and plan games. Check guests' food allergies with parents. Order nonperishable party food and drink (individually packed foods are better than larger packs to avoid waste) and prepare freezable foods. Confirm bookings.

2 DAYS AHEAD Make the cake and any food that can be stored in plastic containers. Fill and assemble party favor bags. Charge your camera battery and get last-minute foods and any extra accessories for the cake.

1 DAY AHEAD Decorate the cake and prepare other food (if hot food, cook and reheat the following day). Discuss the next day's plans with the birthday girl/boy. Decorate your house in the evening and clear the games area. Check the weather forecast if the party is outside.

DAY OF THE PARTY Prepare fresh food: sandwiches (cover with damp tea towels to keep them from drying out), fruit and drinks. Blow up balloons. Decorate your front door or driveway. Play music, put up a sign for the bathroom, set the table and lay out food. Get the birthday child ready and clear a space for birthday presents (have a pen and paper handy to note who they are from).

ORDER OF THE DAY

- *Welcome guests with balloons tied outside the front door or garden gate.*

- *Calm ice breaker or quiet game (page 294).*

- *Lively games (page 300).*

- *Birthday tea and cake (page 282).*

- *Quieter games or activities (page 294).*

- *A few musical games (page 298).*

- *Party favor bags or grab bag (page 304).*

- *Wave good-bye.*

OUTDOOR PARTIES

It's always easier to host children's parties outside, but remember to have a contingency plan in case the weather turns bad. If you live near the ocean, a fun idea could be a trip to the beach with seaside activities, such as building sand castles, kite flying or shell crafts (page 339). You could host a sports party in a nearby park with relays, egg and spoon races and obstacle courses, or a game of Wiffle ball (page 330). Bring mini bottles of water and oranges for halftime. Let parents know if their children need to dress for messy or outdoor activities.

TIMING

Assuming the party is held at home, restrict its length to 2 to 3 hours in an afternoon so that your guests leave in high spirits before they become tired and grumpy (for older children it could stretch a little longer or later). For toddler parties, midmorning works well, although bear in mind that they can get tired after an hour and a half. Make sure you let parents know what meal you will be providing for their children.

NUMBERS

With your child's input, plan how many guests you want to invite and, more important, how many you can manage. For toddlers or children under five years old, keep numbers limited and expect parents to come along too (and perhaps extra siblings). For children aged five or above, any number between eight and twelve guests should be about right, although budget and space will be the deciding factors. Don't feel pressured into inviting the whole class, particularly if it's a large one, and remind your child to keep it low key in front of those who aren't invited. One option is to have a joint party and team up with another family—this is particularly good if a child has a friend in the same class with a birthday around the same time. Alternatively, you might consider inviting just the boys or just the girls for a gender-specific party. This will help to avoid any class upset as well. You can always ask the teacher if your child can bring in a birthday treat, such as cupcakes, for the whole class to make everyone feel included.

HELPERS

Enlist friends, family members or babysitters to act as assistants at the party. Older siblings can also help out. Get them to be responsible for specific elements of the party, such as looking after other parents, running a few games, manning the music station during musical games, making cups of tea or taking children to the bathroom. Have a list of things they can help with beforehand, too, such as preparing sandwiches and laying out the party food, looking after guests' coats and shoes, taking photos or doing face painting.

TIP: *Have plenty of wet wipes for sticky fingers. A first-aid kit might be useful, too.*

CRAFTS AND ACTIVITIES

Children love to use their imaginations, whether it's when creating crafts or making food such as mini pizzas (page 287). You can also get them to help make a few decorations, or plan a quiet activity during the party, like decorating plain paper hats, masks, place mats or party boxes with sequins, stickers, glitter and pasta shapes.

ORIGAMI PLATTER

This is a colorful way to serve children's favorite things. Fill each of the four cones with different sweets.

1: Cut a 20-inch square out of thin construction paper. Fold in all four corners to the center. Turn over and again fold in the four corners. 2: Turn it back over and stick numbers on each square, and decorate. 3: Fold in half between the squares in both directions. Place thumbs and forefingers in each square and bring together so that all the points meet. Turn over and fill the holes with snacks and sweets.

DIY T-SHIRTS

A fun activity for early on so that the decorations have time to dry, ready to take home at the end of the party.

Let them design their T-shirts using fabric markers or fabric paints. You can customize new white T-shirts or revive old ones.

DECORATING COOKIES AND CUPCAKES

Get children to design fun cookie characters or cupcakes to match the theme of the birthday party.

Bake shaped cookies (pages 23 and 225) or plain cupcakes (page 291), then let children decorate them. Have different colored icing and a variety of edible decorations: sprinkles, silver balls, sugar flowers, glitter, glacé cherries and icing pens. Cookie- and cupcake-decorating kits are also quick and easy.

TISSUE TEA LIGHTS

These look beautiful hung out of reach on trees. For a children's party, use battery-powered tea lights.

1: Loop wire around a jam jar, twisting the ends to secure. Attach a second loop of wire to hang the jar from. 2: Cut up pieces of colored tissue paper. 3: Paint the outside of the jam jar with craft glue and stick on the tissue. Place a lit tea light inside.

TIP: *Decorate jam jars or glass tea-light holders with glass paint for a stained-glass effect and as a gift to take home.*

BUTTERFLY LANTERNS

Buy inexpensive plain paper lanterns, then spruce them up with tissue paper butterflies to hang indoors and out.

1: Make a template and cut out two butterflies from colored tissue paper and one from colored construction paper. 2: Stack the three pieces together and crease down the center. 3: Use craft glue along the fold of the card, then place a tissue butterfly on top. Add another line of glue down the fold, and place the last tissue butterfly on the top. 4: Glue the butterflies onto the paper lantern, card side down. 5: Repeat as required.

HOMEMADE MAYPOLE

Make your own maypole using a long stick and colorful ribbons. Children will love dancing around it and weaving their own color in and out. You could combine this with a game of musical chairs.

· 1: Attach five ribbons (each approximately 8 feet in length) to the tip of a long wooden pole using a hammer and nails or a professional staple gun. 2: Wrap heavy-duty masking tape around the top of the pole, then stick on ribbons and felt flowers using a glue stick

MAYPOLE DANCING *This custom stems from a celebration of the end of winter. Historically, in spring, young branches were cut from trees and stuck into the ground and became a focus for festivities. Over the years these tree poles became Maypoles. They were reused each year on May 1st, and dancing children made pretty patterns by braiding colorful ribbons around the poles as they danced.*

PARTY DECORATIONS

Mix and match what you already have at home with store-bought decorations and a few that you might make. There's always plenty of choice for children's parties, so it's the perfect opportunity to go all out with color. Stock up on fun accessories, such as party poppers, streamers, confetti and party hats. Have helium balloons hanging freely from the ceiling with bright curling ribbons cascading down or tied in clusters to the backs of chairs (write names on single balloons as place cards).

BANNERS, BUNTING AND STREAMERS

You can find all sorts of decorations from party shops and online, especially if you have a theme and want matching banners. Hang banners and bunting in the main party room or, if the party's outside, tie them between trees or use them to festoon hedges. Make the most of windows by sticking cut-out shapes and stencils on them (page 14), and hang garlands and paper lanterns from light fixtures or tree branches. Nonmarking poster tack and sticky tape, as well as a hammer and nails, are useful for fixing decorations.

THE PARTY TABLE

Make your table the center of attention but don't go overboard with clutter. A plain-colored or white tablecloth is a good base (and paper or plastic ones are a practical option) to which you can add a few block colors or one prominent theme with your choice of tableware. Fill brightly colored tin buckets with cutlery wrapped in napkins, or use a fun table runner: you can buy paper versions in rolls that can be cut to size or used as oversized place mats (white ones can be doodled on with crayons). To prevent things from being knocked over, attach larger bowls, plates and cake stands to the table using poster tack. If you have limited space or don't have enough chairs, plan a party picnic on a blanket or sheet on the floor with cushions and beanbags scattered around. When setting your party table outside, make sure it's out of the wind and in the shade, and that the tablecloth is fastened with table clips. Individual cartons of juice and water bottles act as useful weights to keep paper plates and napkins from flying away. You could also place bottles of bubbles in paper cups—a practical solution that doubles as presents.

Make the table center an eye-catching one with origami platters (page 274) or large jars filled with candy, pitchers filled with colorful punches or tiered cupcake stands laden with sweet or savory snacks. A birthday cake makes a good centerpiece but set this on a pedestal (a box covered with foil, for example) to enhance its magic. As a finishing touch, fill the empty spaces on the table with handfuls of confetti, sequins or curls of ribbon.

THE BIRTHDAY TEA

Feeding children is often tricky as there will always be some fussy eaters, so keep the party menu simple and don't prepare anything too exotic or spicy. Children tend to eat a little less than usual when they are excited, so it's best not to go overboard. Avoid putting all the sweet and savory foods out at the same time as children will inevitably reach for the sweeter options first. Remember that children love things imaginatively presented—sandwiches cut into shapes, veggies in party cones and fruit juices turned into colorful ice cubes.

CASUAL PARTY PICNIC *For a more informal party setup in a nearby park or garden, lay out a blanket in the shade and bring a tray filled with individually labeled picnic party boxes for each child. Good, portable, packed-lunch-type items include mini filled rolls (easier than sandwiches, which can fall apart), yogurt with plastic spoons, individually wrapped cheeses, cartons of juice, dried fruit or plain popcorn, boxes of raisins or handfuls of grapes. If there's room, include pretty napkins, party blowers and hats.*

PARTY DRINKS AND FUN ICE CUBES

Offer a selection of soft drinks: carbonated drinks, diluted cordials or milkshakes are all popular. Remember to fill cups only when everyone is sitting around the table to avoid spillages. Straws, paper umbrellas and, for older kids, edible garnishes on toothpicks are nice celebratory touches. Make carbonated cordial drinks and plain juices more fun by adding colorful fruit juice ice cubes.

STRAWBERRY MILKSHAKE Serves 4

For a strawberry milkshake, put 14 ounces of washed strawberries in a blender and blend until smooth. Add 2½ cups of milk, 2 tablespoons of superfine sugar and 2 scoops of strawberry or vanilla ice cream and blend again for 1 to 2 minutes. Divide among 4 tall glasses and serve immediately. Almost all fruits work well—make classic single flavors, try tropical fruits or make up combinations, such as peanut butter and banana. For a dairy-free option, replace the milk with almond milk and omit the ice cream. Straws are essential.

OLD-FASHIONED ST. CLEMENT'S Serves 4 (makes 4 cups)

This classic drink is simple to prepare for a crowd and popular with most children. Mix together 2 cups of good-quality orange juice and 2 cups of old-fashioned lemonade (for a homemade recipe see page 355). Orange juice ice cubes are best for this drink.

TIP: *Offer chilled wine, or pots of tea and coffee to parents who are staying to help.*

A SAVORY SPREAD

FUN SANDWICHES

Turn basic sandwiches into something more appealing for your party. For ease, use thinly sliced bread and spreadable butter. Have up to three different sandwich fillings and use paper flags (page 253) as labels to identify each filling, or arrange on tiered cupcake stands.

Snail Pinwheels: Spread crustless bread slices or tortilla wraps evenly with a creamy filling, such as tuna or egg salad. Roll the bread (or wrap) up tightly in plastic wrap and chill. To serve cut into ¾-inch pieces and decorate using a toothpick cut in half for the antennae and peas or corn for the eyes.

Shaped Sandwiches: Cut sandwiches using cookie cutters, such as flowers, hearts or stars. Spreads such as jam or cream cheese or sliced ham are good for these. Take out the middles with a small cutter to let the filling show through, or use gingerbread people cutters and decorate them with food.

Sandwich Boats: Cut sandwiches into triangles (crusts off), and use toothpicks to skewer cherry tomatoes, little lettuce leaves, slices of cucumber or salami as sails.

VEGGIE CONES AND DIPS Serves 8

Present an assembly of crunchy vegetable sticks in paper cones for kids to dip.

Hummus: Blend together 14 ounces of rinsed, canned chickpeas, ½ teaspoon of ground cumin, 6 tablespoons of olive oil, 1 clove of garlic, 1 teaspoon of salt, 3 tablespoons of tahini paste and the zest and juice of 1½ lemons until smooth, then season to taste.

Cheese dip: Melt 2 tablespoons of unsalted butter in a saucepan and stir in 2 tablespoons of all-purpose flour to make a smooth paste, then cook gently for 1 to 2 minutes before gradually pouring in 1¼ cups of milk. Stir for a few minutes more until it thickens, then add 7 ounces of grated cheddar cheese and stir until completely melted. Season to taste.

THINGS ON STICKS

- **Cheese 'n' Tomato Balls:** *Thread cherry tomatoes and mozzarella balls onto toothpicks and stick into a wedge of watermelon. Do the same with other chunky vegetables.*

- **Skewered Sandwiches:** *Shape your bread with a small cookie cutter and "sandwich" together on a skewer whatever your chosen filling is: lettuce, rolled ham and cheese and half a cherry tomato.*

MINI BURGERS Serves 8

Find kid-size mini buns or warm mini pitas, which are flatter and easier to handle.

Place 14 ounces of lean ground beef in a large bowl with 2 teaspoons of Dijon mustard, 1 to 2 teaspoons of Worcestershire sauce, 1 tablespoon of ketchup, 1 small peeled and grated red onion and 1 large egg yolk. Season and mix well to combine. Using damp hands, shape into 8 mini patties and flatten into burgers. Transfer to a tray, cover with plastic wrap and chill for 1 hour.

When ready to cook, preheat the broiler to medium high. Heat 2 tablespoons of olive oil in a nonstick ovenproof frying pan over medium heat and pan-fry the burgers for 3 to 4 minutes on each side or until cooked through and nicely colored. Lay a slice of cheese on top of each burger and place under the broiler until the cheese has melted. Spread a little mayonnaise or ketchup on the bottom half of 8 buns, arrange tomato slices and lettuce on top, followed

HOMEMADE PIZZA DOUGH Serves 8

Get children to help shape and decorate mini pizzas for a fun party activity. Use tomato purée for the sauce, grate lots of cheese and lay out a variety of toppings for everyone to create their own combinations.

Mix together a ¼-ounce packet of quick-acting yeast, 2 teaspoons of sugar and 1 cup of warm water in a bowl and leave to stand for 5 minutes. Place 2½ cups of bread flour and 1 teaspoon of salt in a large bowl. Make a well in the center and pour in the yeast mixture. Add 2 tablespoons of olive oil and mix together to form a soft dough. Add more flour if necessary.

Turn out onto a lightly floured surface and knead well with floured hands for at least 5 minutes, until the dough is smooth and springy to the touch. Place it in a large, lightly oiled bowl, cover with plastic wrap or a damp cloth, and leave it in a warm place for approximately 1 hour, until doubled in size. Knead it on a floured surface.

Divide into 8 equal-sized pieces and roll each piece out to 3-inch diameter circles about ⅓ inch thick. Place on a lightly floured baking tray and add toppings. To cook, drizzle them with extra virgin olive oil and bake in a preheated oven for 10 to 15 minutes at 425°F or until the pizzas are golden, the cheese has melted and the crust is crisp.

TIP : *If you don't have time to make your own dough, buy plain pizza crusts or use English muffin halves instead.*

SWEET THINGS

This is always a popular part of the birthday tea. Buy cake pops, butter bread and cover with sprinkles for fairy bread, swirl bread sticks into melted chocolate and sprinkles to make sparklers, or dip strawberries in chocolate and refrigerate.

KNICKERBOCKER GLORY Make to order

Set out a variety of ice cream flavors, store-bought chocolate sauces or a homemade fruit coulis (page 33) and toppings, such as fresh fruit, crushed malted milk balls or Pop Rocks candy, and get children to create personal concoctions in sundae glasses. Add wafers for a finishing touch.

CHOCOLATE BROWNIES Makes 16

Grease an 8-inch square pan and line with parchment paper. Preheat the oven to 350°F. Melt 7 ounces of dark chocolate and 1¼ sticks of unsalted butter in a pan. In a large bowl, beat 1 cup of packed light brown soft sugar and 3 large eggs with an electric mixer until light and fluffy, then pour in the melted chocolate. Sift ½ cup of self-rising flour into the bowl with 1 teaspoon of salt and fold it in, retaining as much air as possible. Add 3½ ounces of mini marshmallows, ¾ cup of chopped pecans and 3½ ounces of chopped white chocolate. Pour the mixture into the pan and bake for 25 to 30 minutes, until a skewer comes out sticky, but not with raw mixture attached. Let it cool in the pan completely, then serve in squares.

RICE KRISPIES SQUARES Makes 16

Grease an 8-inch square pan and line with baking parchment. Melt 3 tablespoons of unsalted butter in a large pan over low heat, then add 2 tablespoons of golden syrup and 8 ounces of pink and white marshmallows. Once melted, stir and remove from the heat, add 7 cups of Rice Krispies to the pan and mix well to combine. Press the mixture into the pan well and refrigerate until set. Arrange in a checkerboard pattern with brownies.

ORANGE JUICE GELATIN Serves 8

Sprinkle 5 teaspoons of powdered gelatin into ½ cup of cold water to soften. Dissolve 3 tablespoons of superfine sugar in 3⅓ cups of orange juice in a saucepan over low heat. Let it cool slightly, then add the gelatin and whisk to dissolve. Add some canned mandarin segments, pour into containers, then refrigerate until set. Serve with vanilla ice cream. You can also set the gelatin in scooped out orange halves, then cut into wedges.

BIRTHDAY CAKES

The highlight of any children's party is usually the birthday cake, smothered in lots of icing and decorations. The recipe opposite can be used as a handy base not only for a plain sponge cake but for little cupcakes and fairy cakes, too. These can be a visual spectacle, particularly if arranged on tiered cupcake stands as a centerpiece and decorated with mouthwatering delights. If you aren't confident making your own or don't have time, there are lots of quick and easy solutions to help you cheat. Buy plain sponge cakes, such as pound cakes or Swiss rolls (these are also good and firm for carving into novelty cakes) or assemble a store-bought cake mix and ice and decorate it yourself. You can also buy photo cupcakes, customizing the photos according to the birthday boy's or girl's tastes or using their picture on the top. Buttercream icing is best for large cakes or you can buy premade fondant icing in different colors. When you are ready to bring in the cake, close the curtains or dim the lights and make a grand entrance with the candles alight—the "magic" ones that continually relight once you've blown them out were always my favorite.

BASIC SPONGE MIXTURE

Makes enough for 1 deep 8-inch round or 7-inch square cake tin. Cream 1¾ sticks of softened unsalted butter, 1 cup of superfine sugar and 1 teaspoon of vanilla extract in a large bowl with an electric mixer and beat until light and fluffy. Gradually beat in 4 large eggs, one at a time, mixing well after each addition, then carefully fold in 1½ cups of sifted self-rising flour using a large metal spoon. Follow the baking instructions for Fairy Cakes (below), Victoria Sponge (page 253) or Rainbow Cake (page 292).

FAIRY CAKES Makes 12

Line a 12-hole muffin pan with paper cupcake liners and make up a batch of the basic sponge mixture (see above). Divide the mixture among the liners; bake in a preheated 350°F oven for 20 minutes. To decorate, use a simple glacé icing (confectioner's sugar and water, mixed thickly so as not to drip off cakes, or use buttercream (below) and add a few edible sugar decorations.

TIP: *Make butterfly fairy cakes by cutting a round disk out of the top of each cake and filling the hole with buttercream icing. Cut the sponge disk in half and stick the pieces at angles in the icing to create "wings."*

BUTTERCREAM ICING

Makes enough to ice 12 fairy cakes or 1 large sponge cake. Beat 1 stick of softened unsalted butter until light and fluffy. Sift in 2 cups of confectioner's sugar and add 2 teaspoons of freshly boiled water, then beat well until combined. Spread over your cake using an offset spatula.

RAINBOW CAKE

A great friend of mine always had a rainbow cake like this one at her birthday parties and they were the best. The food coloring in this recipe might make you gasp, but you can get natural versions—and, remember, it is a treat and not something your kids will have every day!

SERVES 10–12

unsalted butter, for greasing

3 egg whites

2 batches basic sponge
mixture (page 291)

2 tablespoons milk

2 teaspoons each of food
coloring in red, yellow,
orange, green, blue, purple
and pink, adding more
if required

For the filling

1 quantity buttercream icing
(page 291)

Preheat the oven to 350°F. Grease and line the bottom of 2 shallow 8-inch round cake pans with parchment paper.

Using an electric mixer, beat the egg whites in a large bowl until they form soft peaks. Add the basic sponge mixture and fold together. Add the milk and continue to fold for 1 to 2 minutes to combine.

Divide the mixture into seven separate bowls. Put a few drops of red food coloring in the first bowl and stir, adding more as necessary to get the desired intensity. Repeat with the remaining colors and bowls until you have seven bowls of colored cake mixture.

Divide spoonfuls of the cake mixture between the prepared pans, alternating the colors as you go and keeping each separate in the pan until all the mixture is used up.

Bake for 35 to 40 minutes or until risen and a skewer inserted into each cake comes out clean. Allow to cool in the pans for a few minutes before turning out onto a wire rack and cooling completely.

Turn one cake over onto a plate and spread with buttercream icing before placing the other cake on top.

TIPS : *For a marbled version of this cake, use 1 deep 8-inch cake pan and layer the colored batter, gently swirling as you go. To decorate, cover with buttercream icing and dot with M&M's (page 290).* • *Rather than cutting a round cake into wedges, try cutting it in long slices all the way across, then divide it into finger-sized portions. These will be easier for small people to manage and the cake will go much further.*

TRADITIONAL PARTY GAMES

Have a long list of games you are familiar with or have tried out beforehand and keep to a schedule when planning them—excited children get bored easily. For a two-hour party, you will need at least four to six games and activities. Outdoor games will be weather dependent, and you should have more lined up than you think you'll need; some will go down better than others. Play a selection before the birthday tea and a few after. Remember to buy enough prizes (that will fit into party favor bags) for all the games. Children under the age of four might not understand games in which a child is eliminated and may be upset at having to sit out, so give each participant a prize (a badge, candy or toy). Ask a helper to look after those who don't want to join in or those who are out. Most of the bits and pieces you'll need for these party games are very easy to find in corner stores or large supermarkets and online. To avoid overexcitement, alternate between lively and quiet games.

QUIETER GAMES AND ACTIVITIES

SLEEPING LIONS

Two players (or grown-ups) are chosen to be the hunters. All the other children are lions and must lie down with their eyes closed. Once the lions are sleeping, the hunters move among them, trying to "wake" them. They can move close and whisper in the lions' ears to make them move or giggle, but they cannot touch them. Any lion who moves or makes a sound becomes a hunter until there is just one triumphant sleeping lion left.

ANGELS

This is a lovely game for younger children and requires real concentration from everybody involved. If you're playing indoors, ask everyone to take their shoes off so that the room is as quiet as possible. Two angels are selected, and the rest of the group becomes mortals who must space out across the room, stand still and close their eyes (use blindfolds to ensure no peeking). The angels then walk among the mortals as quietly as they can, each choosing a mortal to stand behind. If a mortal thinks that they sense an angel, they ask, "Is there an angel with me?" The adult in charge replies yes or no. If the mortal is correct, they too become an angel. If they are wrong, or if an angel stands behind a mortal and counts to five (silently!) and then taps them on the shoulder, they must go out. The game ends when everyone is either out or an angel.

PIN THE TAIL...

Draw a tail-less donkey on a large piece of paper and stick it up on a wall or a tree. Ask a child to come forward and stand in front of the picture. Place a neat clump of raffia with sticky tape at the end into the child's hand and then blindfold them. Spin them around a few times and bring them to a stop facing the picture. Ask the child to "pin" the tail on the donkey, then remove their blindfold so they can see where they placed the tail. Initial the point they choose. Award a prize to the player who came the closest.

TIP: *Replace the donkey with another animal to fit the theme of your party.*

THE FLOUR GAME

Prepare the game in advance by filling a medium-sized bowl with flour right up to the brim and press down firmly until the flour is compact. Place a large cutting board over the top of the bowl and then turn it upside down so that the board forms a base. Leave the bowl and board to stand for a few hours, giving the flour time to settle. When everyone is ready to play, bring out the board, place it on a low surface (use a table covered with newspaper if you're playing indoors) and remove the bowl to reveal a smooth, perfectly formed flour mound. This will invariably earn gasps of admiration from everyone. Gently place a square of chocolate on top of the mound. Choose a large knife (a dinner knife or ruler will be safer for younger children) and ask each player to step forward in turn to cut a slice from the flour mound. The aim is to keep the mound from collapsing for as long as possible. You'll be surprised by how many slices the flour can withstand before it finally caves in. When the mound does fall, the piece of chocolate on top will go with it. The player responsible for the collapse must then put their hands behind their back and retrieve the chocolate using just their mouth.

TRAY MEMORY GAME

Before everyone arrives, cover a tray or table with around 20 small objects. These can vary from the mundane to the maverick. Everyday items, such as stationery and cutlery, are good, and so are more unusual knickknacks and trinkets. Variety is key. Once your tray is ready, cover it with a large cloth.

Ask the children to stand around the tray, then remove the cover with a flourish. Allow everyone one minute to remember as many objects as they can. Once the time is up, replace the cloth and give everyone a piece of paper and a pen. Now everyone has five minutes to jot down all they can recall. The person with the longest list at the end wins.

Everyone will have a different way of remembering. Some will have a photographic memory, allowing them to recall the items simply by visualizing them; others might remember them alphabetically. One fun way to jog their memories is to create a story that incorporates as many of the objects as possible.

MUSICAL GAMES

These simple games test the speed of your guests' reactions. You'll need plenty of space or a room cleared of furniture. Wireless speakers are useful if you're outside.

MUSICAL STATUES AND MUSICAL BUMPS

Ask players to spread out, then turn on some music and get them to dance. Whenever the music stops, players must either stay completely still, like statues, or fall down on their bottoms with a bump (depending on which version of the game you're playing). In statues, anyone moving after the music stops is out. In bumps, the last person to sit down is out. Vary the amount of time that the music plays for—a couple of long bursts punctuated by a very short one will often catch people out. When players are out, get them to help you identify the moving statues or the last person to hit the floor until you have a winner.

NEWSPAPER ISLANDS

Give every player a sheet of newspaper and ask them to put their paper down somewhere on the floor. Then turn on some music and get them to dance around the room, taking care not to step on the sheets of newspaper. When the music stops, it means that there is a shark attack: players must find a newspaper island to stand on to avoid being eaten. After each shark attack, take a few pieces of newspaper away and continue playing. Islands can hold only one person at a time, so the next time the music stops there will be a mad dash for safety and some players will find themselves eaten by sharks and out of the game. Repeat until you have a winner.

TIP: *To play musical chairs, set up a circle of chairs, seats facing outward, one fewer than the number of players. While music plays, the children walk around the circle, and, when it stops, they race to find a chair and sit on it. The person left standing is out, one chair is removed and the game begins again. Repeat until you have a winner.*

PASS THE PARCEL

This takes a bit of preparation before the party, but is worth it and is an excellent way to calm things down. Wrap a small gift in many layers of paper—use newspaper or brown paper instead of wrapping paper on the outer layers, but try to make the layers closest to the prize a bit more interesting. Between every layer include a candy or another tiny prize. You could also include a question on a piece of paper so that the person unwrapping the parcel must ask it, and the first person to give the correct answer gets the candy. To play, sit everyone in a large circle and ask them to pass the parcel around as the music plays. Every time the music stops, the person holding the parcel gets to unwrap a layer. Make sure that everyone gets a chance to unwrap a layer and get a candy so the whole party will really enjoy the game.

LIVELY GAMES

As well as the games below, Simon Says is a great time filler and easy to play between other games. Call out commands, with accompanying actions, using the phrase "Simon says," for example, "Simon says pat your head." Everyone must do as Simon says until the next direction is called. Occasionally, the leader gives an instruction *without* the words "Simon says" and then players should do absolutely nothing. Anyone who follows the order is out—you'll be surprised by how easy it is to fool them! To make things more difficult, give your orders in very quick succession. Another good activity is to fill an empty piñata with goodies and get children to take turns trying to break it with a stick.

CORNERS

This game is perfect for large groups of children and bigger venues like a backyard or gym. Number the four corners of the room one, two, three and four (or color code each with balloons). Give a quick guided tour, pointing out the numbers. Choose someone to be "it" and blindfold them. They stand in the middle of the room while everyone else scatters, with each player deciding on a corner to move to. Once everybody is in their corner of choice, the blindfolded player calls out a number: one, two, three or four. All the children at that corner are then out. Everyone left in the game scatters again and the whole process is repeated. When there are four or fewer players left, they must all choose different corners. The final player left in the game is blindfolded for the next round. Although it's total chance, the winner can congratulate themselves for excellent guesswork!

GRANDMOTHER'S FOOTSTEPS

Someone is chosen to be Grandmother. This person stands at the end of the room or the garden with their back to the other players. Everyone else arranges themselves along a starting line. On "Go!," players begin to make their way toward Grandmother. She can turn around at any point in the game and when she does the other players must freeze for as long as she is looking at them. If she catches anyone moving, they are sent back to the starting line. The aim is to reach Grandmother first and tag her on the shoulder. The player who successfully tags her becomes Grandmother in the next round. There are a number of fun variations on this game. You can lay out a set of chairs and demand that players climb over one of them before they can tag Grandmother. If she turns around midclimb, players will inevitably struggle to maintain their balance. The more obstacles the better!

THE CHOCOLATE GAME

For this game, you'll need a large chocolate bar, a knife and fork, some winter layers (hat, gloves and scarf) and dice. The chocolate bar is unwrapped and placed on a chopping board. Players form a circle around the chocolate and take turns rolling the dice. When a six is thrown, the player who rolled it shouts "SIX!" and puts on the layers as fast as they can. If you want to make things harder, add extra layers, such as leg warmers, fake mustaches or sunglasses. Once the player who threw the six is dressed, they must pick up the knife and fork and cut and eat a square of the chocolate bar. This is much easier said than done. All the while, other players continue to pass the dice around the circle and when another six is rolled, the person in the center must stop what they're doing—whatever stage of dressing or cutting they have reached—and hand over the clothes and cutlery. The chocolate is remarkably difficult to cut through, especially when the knife is held through woolly winter gloves; for younger children, use individual chocolates to pick up with their fingers instead.

OTHER LIVELY GAMES FOR CHILDREN'S PARTIES

- *Doughnut tree (page 43)*
- *Egg and spoon races (page 242)*
- *Pass the orange (page 129)*
- *Kick the can (page 381)*
- *Three-legged race (page 332)*
- *Wheelbarrow races (page 346)*
- *Cup and ball (page 332)*
- *Tug-of-war (page 332)*
- *Bowling (page 39)*
- *British bulldogs (page 346)*
- *Limbo (page 332)*
- *Capture the flag (page 381)*

SACK RACE

The sack race tends to join the egg and spoon race at parties and school sports days. Players put both their legs inside a sack or pillowcase. The higher the sack reaches on the players' bodies, the harder the game becomes. Beginners might want to start with sacks that reach waist high, but for the more ambitious and experienced sack racers you can provide ones that come all the way up to the neck to keep their arms inside. Everyone stands along a starting line and, on "Go!," players start jumping in their sacks toward the finish line. Overenthusiastic racers will most likely get themselves in a tangle and fall. Watching them try to get up again inside their small sacks is especially amusing for spectators. The first person to cross the finish line is the winner.

GOOD-BYES

PARTY FAVOR BAGS

Assemble party favor bags in advance and keep them on a large tray or in a basket well hidden to avoid any peeking. Personalize them with stickers or labels to avoid confusion and to make sure you haven't forgotten anyone. Keep the contents the same to prevent squabbling over who gets what, unless you differentiate between boys' and girls' bags. The best party favor bags are often those that have been well thought about with fillers chosen to fit a particular theme, age group or gender—they needn't be expensive.

There are lots of cheap present ideas that are great for younger children. Older ones might prefer an individual keepsake gift, such as a plant, storybook, craft or baking kit. "Loot" or paper bags are the most practical and popular (prefilled ones can save the day), but you can use all sorts of other bags and even containers: fill plastic cups or mugs with treats, wrap them in cellophane and tie them with ribbon; fabric bags or organza bags are useful as they can be kept afterward; even party picnic boxes can be used, with tissue paper and confetti to make it more of a surprise. Another option for going-home presents is to have a grab bag—a box or container filled with shredded paper or straw into which children can dive and pick out a colorfully wrapped present to take home. Have a few bags or prizes handy for siblings.

GOOD FILLERS

- *Pocket-size gadgets, puzzles, badges or medals.*

- *Foam gliders, pull-back cars and spinning tops.*

- *Stuffed animals, slinky snakes or finger puppets.*

- *Bubbles, bouncy balls, yo-yos.*

- *Stationery sets, notepads, activity books and stickers.*

- *Modeling clay, play dough or Etch A Sketch.*

- *A cupcake or piece of birthday cake in an organza bag.*

- *Jewelry sets, hairclips, sunglasses, paper fans.*

- *Sweets such as Pop Rocks, marshmallows, M&M's, gummy sweets and sherbet sticks or flying saucers.*

I question not if thrushes sing
If roses load the air;
Beyond my heart I need not reach
When summer all is there

"Love's World," John Vance Cheney

BARBECUES

Nothing says summer quite like a barbecue. People all over the world have been grilling pieces of meat over fire for thousands of years, but barbecues as we recognize them today are thought to have originated in the Caribbean, a region that to this day remains passionate about outdoor cooking. Grilling food outdoors and sharing it with others has become an essential part of modern living and a way to enjoy and celebrate the warm summer months.

It's true that the British climate is not ideally suited to cooking outdoors: the weather is often a gamble, making a day of soaring temperatures, unbroken blue skies and a balmy evening a thrilling rarity. But even with cloud-ridden skies, there is always good British cheer that the weather has held and—most important—it's not raining! Canceling a barbecue celebration is unheard of, unless it's actually forecast to thunder all day and night. Most guests will, without doubt, still relish the chance of eating outside wrapped up in blankets and coats. Optimism never wavers, even if, in the end, you have to eat indoors.

Cooking on the barbecue offers those who prefer more casual entertaining an opportunity to host something without the pressures of formal courses or culinary etiquette. No one expects to sit down at the table—a bench, garden chair or even standing will do. It's a meal that no one really seems to mind waiting for. The billows of smoke set the atmosphere, wafting over garden fences, hedges and walls and whetting the taste buds. A glass of something cold—a pale pink rosé or a heady punch—and a few outdoor games that can be played barefoot in the grass will keep everyone happy on this most laid-back of occasions.

Whether it's a planned affair or a more spontaneous shindig, the joy of cooking outside is that you don't have to slave away and overheat in the kitchen. That's not to say no preparations are needed, but it's how and what you choose to barbecue that is the key here, where possible making and marinating in good time to lock in the juicy flavors. Side dishes can be preassembled in bowls, made up of all the fresh, seasonal and colorful ingredients you have missed in the winter, and dessert might be just a combination of ripe berries and cream, Britain's signature summer dessert. Whatever the menu or occasion, we can all enjoy a barbecue, making it one of the most all-embracing celebrations ever.

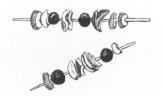

SUMMER FLOWERS

Bring bursts of color to your setting with delicate scented blooms such as sweet peas. Bright hydrangea heads look lovely floating in a globe vase with a little water, and peonies come in all shades of pink, white and coral. Dahlias grow in more vibrant tints, and stocks, delphiniums and gladioli add height, creating a country-garden feel wherever you are. For more celebratory occasions, line pathways with shepherd's crooks and hang them with jam jars filled with posies, or thread colorful flower heads such as gerberas on fine florist wire to make garlands (these will probably last only the day, so spritz them with water to prevent them from wilting). If your gathering goes on into the evening, fill storm lanterns with an inch or two of water, add pillar candles and decorate with a few sprigs of fresh herbs or flowers; rosemary and lavender both smell wonderful.

GARDEN TABLES

There is no real need for decorations when throwing a barbecue party—let the summer garden, in all its vibrant and luscious splendor, speak for itself. For garden parties at home, we often bring one of our indoor tables outside so we can seat more people. Arrange extra benches and seats close by for children to sit on if you don't have enough places at the table. Use tablecloths or runners in fresh colors (overlap a few if need be) to bring out the natural surroundings. A burlap runner will look rustic. If it's a long table, line the center with a variety of inexpensive flowers; daisies or achillea are perfect base colors for a summer party paired with soft green foliage, such as alchemilla mollis (lady's mantle) or cow parsley, picked from the wild.

For place settings, write names on dried bay leaves and skewer them with toothpicks into lemons or other fruits. Tie napkins folded around individual sets of cutlery with jute twine, and decorate with sprigs of fresh herbs or flowers. Use table clips or thumb tacks to keep the tablecloth from flying away and make sure any decorations are firmly secured against the wind (fill the bottoms of smaller vases with handfuls of stones to keep them sturdy). Colored glasses, patterned bowls and tableware will create a Mediterranean feel, and an umbrella will provide much-needed shade on a hot day. For later in the afternoon, have tea lights, lanterns, garden torches, braziers or fire pits ready for warmth as the light fades. Use citronella candles and antimosquito coils to keep bugs away.

STARTERS AND SNACKS

CRUDITÉS WITH ANCHOVY DIP Serves 8–12

A selection of fresh vegetables makes for a stunning and colorful centerpiece. Use whole baby carrots, radishes (scrubbed but with the tops left on), blanched asparagus, yellow and red pepper strips, baby corn and a few grissini breadsticks (wrapped in prosciutto). Keep prepared crudités cold and crisp in a bowl of iced salted water.

To make the dip, put 4 garlic cloves in a small blender with 7 ounces of drained canned anchovies and blend until you have a rough paste. Add 2 tablespoons of olive oil and stir in ½ to ¾ cup of crème fraîche. Season well. Arrange prepared vegetables on a large platter or in a large bowl and serve alongside.

GAZPACHO Serves 8

This fresh soup is really refreshing on a hot summer's day and makes a wonderful starter.

Place 2½ pounds of chopped ripe plum or vine tomatoes, 1 peeled and chopped small red onion, 2 peeled and chopped cloves of garlic, 1 seeded and chopped red pepper and ½ a peeled and seeded cucumber in a blender and mix until smooth. Add 1 to 1¼ cups of tomato juice, 2 tablespoons of sherry vinegar, 4 tablespoons of dry sherry, 1 tablespoon of sugar and a pinch of cayenne pepper and season well with salt and freshly ground black pepper. Blend again until well combined and smooth (in two batches if necessary). Pass the mixture through a sieve into a large pitcher or bowl, pushing through the sieve to make sure you get all the juices from the pulp. Chill in the fridge for at least 1 hour. Serve in bowls and garnish with finely diced hard-boiled eggs, yellow, green and red peppers, cucumber and scallions.

BARBECUED CAMEMBERT Serves 8–12

Delicious cooked straight on the barbecue or in the oven and served as a starter with red-onion marmalade (page 388).

Light a barbecue and allow the flames to settle until the charcoal has turned white and is piping hot. Remove two 8-ounce Camembert wheels from their boxes and paper wrappings and make incisions in the tops of the cheeses. Stud with rosemary sprigs and 2 peeled and finely sliced garlic cloves. Place the cheeses back in their boxes (no lids) and onto a sheet of foil. Drizzle the tops of the cheeses with olive oil and season with salt and pepper. Wrap the foil around both boxes to make a secure parcel. Place on the barbecue and cook for 10 to 15 minutes until the center is melted and oozing.

A chilled Provençal rosé or a Chilean sauvignon blanc is lovely with Mediterranean-style summer starters.

MEATS AND MARINADES

During summer, food preparation should reflect the mood of the season. Everything should be easy to assemble as the last thing anyone wants to do is slave away inside on a hot, lazy day. Sausages and burgers are staples of most barbecues, while marinated chicken thighs are inexpensive and probably my favorite. Marinate meats in the fridge for at least 1 to 2 hours, but preferably overnight so the flavors develop. For a hungry crowd a marinated leg of lamb is always a popular choice, sliced and served in wraps with a variety of salads.

PRACTICAL TIPS FOR BARBECUING

- *A charcoal barbecue is traditional and provides that unique, hands-on satisfaction of building and starting a fire, but a gas grill is quick, clean and convenient—better for catering on a larger scale.*

- *A useful kit includes tongs, skewers to cook food on (always soak wooden ones in water beforehand so they don't burn), aluminum trays and disposable foil platters to keep food warm on (don't use the same plate or board for uncooked and cooked foods). Always cook meat from room temperature rather than directly from the fridge.*

- *When cooking over coals, allow the flames to settle on the barbecue and wait until the charcoal has turned white.*

- *An oven can be useful to start cooking larger pieces of meat and is another place to keep food warm.*

- *Cook on a clean grill each time. Use a wire brush while the grill is still hot so the food comes off easily.*

MEDITERRANEAN MARINADE Serves 8

These flavors are wonderful with a butterflied leg of lamb. Cook for roughly 6 to 8 minutes per pound, plus an extra 20 minutes. Allow the lamb to rest to give you juicy pink meat. As a guide, a 4-pound leg will feed 8 people.

Mix together ½ cup of olive oil, the finely grated zest and juice of 2 lemons, 2 tablespoons of anchovy paste (or 1 ounce of finely chopped anchovies), 4 tablespoons of chopped fresh rosemary, 4 peeled and crushed cloves of garlic, and season well.

SPICY YOGURT MARINADE Serves 8

This is a lovely marinade for up to 16 chicken thighs or drumsticks. As a guide, bone-in chicken thighs will need about 15 minutes on each side to cook through, and boneless ones around half that time.

Mix together 3½ cups of Greek or plain yogurt, 4 peeled and crushed cloves of garlic, 4 tablespoons of mango chutney, the finely grated zest and juice of 2 oranges, 4 tablespoons of mild curry powder, 4 tablespoons of chopped fresh cilantro, and season well.

HOMEMADE BURGERS

Homemade burgers are very easy to make in advance using good-quality ground meat with lots of seasoning. Classic beef burgers (page 286) are a safe choice, especially mini ones for children, but adults will appreciate more interesting flavor combinations. Avoid turning your burgers too often on the barbecue, otherwise they will fall apart. For an extra surprise, cram a chunk of your favorite cheese into the middle of the patty and let it melt as the burger cooks. Yum!

SERVES 8 (MAKES 8–10 OF EACH)

LAMB AND MINT

2 pounds ground lamb

1 small red onion, peeled and finely chopped

2 garlic cloves, peeled and finely chopped

2 tablespoons mint sauce

a small handful of chopped fresh mint

1 large egg yolk, to bind

salt and freshly ground black pepper

PORK AND HERB

2 pounds ground pork

1 small onion, peeled and finely chopped

2 garlic cloves, peeled and finely chopped

3 tablespoons applesauce

2 tablespoons whole-grain mustard

4 tablespoons chopped sage leaves

2 large egg yolks, to bind

salt and freshly ground black pepper

To make the burgers, place all the ingredients in a large bowl, season well with salt and freshly ground black pepper and mix together well to combine. Using clean, wet hands, shape the mixture into 8 equal patties, pressing down to make burger shapes. Place on a baking sheet, cover with plastic wrap and chill in the fridge for 1 hour. Light a barbecue and allow the flames to settle until the charcoal has turned white and is piping hot. Drizzle the burgers with a touch of olive oil and then grill on the barbecue for 6 to 8 minutes on each side, until cooked through.

 Red wines, such as Australian Shiraz or Cabernet Merlot.

BUILD YOUR OWN BURGER *The joy of a well-made burger is in being able to customize it to your particular taste. Make sure you buy a good selection of breads: white, brown and seeded rolls, as well as ciabatta, pita and whole-wheat wraps. This can make or break a really good burger (remember, the buns need to be the right size for the burgers). Offer a wide selection of fillings: different cheeses, such as cheddar, emmenthal, mozzarella and blue cheese, sliced tomatoes, avocados, gherkins and lettuce. As well as standard condiments, offer other garnishes such as fresh pesto, chili sauce and garlic mayonnaise, or for ease, mix up an all-in-one combo sauce of equal parts mayonnaise, ketchup and mustard.*

FOIL-WRAPPED FISH

Wrapping and steaming in foil is a great way to cook delicate fish on the barbecue as you seal them up like tasty presents. These neat parcels serve 8 as part of a barbecue spread, or 4 as a main course. Light the barbecue and allow the flames to settle until the charcoal has turned white-hot. To prepare any of the fish parcels below, arrange two large sheets of foil on a flat surface in a double layer. Brush the top layer with olive oil to prevent the fish from sticking as it cooks.

A dry white Bordeaux is a good choice for barbecued fish.

SEA BASS WITH FENNEL, LEMON AND CAPERS

Thinly slice 1 fennel bulb, 2 celery stalks and 1 lemon and spread half the slices over the center of the foil in a single layer. Place one 2-pound whole sea bass, scaled and gutted, on top and fill the cavity with the rest of the fennel, celery and lemon. Scatter ½ cup of drained capers and 2 teaspoons of fennel seeds in and around the fish. Fold the edges of the foil inward, to ensure no juices escape. Pour in ¾ cup of dry white wine, 4 tablespoons of vermouth and ½ cup of fish stock. Season well, dot with butter and wrap securely. Barbecue for 30 to 35 minutes until the flesh is opaque, the skin comes off easily and the flesh flakes away from the bones.

TIP: *Follow the method above, but replace the sea bass with 2 rainbow trout, flavored with lemon and herbs.*

MACKEREL WITH LIME, GINGER AND CHILI

Score 8 pin-boned mackerel filets and place in a shallow dish. For the marinade, whisk 2 tablespoons each of honey, fish sauce, and soy sauce with 4 tablespoons of sesame oil, 2 peeled and crushed garlic cloves and the finely grated zest and juice of 2 limes in a bowl and season well. Peel and finely grate a 1-inch piece of fresh ginger and add to the marinade with 1 seeded and finely sliced red chili. Pour the mixture over the fish and allow to marinate for 3 to 5 minutes. Transfer the filets to the center of the foil. Fold the edges of the foil inward, to ensure no juices escape. Pour the remaining marinade over the fish and wrap securely. Barbecue for 4 to 5 minutes until cooked through. Alternatively, barbecue the mackerel filets directly on a well-oiled grill for 3 to 4 minutes on each side until nicely charred for crispy skin.

TIP: *As an alternative, wrap salmon filets with sun-dried tomatoes, black olives, capers, lemon juice and parsley.*

VEGETARIAN SIDES

Asparagus is delicious cooked straight on the barbecue grill for 5 to 7 minutes. Corn on the cob can also be cooked on the grill until its outsides are nicely charred, and is wonderful dripping with melted flavored butter (page 376).

TOMATO, RED ONION AND BASIL TART Serves 8

This tart is quick and easy to prepare, it's also tasty sprinkled with crumbled feta cheese. Eat it hot or cold.

Unroll 1 sheet of thawed frozen puff pastry, score a ½-inch border around the inside and prick all over. Chill it while you prepare the filling. Preheat the oven to 400°F and place a baking sheet in the oven to heat up. Heat 2 tablespoons of olive oil in a large frying pan. Add 3 peeled and sliced red onions, season well and fry over medium heat, stirring frequently, for 10 minutes or until the onions have softened. Add 3 cloves of peeled and finely chopped garlic and fry for another 2 minutes. Remove from the heat and leave to cool slightly while you prepare the rest of the ingredients.

Thinly slice 14 ounces of plump ripe tomatoes. Spread 2 tablespoons of sun-dried tomato paste evenly over the chilled puff pastry, being careful not to cross over the scored edge, followed by the onions, then place the tomato slices on top in rows. Drizzle with 1 tablespoon of basil-infused olive oil, season well and bake for 15 to 20 minutes or until the pastry is golden brown and well risen. Scatter 2 ounces of soft goat cheese over the top and bake for another 5 minutes. Sprinkle a handful of basil leaves over the tart, drizzle some balsamic vinegar over it and cut into slices before serving warm.

RATATOUILLE VEGETABLE SKEWERS Serves 8

Soak 8 wooden skewers in water for 30 minutes, or use metal skewers. Light the barbecue and wait until the charcoal has turned white and is piping hot. Chop and seed 4 mixed color peppers into bite-sized pieces, along with 1 zucchini and 1 large red onion cut into wedges. In a large bowl, mix 4 tablespoons of olive oil, 2 tablespoons of red wine vinegar, 2 peeled and crushed cloves of garlic, 1 tablespoon of herbes de Provence and season until combined. Add 16 cherry tomatoes, the peppers, zucchini and onion, and toss to coat. Marinate for 30 minutes. Thread the vegetables onto the skewers, and cook directly on the barbecue for 3 to 4 minutes on each side, until they are nicely charred and the vegetables have softened.

TIP: *For a quick ratatouille, heat 2 tablespoons of olive oil in a large pan, sauté the cut vegetables for 4 to 5 minutes until soft. Season, add a little vegetable stock and a dash of sherry vinegar. Simmer for 15 to 20 minutes, then add a handful of shredded basil and cook for another minute before serving.*

COLORFUL SALADS

A selection of vibrant salads complements the caramelized smoky foods at a barbecue. Try the suggestions below, or toss fine ribbons of carrot and toasted cumin seeds with orange juice and a mustard vinaigrette. Keep your dishes covered until needed to deter insects (beaded net food covers are useful), and dress salads lightly just before serving, otherwise the leaves will wilt.

LENTIL AND GRILLED PEPPER SALAD Serves 8

The base of this salad can be made well in advance. Use dried Puy lentils for a nutty bite, or buy good-quality precooked lentils. Peeling the skins off the peppers isn't essential but will make all the difference; as soon as they are cooked put them in a freezer bag and seal for a few minutes, then open and peel off the skin.

Preheat the grill or griddle or wait until the barbecue coals are red hot. Seed and quarter 1 red, 1 green, 1 yellow and 1 orange pepper, drizzle a little olive oil over them and season. Grill or barbecue for 6 to 8 minutes on each side until nicely charred and softened. Once cool, cut into strips or bite-sized pieces.

Heat 1 quart of vegetable stock in a large pan and add 1½ cups of Puy lentils and 2 bay leaves. Boil for 10 minutes, then simmer for 15 minutes or until tender. Drain and rinse the lentils in cold water, discard the bay leaves and transfer to a large serving bowl. Add the peppers and a small handful of chopped herbs such as basil, parsley and chives. Season to taste and mix together with 5 ounces of cubed soft goat cheese and 3 tablespoons of olive oil.

PEA, MINT, BROAD BEAN AND RADISH SALAD Serves 8

Combines sweet emerald peas and fresh, slightly bitter broad beans (shell them by gently squeezing the cooked pods between your finger and thumb).

Boil a large pan of salted water and cook 1⅓ pounds (unpodded weight) of shelled fresh broad beans for 2 minutes, then add 10 ounces of shelled garden peas and cook for another 1 to 2 minutes until tender. Drain and rinse under cold water, pod the broad beans, then place the beans and peas in a large bowl. Add a small bunch of fresh chopped mint, 5 ounces of crumbled feta cheese and 6 radishes cut into quarters.

For the dressing, whisk together the juice and finely grated zest of ½ a lemon, 1 peeled and crushed garlic clove, 2 teaspoons of Dijon mustard, 1 teaspoon of honey, 6 tablespoons of extra virgin olive oil and salt and freshly ground black pepper to make a light vinaigrette, adding more oil if necessary until you achieve the desired consistency. Pour the dressing over the salad and toss to combine. Serve garnished with baby mint leaves and a little lemon zest.

SUMMER BERRIES

Nothing could be more symbolic of British summer afternoons than strawberries and cream. Eton Mess, a delicious combination of meringues, strawberries and whipped cream, is always popular. For a twist, freeze the mixture for 5 to 6 hours in a loaf pan and allow to soften slightly before serving as an ice cream slice (see picture opposite).

SUMMER PUDDING Serves 8

Place 1¾ pounds of mixed summer berries in a large saucepan, add ½ cup of superfine sugar, 4 tablespoons of fruit liqueur (Framboise or Cassis) and 4 tablespoons of water. Bring to a simmer and add sugar to taste. Cook for a few minutes until the fruit has slightly softened and the sugar has melted. Allow to cool and strain, reserving the juices and fruit.

Remove the crusts from 8 slices of thick white bread. Cut one slice into a circle to fit the base of a 1-quart deep bowl and another two slices to fit the top of the basin. Cut the remaining slices in half lengthwise. Dip the smaller bread circle into the fruit juice so it absorbs the juice (use this to line the pudding basin). Dip the bread halves into the juice, lining the sides of the basin, overlapping as you go and pressing the edges together until all the bread is used up. Spoon the fruit into the center. Dip the bread for the top of the pudding into the juice and use it to cover the top. Place a small plate over the pudding, top with a heavy weight and refrigerate overnight. Invert the pudding onto a plate and serve with heavy cream.

GOOSEBERRY FOOL Serves 8

This dessert is simple, elegant and light. Gooseberries are the classic British ingredient, but all berries work well. Its name derives from the French term "fouler," meaning "to mash."

Place 1¾ pounds of fresh or frozen gooseberries (reserving a few for a garnish) in a saucepan with 1 cup of superfine sugar and the seeds from 2 vanilla beans. Heat gently for 4 to 5 minutes until softened (allow 10 to 15 minutes if using frozen fruit, and drain off excess liquid). Transfer to a food processor and blend to a smooth purée, then pour into a large bowl and cool. Lightly mix 14 ounces of Greek yogurt with 14 ounces of premade vanilla pudding, then gently fold into the gooseberry purée to give a rippled effect. Spoon into serving glasses, drizzle with 2 tablespoons of honey and garnish with berries and lime zest.

STRAWBERRY AND ORANGE GRANITA Serves 8

The tangy flavors in this deep-orange-hued granita are almost too good to be true. Each mouthful tastes like a tart, fruity sorbet and makes a cool palate cleanser after eating charred, barbecued foods.

Place 11 ounces of washed and hulled strawberries, the finely grated zest and juice of 2 oranges, ¾ cup of superfine sugar and ½ cup of water in a food processor and blend until smooth. Transfer to a freezerproof plastic box with a lid and freeze for 2 hours. Stir, using a fork to break up the ice crystals, and return to the freezer for another 2 to 3 hours or until completely frozen.

Remove from the freezer and allow to stand for 5 to 10 minutes at room temperature. Stir using a fork to fluff up the mixture and spoon into serving glasses (you could also use an ice cream scoop to create perfect balls). Garnish with mint leaves.

HAZELNUT ROULADE

This was one of my granny's signature desserts, which she would always serve with a berry compote made with fruits from her garden. I always think of her when I eat it. It's a great buffet-type dessert that can be made in advance. Serve alongside a pitcher of passion fruit coulis to add a burst of color.

SERVES 8

4 medium egg whites

1 cup superfine sugar

2 teaspoons vanilla extract

½ teaspoon cornstarch

1 teaspoon white wine vinegar

½ cup toasted hazelnuts, chopped

For the roulade

3 ounces Dulce de Leche or caramel sauce

½ teaspoon sea salt

½ cup heavy cream, softly whipped

For the coulis

8 passion fruit

1¼ cups confectioner's sugar, sifted

Preheat the oven to 325°F. Cover a lightly buttered 9 x 13-inch jelly roll pan with baking parchment. Whisk the egg whites in a large bowl until they form soft peaks, then gradually add the sugar, continuing to whisk as you do so. Add the vanilla extract, cornstarch and vinegar and whisk until the mixture is stiff. Spread the meringue mix evenly over the lined pan. Scatter the hazelnuts over the batter, reserving some for the filling and garnish. Cook in the oven for 25 minutes, then remove from the oven and allow to cool.

To create the roulade, place a sheet of wax paper on a work surface and put the meringue facedown on it. Peel the parchment off the cake. Using an offset spatula, spread an even layer of the caramel over the cake, allowing space along the sides for the filling to spread out, and sprinkle sea salt on the caramel. Spread whipped cream over the caramel and finally scatter some hazelnuts over the filling.

Starting with the longer side closest to you, roll the roulade up, using the wax paper to help you. Once completely rolled, rotate it so that the seam is on the bottom. Wrap in foil until ready to serve, then garnish with the remaining hazelnuts.

To make the coulis, scoop the passion fruit contents into a food processor. Pulse a few times to loosen the pulp from the seeds, then press the pulp through a sieve to extract all the juice. Add the confectioner's sugar a little at a time and whisk until smooth, adding more sugar to taste.

SUMMER DRINKS

Summer drinks should be cooling, refreshing and packed with plenty of ice. Nothing celebrates the start of summer better than Pimm's. There are lots of variations but the basic recipe is on the bottle (one part Pimm's No. 1 to three parts lemonade). I prefer the vodka-based No. 6 Cup. If you find the mix too sweet, replace some or all of the lemonade with ginger ale. For a Pimm's Royale add a splash of Pimm's to a Champagne flute and top with Champagne.

THE WIMBLEDON Serves 8

A fruity white-wine spritzer. Pour 1 cup of strawberry cordial into a large pitcher or bowl. Add 6 cups of chilled dry white wine, 3½ cups of soda water, a handful of fresh mint leaves and the juice of 2 lemons. Mix together well. Serve over ice cubes in tall glasses.

MUSTIQUE RUM PUNCH Serves 8

This recipe is so good it has been renamed Pum Runch in my family due to its after-effects, probably because the typical rum used in Mustique is an 80-proof Sunset rum. For this slightly less potent version, mix together 3 cups of white rum and 3 cups of dark rum with 1 quart each of orange juice and pineapple juice. Add 2 cups of passion fruit juice and the juice of 4 limes (adjusting quantities to taste). Add a dash of Angostura bitters and grenadine syrup to achieve the desired color along with a generous grating of nutmeg. This will keep for 1 month if refrigerated, so make a batch in advance and store in large plastic water bottles to prep for a party.

SUMMER PUNCH Serves 8

A light, refreshing drink for a summer's day that can easily be doubled if you're serving a thirsty crowd. Pour ¾ cup of elderflower cordial (page 389) into a large pitcher or bowl and add ¾ cup of vodka, 6 cups of chilled Prosecco and 3½ cups of soda water. Stir to combine. Garnish with slices of lime and cucumber. Serve over ice cubes in tall glasses.

"ONE OF SOUR. . ." *Punch is a mixed drink that usually contains fruit juice. The name is derived from the Hindi word* **panch,** *meaning "five," a reference to the number of original ingredients—spirits, water, lemon juice, sugar and spices. Employees of the British East India Company introduced punch to England from India during the early seventeenth century. For homemade concoctions, stick with the rhyme "one of sour, two of sweet, three of strong and four of weak." This should get everyone nicely in the mood!*

SUMMER SPORTS

Choose games that are suited to the space you have around you: play boules on gravel driveways while croquet, short tennis and badminton can be set up temporarily for a few weeks on grassy patches in the garden. Skipping games with giant ropes, hopscotch, tug-of-war and three-legged races can be enjoyed absolutely anywhere, on any surface, providing there is plenty of space, and if you are lucky enough to have one of those big trampolines, they are fun for young and old alike.

WATER, WATER EVERYWHERE...

For children, water-fueled games can save the day in hot, muggy weather. Provide a wide selection of water pistols and water guns in various sizes, which offer the possibility for both sustained and staccato squirting. The water balloon is also a firm favorite and can be used as defense in water fights, with the potential for soaking multiple players in one go. Finally, the garden hose or sprinkler is not be underestimated. If your venue allows it, turn a slope into a slippery slide using a sheet of plastic and a running hose.

BALLOON DASH

Split everyone into pairs. Ask partners to arrange themselves along a starting line, standing back to back with their arms interlocking. Place a large water balloon in the small space between each pair's backs and when everyone is ready, call "Go!" The pairs must then make their way to the finish line without dropping or breaking the balloon between them. If a balloon does break, then the pair responsible must head back to the starting line—a little wetter than before—to get a new balloon and start again. The first pair to complete the race with their balloon still intact wins.

WIFFLE BALL

Wiffle Ball (or rounders, as it's known in Britain) is a firm favorite for kids and adults alike. I feel nostalgic whenever I think about this childhood game and it's a great game to play in the park or on the beach on sunny Sunday afternoons. Grab a wiffle ball or baseball bat and ball, divide into teams and set up four "bases" in a large open space (ideally these should be tall wooden poles pushed into the ground but shoes and clothing will do just as well). Look online to brush up on the rules, and let the competition commence.

TRADITIONAL FAVORITES

THREE-LEGGED RACE

This is an old favorite from primary-school sports days but it can be enjoyed by all age groups. Ask everyone to get into pairs and give each pair a scarf or old pair of tights. Tie one player's left leg to the other player's right leg. Give everyone a few minutes to practice walking together, then line them up at the starting line. On "Go!" everyone has to run to the finish line. The first pair over the line is the winner. Make the race more difficult by forcing the pairs to walk sideways, like crabs. With adults you can make them face each other and tie the scarf around their waists. One person will be walking forward while the other has to walk backward.

TUG-OF-WAR

Lots of English villages used to have a tug-of-war every year as a ritual to bring the community together. Divide your group into two evenly matched teams. Each member of the team stands in a line, one behind the other, with the two teams facing each other, about 10 feet apart. Draw a horizontal line or leave a length of ribbon at the midpoint between the teams and pass a long length of thick rope between them. On the starter's signal the two teams should begin to pull as hard as they can on their side of the rope. The object of the game is to pull the opposing team over the line. Make the contest the best of five.

CUP AND BALL

This is a variation on the ever-popular egg and spoon race. Give each player a plastic or paper cup and a tennis ball. Ask them to put the ball inside the cup and to balance it on their head. The weight of the tennis ball should hold the cup in place but you have to keep your back very straight and move very smoothly to stop it from slipping off. Line your players up, and on "Go!" they must make their way to the finish line without the cups falling off their heads. Every time they drop the ball they have to go back to the beginning. To make this game more "refreshing," you can replace the tennis ball with water.

LIMBO

You'll need something to act as your limbo stick, such as a piece of bamboo, a kitchen broom or simply a length of string pulled taut. Everyone takes it in turns to pass underneath, leaning their shoulders backward and turning their face up toward the limbo stick, without falling or putting their hands on the ground for balance. At head height, everyone should make it to the other side. The bar is then lowered a few inches and players take another shot at limboing under it. Anyone who touches the stick or the ground is out. It gets harder as the bar continues to lower: the person who can limbo the lowest is declared the winner.

"Hold hard a minute, then!" said the Rat. He looped the painter through a ring in his landing-stage, climbed up into his hole above, and after a short interval reappeared staggering under a fat, wicker luncheon-basket.

"What's inside it?" asked the Mole, wriggling with curiosity.

"There's cold chicken inside it," replied the Rat briefly;
"coldtonguecoldhamcoldbeefpickledgherkinssaladfrenchrollscress-
sandwichespottedmeatgingerbeerlemonadesodawater—"
"O stop, stop," cried the Mole in ecstasies: "This is too much!"

The Wind in the Willows, *Kenneth Grahame*

PICNICS

Being outside in the open air, lazily picking at foods while surrounded by nature, is what I love about picnics. Eating *al fresco* seems to heighten the senses; food tastes better, air smells cleaner, birds sing louder and you notice little things like the wildlife passing close by. The earliest picnics were in the form of medieval hunting feasts where people ate pastries, hams and other cooked meats, but the practice became popular during Victorian times. The development of the railways encouraged rambling in the countryside, and the decline of coaching inns—until then relied upon for a decent meal—meant people had to cater for themselves. Today, the possibilities of picnicking are endless, and it has become a more accessible activity than ever before; be it close to home, faraway or abroad, each picnic spot is unique and evocative in its own way. Perhaps the best locations for these movable feasts are those that are unexpected and random—maybe reached by bike, or stumbled across on a walk: little pieces of previously undiscovered paradise.

You can picnic almost anywhere and in any scenario; a favorite secret place in a local park under the shade of intertwining tree branches; a spot in a wild meadow hidden among lush long grass, surrounded by dandelion clocks and visited by wayward insects; or perhaps on the beach alongside bats and balls, sand castles and swimming—the seaside in all its glory with seagulls swooping down on crumbs after you've left. Picnics can also be part of a sociable and celebratory occasion: at the side of a cricket pitch, at an outdoor concert or after a school's sports day.

Some of my fondest family memories are of picnics while on walks in the Lake District, perched on the brow of a hill with strikingly beautiful views, miles from anywhere, the landscape punctuated by mountains, tarns and the speckle of Cumbrian villages. There was always a flurry of activity before we set off as we prepared the picnic as efficiently as possible so as not to lose the best of the day. One would butter the bread slices, another would fill them and someone else would gather bits and pieces, such as chocolate bars, fruit and drinks, making sure nothing was forgotten. The challenge was to be able to fit everything neatly into a few backpacks so that it would travel well on our backs and in such a way that an essential reward, such as Chocolate Tiffin or Banana Bread, might be savored toward the end of our expedition to fuel the last steps home.

OUTDOOR EXCURSIONS

Choosing the perfect spot always takes time if you're anything like me, but it's primarily about finding the flattest ground possible. The type of excursion will also determine what you can bring; if you are transporting the food on your back you need your picnic to be practical and minimal, but if you are driving to, say, the beach and are planning to settle in for the afternoon, you can bring plenty of food, utensils, wicker bags and baskets, as well as items to give shelter, shade and comfort.

Picnics are by nature casual affairs and the key is to reflect that when it comes to the contents of your hamper, bag or backpack. The food needn't be elaborate; somehow the simplest food looks mouthwatering and delicious when eaten outside in the elements. Figure out in advance how long you plan to picnic for—be it an excursion where you'll have half an hour to refuel (while admiring the view), or a more lazy, casual affair that often turns into an afternoon's grazing as you while away the time exploring the surroundings or gently dozing off in the heat of the day.

A COMMUNAL FEAST

Foods that don't need cooking and require only a knife to divvy up are the best, or those that come in their own packaging will guarantee minimal fuss. Get fellow picnickers to contribute something special to the spread, be it homemade or grabbed from their local market. Each exciting parcel can be carefully unveiled—a parade of treats and surprises, each simple component a wonder in itself. Washed down with chilled white or rosé wine, or a cold beer, this is the way to stop for lunch.

PICNIC ESSENTIALS

- **A picnic blanket**: *the focal point of any picnic; everything centers on this.*

- **A wicker hamper**: *complete with creaking hinges, the perfect accessory for a fancy picnic.*

- **A cooler with ice packs**: *ideal for drinks and perishable foods. Cool drinks in streams or rock pools and freeze fruit juices beforehand so they become slushes by the time you want to drink them. Store homemade drinks in stoppered bottles and thermoses.*

- **Containers and crockery**: *Tupperware and tins (good for stacking), melamine plates and cups that can take bashing about; or ecofriendly bamboo picnic ware. Use party boxes for kids.*

- **Utensils**: *bottle opener, cutlery, napkins, mini chopping board with pocket knife, garbage bags.*

- **Beach luxuries**: *deck chair, beach cushions, parasols and wind breakers, beach bag with games kit and towels or sarongs.*

BEACH PICNICS

There is something about the seaside—the salty air, the sand and sea between your toes and the liberating feeling of wide-open space under big blue skies—that conjures up a sense of holiday and adventure. It provides the perfect location for picnicking, either hidden away between the rolling dunes or set back in a sandy inlet. Make paper windmills in advance to mark your picnic spot or bring a bit of the beach back home with you in the form of a handful of pretty shells to make things with.

BEACH CRAFTS

PAPER WINDMILLS

In the run-up to your trip, build the excitement for children by making these windmills to take to the beach.

I: Glue (with a glue stick) 2 sheets of brightly colored paper together. 2: From each corner, cut a 4-inch incision toward the center of the paper. Gently bend every second point into the center of the paper. 3: When all four corners are folded, secure them at the center by pushing a straight pin through them. (Use Super Glue to attach the pin to a cork.) 4: Glue a thin, short bamboo cane to the cork on the back of the windmill.

SEASIDE JEWELRY

Rock pools and shorelines are treasure troves for discovering interesting objects to make keepsake jewelry out of.

I: Buy a friendship bracelet kit that includes colored yarns and mixed beads or collect cut ribbon, raffia and leather. 2: Using a thick darning needle or the point of a pair of scissors, make a hole in the shells or other seaside objects. 3: Thread onto lengths of yarn and other materials to make bracelets and necklaces.

SHELL SKEWERS

These are ideal for serving shrimp, scallops or other seaside-themed foods on, and as a fun canapé-serving idea.

I: Wash any shells collected from the beach to thoroughly remove any sand, grit or salt from the surfaces. 2: Using Super Glue or a glue gun, glue each shell to the top of a skewer.

PICNIC HAMPER FARE

Pasties and sausage rolls make ideal portable picnic snacks; the sausage rolls are prespread inside with condiments and the pasties are mini versions. Uncooked they can be frozen for up to 3 months (add to the cooking time until piping hot). Serve with real ale or lager.

CORNISH PASTIES Makes 8

To make the filling, place 2 tablespoons of Worcestershire sauce, 2 teaspoons of English mustard (optional), 2 to 3 tablespoons of cornstarch, 2 teaspoons of superfine sugar and 1¼ cups of beef stock in a saucepan, then bring to a boil and simmer, stirring continuously, until thickened. Peel and dice 1 small potato, 1 small onion and ¼ of a turnip and mix in a bowl with 7 ounces of beef chuck steak, trimmed of fat and finely chopped, and season well. Pour the sauce over the meat and vegetables and stir to combine. Leave to cool completely.

Preheat the oven to 425°F. Unroll two 8-ounce refrigerated pie crusts on a work surface. Using a round pastry cutter, cut into 8 circles (approximately 4 inches each). Spoon the filling into the center of each pastry circle and spread it out, leaving a ⅓-inch border at the edges. Brush the edges with a beaten egg yolk mixed with a little water and draw up the sides so they join at the top. Using your fingers, crimp together to seal, forming a pocket. Transfer them, seam up, to a baking sheet, making sure to space them out. Brush all over with the rest of the egg yolk mixture. Chill for at least 20 minutes. Bake in the oven for 10 minutes at 425°F, then reduce the heat to 350°F and cook for another 15 minutes, or until golden.

SAUSAGE ROLLS Makes 8

Preheat the oven to 400°F. Unroll 1 thawed sheet of frozen puff pastry on a lightly floured surface and roll out to make it slightly bigger. Cut into 8 equal rectangles, each a little longer than the sausages you are using. Lightly spread each rectangle with ½ teaspoon of mustard. Place a sausage in the center of each rectangle and top with a tablespoon of tomato chutney or red-onion marmalade (page 388). Brush the edge of the pastry square with a beaten egg yolk mixed with a little water.

Roll out a second puff pastry sheet to the same size as the first. Cut into 8 equal rectangles, placing one on top of each sausage. Press around the sausage firmly to make sure it is well sealed and then trim the edges (leaving a ¼-inch border) with a sharp knife. Place on a baking sheet lined with baking parchment and crimp the edges of each sausage roll using a fork. Prick the top with a fork, brush the pockets with the rest of the egg-yolk mixture and chill for at least 20 minutes. Bake for 20 to 25 minutes, until the pastry is golden brown.

THE CORNISH PASTY *This traditional British pie has attained iconic and protected status and is instantly recognizable by the distinctive shape of its pastry casing. By the end of the eighteenth century it had become a staple lunch for farmers and miners in Cornwall because it was nutritious (the traditional filling is beef, potato, turnip and onion seasoned with salt and pepper) and portable. Some accounts say that the crimping across the top acted as a convenient handle that could be discarded without being eaten to ensure that dirty hands didn't touch the food.*

WATERCRESS AND GOAT CHEESE QUICHE Serves 8

For more civilized picnics, transport this quiche whole in its pan. Preslicing it will make it easier to dish out, or make individual versions in mini tart tins and store in a large plastic container layered with parchment paper. You can make this up to 3 days in advance.

Roll an 8-ounce refrigerated pie crust out on a floured surface and use to line a 10-inch removable bottom tart pan. Press the pastry into the pan, allowing a slight overhang. Prick with a fork and chill in the fridge for 30 minutes. Preheat the oven to 400°F. Line the pastry with parchment paper or foil and fill with ceramic baking beans or rice. Bake blind for 20 minutes. Remove from the oven, remove the foil and baking beans and brush the pastry surface with beaten egg. Return to the oven to cook for another 5 minutes, until golden. Allow to cool and then carefully remove the pastry overhang using a small, serrated knife. Reduce the oven temperature to 350°F.

For the filling, heat 2 tablespoons of olive oil in a pan and gently cook 2 trimmed and sliced leeks (approximately 5 ounces), for 10 minutes until softened. Stir in 5 ounces of trimmed and roughly chopped watercress sprigs, and allow to wilt. Remove from the heat and allow to cool. In a large bowl, beat 6 medium eggs and 1¼ cups of heavy cream together until combined. Stir in 1 teaspoon of freshly grated nutmeg and 4 tablespoons of store-bought green pesto and season well with salt and freshly ground black pepper. Stir in the cooked watercress mixture. Place the tart shell on a baking sheet and pour in the filling. Arrange 5 ounces of thinly sliced or crumbled goat cheese on top and bake in the oven for 30 minutes, until light golden and set. Remove from the oven and allow to cool slightly if removing from the pan.

TIPS: *The uncooked pastry case can be blind baked from frozen. Add a few more minutes to the cooking time until golden brown and crisp. • You can replace the watercress with cooked, drained spinach.*

SMOKED MACKEREL PÂTÉ Serves 8 (makes 14 ounces)

This provides an authentic taste of the sea and can be made in a flash. Decant into a sealable plastic tub for dipping or spread straight onto mini buns with a few lettuce leaves and wrap in plastic wrap to keep fresh. It makes a delicious starter, served in quenelles with red-onion marmalade (page 388).

Place 4 filets (approximately 8 ounces) of smoked mackerel, the finely grated zest and juice of ½ a lemon, 1 tablespoon of prepared horseradish and ½ cup of crème fraîche or light cream cheese in a food processor. Add a generous pinch of cayenne pepper and season with salt and freshly ground black pepper. Blend until smooth and transfer to a serving dish. Place in the fridge and chill for at least an hour. Sprinkle with 1 to 2 tablespoons of chopped chives, cayenne and cracked black pepper to serve. This will keep in the fridge for 3 days.

A SHELLFISH FEAST

There's something wonderfully satisfying about cooking fish or shellfish fresh off the boat. Peeling the shells, dipping the sweet flesh into garlic mayonnaise (just add crushed garlic to your favorite brand and combine) using only your fingers brings out the hunter-gatherer feeling. Live, freshly caught lobster, crab and shrimp should all be cooked in rapidly boiling salted water. Cook lobster for 6 minutes per pound, crab for 10 to 15 minutes until they float, and shrimp for 2 to 3 minutes.

POTTED SHRIMP Serves 8

These tiny shrimp set in butter have a sweet, distinctive flavor and are delicious spread on bread or oat cakes. Alternatively, serve these as a starter with Melba toast. Picked white crabmeat can also be used in place of the shrimp.

Clarify 2½ sticks of salted butter by melting them in a pan over low heat. Allow the butter to simmer very gently until foam forms on the surface, then use a spoon to skim off the foam, until you are left with a clear butter. Once it has settled, pour it into a pitcher, discarding any sediment left behind. Place 1 pound of cooked and peeled small shrimp in a large bowl and add ½ teaspoon of ground mace, ½ teaspoon of freshly grated nutmeg, 1 teaspoon of anchovy paste, the finely grated zest and juice of 1 lemon, salt and freshly ground black pepper and a generous pinch of cayenne pepper. Stir together to combine. Spoon the shrimp into eight ramekins. Pour the clarified butter over the shrimp so they are just covered. Chill in the fridge for 1 hour or until set. These will keep in the fridge for 3 to 4 days.

MUSSELS IN WHITE WINE Serves 4 (or 8 as a starter)

Aside from time cleaning them (debearding), they're quick to cook and can be wrapped in foil and steamed.

Melt 2 tablespoons of butter in a large, deep saucepan that is big enough to hold all the mussels, then add 6 peeled and finely chopped round shallots and 4 crushed garlic cloves. Cook for a few minutes until softened but not colored. Add 4 pounds of cleaned mussels to the pan with 1¼ cups of white wine and cover with a lid. Cook for 4 to 5 minutes over high heat, shaking the pan occasionally, until the mussels have opened. Discard any that do not open. Spoon out the mussels, keeping them warm in another pan and simmer the liquid briefly until reduced. Add a squeeze of lemon juice, ¾ cup of heavy cream, some chopped flat-leaf parsley, and season. Heat for another 2 to 3 minutes to thicken slightly. Serve in bowls with the sauce poured over the mussels, with a French baguette on the side to dip into the sauce.

A cold Meursault, Muscadet or Champagne goes well with shellfish.

BEACH GAMES

There's a whole host of fun to be had on a wide-open beach with a bat and ball, a kite to fly, traditional horseshoes or diabolo juggling.

WHEELBARROW RACES

Divide players into pairs. One in each pair needs to get on all fours, to be the "wheelbarrow," while the other holds their legs and is the "driver." You can devise a huge variety of races. An obstacle race involves more skill and can include negotiating sand castles, spades stuck in the sand and cricket stumps. The average beach bag is bound to contain everything you need for props.

BRITISH BULLDOGS

Two "home" areas are marked out at either end of the space, and one or two people are chosen as bulldogs. They stand in the middle of the space; everyone else lines up in a home area. When the bulldogs shout "British Bulldogs!" the players must run across the field to the opposite home area. If they are caught by a bulldog who manages to hang on to them long enough to shout "British Bulldog one, two, three," they must become a bulldog too in the next round, and so it goes. The last player to be caught is the winner.

ULTIMATE FRISBEE

Split into two teams of between four and ten people. Mark out two "end zones," or goals, at either end of a large, rectangular playing space. To start, teams line up within the end zone they are defending. A player on the starting team throws the frisbee to someone on the other team in the opposite end zone. This first catch marks the beginning of play and everyone is now free to run into the middle of the field to attack and defend, intercepting the frisbee when it comes their way. A goal is scored when a team completes a pass to a player standing in the end zone that they are attacking. Players cannot run with the frisbee; they can only pass it. If the team not in possession intercepts the frisbee by catching it or knocking it to the ground, they can start heading toward their end zone. Agree on a number of goals to aim for to decide the winning team.

ROUNDING OFF THE DAY

When the heat has gone from the sun and the light turns golden, mix up some seaside-inspired sundowners. Once home, with sand still sticking to your hands and feet, a sand castle cake is the perfect solution to flagging spirits, especially if you happen to have missed the passing ice cream truck.

ICE CREAM SAND CASTLE CAKE

To re-create your day at the beach, buy a tub of vanilla ice cream on your way home. Just before serving, run a knife around the ice cream and cut it out of the tub with scissors before turning it out on a serving plate. Scatter crushed graham crackers or cookies over the surface of the ice cream.

TIP: *Use mini ice cream tubs for individual servings, varying the flavors and cookie type.*

SEA BREEZE Serves 4

Pour ½ cup of vodka, ¾ cup of cranberry juice, ¾ cup of grapefruit juice and the juice of 1 lime into a cocktail shaker, thermos or pitcher. Shake or mix together well to combine. Divide ice cubes among four glasses and pour the cocktail over the ice. Stir well. You can garnish with lime wedges.

TIP: *Keep drinks really cold in thermoses or coolers and bring along a few salted nuts as nibbles to go with them.*

DARK AND STORMY Serves 4

Mix ½ cup of dark rum with the juice of 1 lime in a cocktail shaker, flask or pitcher and shake or mix well to combine. Pour into four glasses over ice cubes and top each with ginger beer. Stir well. You can garnish with lime wedges.

TIP: *A rum punch is another classic sunset cocktail (page 328).*

COUNTRYSIDE PICNICS

Walking or cycling to a picnic spot brings a real sense of achievement and satisfaction; the food is more enjoyable eaten in the fresh air, mid-expedition. However limited the space is in your backpack, include a few luxuries to make the excursion worthwhile.

PACKING ESSENTIALS

- **A backpack**: *practical for longer expeditions. Pack a couple of picnic blankets and wrap foods well to avoid leaks, spillages and things getting squashed.*

- **Snacks**: *scrubbed radishes, a bunch of carrots, tomatoes on the vine, hard-boiled eggs, Scotch eggs, pork pies, cheese sealed in its rind, energy-rich treats (page 358).*

- **Drinks**: *homemade infusions in stoppered bottles (page 355), cans of beer, individual juice cartons and miniature screwcap wine bottles (easy to open and more practical to pack and chill quickly).*

- **Sandwiches**: *wrap tightly in wax paper, plastic wrap or foil so they don't fall apart. Rolls are good because they are squashable and are less likely than slices of bread to fall apart. See page 253 for some filling ideas.*

- **Fruit**: *shiny cherries still in their brown paper bag, bunches of grapes, watermelon slices, whole strawberries, plums, apples and bananas. Store soft fruit in hard plastic containers to avoid bruising and squashing.*

COUNTRYSIDE PICNIC FOOD

When I think of idyllic picnics in the countryside, the sorts of foods I enjoy have a Mediterranean feel to them. If you're on an excursion, then of course sandwiches are practical, but elevate them from the ordinary by making a giant filled picnic loaf that can be cut into hearty slices (page 353). Let your menu be dictated by what's in season: take a trip to a farmers' market for fresh fruits and vegetables, and choose interesting local cheeses and wines. If the picnic spread is for a summer sports day or a cricket-match tea and you're catering for a crowd, homemade foods, such as a prepare-ahead roulade, a vegetarian quiche (page 343) or a pork terrine (page 357) are always appreciated. Make your picnic buffet spread as exciting as the action on the field.

 Keep it light, with Beaujolais and cool, crisp whites such as Pinot Grigio, Gavi and Sancerre.

SPINACH ROULADE Serves 8

This looks really impressive, but tastes surprisingly light. Make it the day before or freeze the unfilled roulade ahead for up to 1 month (defrosting it fully before filling it). Transport it tightly wrapped in plastic wrap or in a loaf pan.

Preheat the oven to 425°F. Lightly butter a 9 x 12-inch jelly roll pan and line with parchment paper greased with butter. Wash 1 pound of baby spinach, stalks removed, and put in a pan without draining. Cook over a gentle heat for 1 to 2 minutes until the spinach has just wilted. Drain well, squeezing out any excess water, then coarsely chop it in a food processor. Separate 4 eggs. Transfer the spinach to a large bowl and beat in 2 tablespoons of softened butter, the egg yolks and a generous grating of nutmeg. Season with salt and pepper. In another bowl, whisk the egg whites until firm but not dry, then fold gently into the spinach mixture. Pour into the prepared pan and bake for 10 to 12 minutes.

For the filling, mix together 7 ounces of ricotta, ¼ cup of grated Parmesan, the finely grated zest and juice of 1 lemon and a small handful of chopped basil, and season well. Spread in an even layer over the roulade. Scatter 3 ounces of chopped sun-dried tomatoes over the filling and then roll up from one long side. Cover and chill for 30 minutes. Allow the roulade to come to room temperature and sprinkle with a little grated Parmesan before cutting into slices to serve.

TIP: *Experiment with different fillings depending on what's in your fridge at the time, such as sun-dried tomatoes, a combination of crème fraîche with mushrooms, smoked salmon, shrimp, blue cheese or a garlic and herb cheese.*

PICNIC LOAF Serves 8

This loaf packs everything in and you can make this the night before and refrigerate it to let the flavors develop. Combine 2 tablespoons of grainy mustard and 6 tablespoons of good-quality mayonnaise in a small bowl with a squeeze of lemon juice. Mix together 3 ounces of sliced artichoke hearts, 3 ounces of finely chopped sun-dried tomatoes and 3 tablespoons of chopped basil and season well. Cut a "lid" off a medium round bread boule, then scoop out the bread from the inside to make room for the filling. Spread the mustard mayonnaise around the inside of the bread, then start to layer up the fillings with the artichoke/tomato mix, 7 ounces of thickly sliced cooked ham, 7 ounces of sliced Brie cheese and 3 ounces of picked watercress leaves. Press together gently, put the lid back on the bread, secure with string like a parcel and wrap it tightly in plastic wrap to pack in your backpack.

PEA AND MINT SOUP Serves 8

Gently heat 1 tablespoon of olive oil in a large saucepan, then add 1 bunch of roughly chopped scallions, and cook over low heat for 3 to 4 minutes. Add 1 crushed garlic clove and cook for another minute. Add 2 pounds of frozen peas, 1 bunch of fresh mint leaves, 1½ tablespoons of sugar (optional) and 3½ cups of chicken stock. Cover with a lid and simmer for 5 to 6 minutes, then put aside to cool slightly. Remove the mint from the pan, transfer the soup to a food processor and blend. (It can be frozen for up to 3 months. Defrost before reheating and adding the crème fraîche.) Return to the pan, and stir in 3 tablespoons of crème fraîche. Warm through, add a squeeze of lemon juice and season to taste. Serve hot or cold with crusty fresh bread.

REFRESHERS

OLD-FASHIONED LEMONADE Makes 2 quarts

Put 1 cup of superfine sugar, 1¼ cups of water and the zest of 1 lemon in a large saucepan.
Stir over medium heat for 4 minutes until the sugar dissolves. Remove from the heat. Stir
in the juice of 6 lemons and 7 cups of water. Strain into a pitcher and chill. This will keep
for 3 days in the fridge.

HOMEMADE GINGER BEER Makes 2 quarts

Finely chop 18 ounces of peeled ginger in a food processor. Put in a large saucepan with
2 cups of packed brown sugar and 2 quarts of water and bring to a boil. Boil for 1 minute,
turn off the heat and cover loosely. Let the mixture cool to room temperature. Strain the
ginger liquid through a fine sieve into a large pitcher; discard the solids. Add the juice of 1
lemon. Fill glasses with ice cubes and pour in the ginger beer. Top off with soda water and
garnish with lime wedges. This will keep for 3 days in the fridge.

PORK TERRINE

This rustic terrine is really worth the effort. It's a luxurious addition to any picnic. Serve in thick slices with a squash chutney (page 388) or red-onion marmalade (page 388). You can make this 4 days in advance and keep covered in the fridge, but leave out the egg as it will turn gray at the edges.

SERVES 8

2 ounces smoked bacon, cut into small rectangular pieces

3½ ounces chicken livers, roughly chopped

14 ounces lean ground pork

1 duck breast, skinned

½ cup dried bread crumbs

3 tablespoons milk

1 tablespoon salted butter

2 shallots, peeled and chopped

1 large garlic clove, peeled and chopped

1 tablespoon coriander seeds

1 teaspoon black peppercorns

1 to 2 tablespoons Cognac

2 medium free-range eggs, whisked

¼ cup dried sour cherries, chopped

¼ cup pistachios, chopped

salt

one 8-ounce package bacon

4 medium eggs, boiled for 5 minutes and peeled but kept whole (optional)

Preheat the oven to 325°F. In a food processor, pulse the bacon, chicken livers, pork and duck in batches to a coarse texture, then transfer to a large bowl. Place the bread crumbs in a separate bowl, add the milk and allow to soak for 5 minutes. Melt the butter in a small skillet over low heat, add the shallots and garlic and cook for 2 to 3 minutes, until softened. Cool slightly, then add to the food processor with the milk and bread crumbs. Process until coarsely chopped, then add to the bowl with the meat, mixing well.

Grind the coriander seeds and peppercorns to a coarse powder using a mortar and pestle or spice grinder. Add to the meat along with the Cognac, eggs, cherries and pistachios and season well with salt. Mix together very thoroughly until combined.

Line an 8½ x 4½-inch loaf pan with bacon strips, reserving 3 slices for the top. Put half the terrine mixture in the tin, pressing it carefully into the corners. If using them, sit the cooked eggs in a line along the center. Carefully spoon the remaining terrine mixture on top, pressing into the corners again. Arrange the reserved bacon slices over the top, tucking in the ends. Cover the dish tightly with foil, then put in a roasting pan with high sides. Pour boiling water into the pan to come halfway up the sides of the loaf pan. Bake for 2 hours, remove the foil, then bake for another 15 minutes to brown the top. Cool completely, then wrap in fresh foil and chill overnight. Serve cold or at room temperature.

*A chilled Beaujolais.*

REFUELING SNACKS

Ideal on a walking or biking adventure, these energy-giving bites are just the sort of thing you'll need to get you to the top of that next hill or settle into a satisfied sugary slumber. These will all keep for 3 days in an airtight container.

GRANOLA BARS Makes 16 squares

Preheat the oven to 350°F and grease and line a 9-inch square cake pan. Put 1½ sticks of unsalted butter, 1 cup of packed soft light brown sugar and 7 tablespoons of golden syrup (or honey) in a saucepan and heat, stirring occasionally, until the butter has melted and the sugar has dissolved. Add 4½ cups of old-fashioned rolled oats, 4 ounces of dried fruit (such as a mixture of dried apricots, dried cherries, golden raisins) and ½ cup of dried coconut (or mixed seeds), then mix well. Transfer the oat mixture to the pan and smooth down using the back of a tablespoon. Bake in the oven for 25 to 30 minutes, until light golden. Cool in the pan, turn out and cut into squares.

TRIPLE CHOCOLATE TIFFIN Makes 16 squares

Line an 8-inch square cake pan with parchment paper. Place a large bowl over a pan of simmering water, and put 7 tablespoons of unsalted butter, 11 ounces of chopped milk chocolate and ½ cup of golden syrup (or honey) in it. Stir together with a wooden spoon and, once melted, remove the bowl to cool for a few minutes.

Place 3½ ounces of chopped good-quality dark chocolate (70 percent cocoa solids), ⅓ cup of white chocolate chips, ½ cup of raisins and 10 ounces of crushed animal crackers or graham crackers in a large bowl and stir together with the melted chocolate sauce. Pour into the lined pan, pressing into the edges and leave to set in the fridge for a minimum of 2 hours. Remove from the pan and slice into squares.

BANANA BREAD Serves 8–10

Lightly grease an 8½ x 4½-inch loaf pan and preheat the oven to 350°F. In a large mixing bowl, beat together 7 tablespoons of softened, unsalted butter and ¾ cup of packed light brown sugar. Sift 2 cups of self-rising flour and 1 teaspoon of baking powder into the bowl and mix together. Peel and mash 3 large bananas and stir them into the mixture with 1 large egg, and mix well again. Pour the mixture into the pan and sprinkle the top with brown sugar, then bake for 50 minutes until the cake is well risen. Leave to cool slightly in the pan for 5 to 10 minutes, then remove from the pan and allow to cool completely on a wire rack. It can be frozen for up to a month.

Ging, gang, goolie, goolie, goolie, goolie, watcha
Ging, gang, goo, ging, gang, goo
Ging, gang, goolie, goolie, goolie, goolie, watcha
Ging, gang, goo, ging, gang, goo

"Ging Gang Goolie," *Robert Baden-Powell*

CAMPING

Camping is a celebration of being outdoors—rather like a picnic, but it brings an extra sense of camaraderie and adventure. Sleeping under canvas makes you feel removed from everything, whether you are pitching a tent at the bottom of the garden or in the wilds of the countryside, by a wood or in a field. Most of my childhood camping memories take me back to sleepovers in my parents' garden or those of my friends. Of course, we were never that far from the house, so perhaps not quite as courageous as we thought we were, but there was a certain novelty and excitement about sleeping outside, surrounded by the slightly spooky sounds of nature, sharing midnight feasts in the dark. We would spend the entire day preparing for it, gathering ingredients from the kitchen and foraging outside, setting up our camp. We would roast sticky sweet snacks on the fire, then at night we would talk around a lit flashlight until way past our normal bedtime— our chatter occasionally interrupted by the sound of the rain gently hitting the canvas, or of some nocturnal creature nearby. If the night was particularly warm, we'd start off outside in our sleeping bags until the dew started to fall. Being out in the open air, exposed to the elements, brought a real sense of exhilaration . . . even if we had set up camp just yards from the backdoor (our parents would leave us the spare key, just in case).

Away from modern comforts and often with no cell phone service, camping can be therapeutic and provide a break from routine. There are no rules. The pace of day-to-day activities is dictated by nature's clock—falling asleep with the rising moon, the air chilled in the blackened night, and waking with the morning light. There is something quite charming about a simple, nomadic existence, making a home away from home and tuning in to the rhythms of the earth. Life slows down, and even the smallest chores can turn into adventures: boiling water for tea, toasting bread or baking a banana in the embers of a fire.

Camping means different things to everyone, but it is almost universally accessible and can be enjoyed by all. It's not only affordable, but can be tailored to suit most needs, be it a bells-and-whistles "glamping" experience, a backpacker-style adventure in the wilderness, a family holiday at the beach, or a children's sleepover party in a garden. Whatever form it takes, camping is earthy, soul enriching and character building, and there can be few such satisfying moments as having your tent pitched and the smoke rising from your campfire as the golden sun sets on the horizon—even if it's just for a fleeting moment before the rain spoils everything.

PLANNING AND EQUIPMENT

If you are going on a backpacking adventure, it's particularly important to ensure that you have everything you need and that it's compact and lightweight. If you have your car nearby or are in sight of the house, then you don't need to be quite so organized.

THE CAMPSITE

Check that your camping spot is not on restricted land and familiarize yourself with any rules and regulations. If you're planning to walk to your campsite, backpacks are the most practical way of transporting everything. Always carry bags for trash. You should leave the campsite without any traces of your having been there.

PACKING

Check your tent before you leave in case you need to make repairs. Traditional tents and teepees can be rented and purchased online. Bring the right equipment for the weather conditions (check before you go): sunscreen, a hat, and a towel for swimming, or rain gear. Pack layers for when it gets cooler: fleeces, blankets, wool socks and hats (even hot water bottles). Make a checklist—it's otherwise too easy to forget essentials, and it's useful to have when you arrive home to make sure nothing is missing.

USEFUL EQUIPMENT

- *Tents, tarps, sleeping bags and blankets.*
- *Fire starters and matches.*
- *Flashlights (headlamps are best!) and an LED hook light.*
- *All-weather kit.*
- *Swiss Army knife with can and bottle opener, trash bags.*
- *First-aid kit.*

FOOD AND DRINK

Plan what utensils you'll need (a ladle for serving stew, tongs for a barbecue or thermoses to keep hot drinks warm). Rather than taking whole packages and bottles of food and drink, measure out what you'll need into smaller containers. Enamel, plastic or biodegradable plates, bowls and mugs are most practical. Aluminum foil is great for cooking and to keep things warm, and use resealable plastic bags for marinades and dressings. Bring plenty of water and insulated coolers. A "brewing kit" for hot drinks with individually wrapped sachets will help guard against things getting damp. Shelf-stable milk is more practical than fresh milk that requires refrigeration.

TIPS: *Wrap cutlery in bandannas, which are useful as napkins, neckties, pot holders, dish rags or even eye masks if you want to sleep past dawn.* • *Pack after-dinner grub in paper bags fastened with clothes pins to keep insects and prying hands from creeping in.*

SETTING UP CAMP

It's imperative to pick a camping spot that is flat, well drained and free from stones or sharp objects—grass is ideal. Test this out by lying on your chosen territory.

PITCHING THE TENT

Your tent needs to be sheltered from the wind, but if the weather is hot, angle it so that the breeze can flow through. If a slope is unavoidable, make sure your feet are facing down the hill to sleep. Hammer pegs in with a wooden mallet, and check that they're secure. It can be fun to have an encampment of several tents with bunting strung between them if you're celebrating a particular occasion; pitch them in a semicircle with a campfire in the middle, downwind. It's worth taking the time to practice putting up new tents beforehand, or to check for damaged or missing parts on old ones.

> CAMOUFLAGE DENS *This is a great activity to keep kids busy while you set things up. Divide them into pairs and give them a limited time to create a camouflaged den or teepee using natural materials: pieces of wood, netting, rope, string, leaves and branches (anything they can find). If you like, pick a winning design based on how well camouflaged it is, how comfy inside, how waterproof and so on, but it doesn't have to be competitive.*

INSIDE THE TENT

When I used to camp in our garden, Dad would always use an outdoor extension cord and plug in a lamp inside the tent, making our nights on our own a lot less scary—in hindsight, it was cheating a bit! Battery lanterns and flashlights are portable and authentic, while LED tent lights have useful hooks so you can hang them up. Try laying old blankets on the floor, or use sleeping mats, airbeds or camp beds. Hot water bottles are a welcome luxury; place them inside sleeping bags early in the evening to keep them warm until bedtime. Nothing can replace pillows, but choose special camping versions if you're pushed for space. Folding tables are useful for meals and games, but even an upside-down wooden box covered with a cloth will do the job.

TIP: Cut out shapes of stars and crescent moons to stick to the inside of the tent with double-sided sticky tape; when it gets dark and the tent is illuminated inside, you'll feel closer to the heavens.

CAMPING CRAFTS

With adult help, these crafts are good for children to enjoy outdoors. They can communicate between tents with tin can phones and mark their campsite with a homemade flag.

TIN CAN PHONES

I : Pierce a hole in the base of two tin cans (best to get an adult to help with this). 2 : Thread the ends of a 9-foot length of thin rope or string through the holes in the cans. Tie knots at each end on the inside of the cans to secure. 3 : Keep the cord taut to speak and listen.

HOMEMADE FLAGS

I : Cut a rectangle out of muslin, canvas or any plain, medium-weight cotton fabric. 2 : Fold one end around a straight branch or bamboo stick and get an adult to hand sew to secure, or stick with craft glue. 3 : Paint designs on the fabric with waterproof acrylic paint.

CAMPING FOODS

Camping provides a great excuse to enjoy food away from the constraints of sitting at the table and your typical routine, but it needs to be simple and easy to eat—especially if you are going to be eating at dusk. The main meals I have included are ideal for camping—one-pot dishes that should suit the mood and the occasion at the end of a day's adventure. They can be prepared at home beforehand and warmed up (if only for authenticity's sake). Dish out with a soup ladle into enamel bowls or hollowed-out bread rolls to capture all the juices. Bring a small bottle of Tabasco to add a fiery finish! Thread some rope through a roll of paper towel and tie it up near your campfire for cleaning sticky fingers. Wet wipes, tea towels and bandannas are also useful to have to hand.

COOKING ON A FIRE

If you are a serious camper and plan to prepare your food and drink on the fire, build a campfire (assuming you're allowed to build one at your site). Check that the area is free from any dry tinder or overhanging wood. If it's windy, or you are on a beach, dig a pit and surround the fire with stones or bricks to keep it from spreading. Keep your campfire a manageable size, making sure water is always nearby just in case. Light the fire early in the evening as it will take time to give off any real heat, and, before you go to bed, check that it is completely out.

The best time to cook is when the flames on the fire are low and the embers are red hot (high yellow flames are dangerous and will blacken pans). The main disadvantage of cooking on the fire is that it will give out less light; however, you can always stoke up the flames again after you've cooked everything. You will need a grill rack from your oven and two robust logs or stones on either side of the fire to lay it across to make a sturdy cooking platform. You can find or make a tripod that sits above the fire with a hook from which to hang a cooking pan. Alternatively, use a Dutch oven, which can stand directly in the embers. For more about cooking over an open fire see the Barbecue chapter (page 306).

If you'd rather not use an open fire for cooking, a portable stove or disposable barbecue can provide a more consistent heat source and is worth considering.

CAMPING SAUSAGES AND BEANS Serves 8

Kids will love this cowboy-style casserole, and for grown-ups you can add spices and chilies to give it extra bite. Alternatively, wrap strips of bacon around the sausages before cutting them up.

Heat 2 tablespoons of olive oil in a large pan with a lid, add 1 peeled and roughly chopped onion and 2 peeled and crushed garlic cloves and sauté for 4 to 5 minutes, until softened. Add 6 sausages cut into chunks and 10 mini chorizo sausages cut in half and fry for several more minutes, stirring from time to time. Stir in 1 teaspoon of smoked paprika and 2 tablespoons of tomato purée and mix well. Cook for another minute. Add 7 ounces of roasted red peppers from a jar, cut into bite-sized pieces, a 14-ounce can of chopped tomatoes and a 14-ounce can of drained green beans. Pour in 1 cup of chicken or vegetable stock, then bring to a boil and reduce the heat to a gentle simmer. Cover with a lid and allow to simmer gently for 25 to 30 minutes, removing the lid for the last 5 to 10 minutes to reduce the liquid and thicken the sauce. Stir in 5 cups of baby leaf spinach, season with salt and freshly ground black pepper to taste and serve with baked potatoes cooked in the embers of the fire, corn on the cob (page 376) or flat breads and pita.

CHILI CON CARNE Serves 8

This is ideal spicy food for the great outdoors and can be prepared in advance, requiring just last-minute heating. Serve in tacos with boil-in-the-bag rice or corn fritters (page 376).

Heat 1 tablespoon of olive oil in a large pan and, once hot, cook 1¾ pounds of ground beef for a few minutes, until nicely browned. Remove from the pan, drain off the excess fat and set aside. Wipe the pan clean and add 2 tablespoons of olive oil. Sauté 2 large peeled and finely chopped onions and 4 peeled and crushed garlic cloves for a few minutes until softened. Add 1 red and 2 green seeded, and finely chopped chilies and cook for another minute. Stir in ½ teaspoon of chili powder, 1 teaspoon each of cayenne pepper and ground cumin and 3 teaspoons of paprika and cook for 1 to 2 minutes, then add the ground beef back to the pan. Stir in 4 tablespoons of tomato purée and heat for 1 minute. Add 1½ cups of red wine, simmer over high heat for 2 to 3 minutes to burn off the alcohol and then add two 14-ounce cans of chopped tomatoes, ¾ cup of beef stock and 2 cinnamon sticks. Bring to a boil, then reduce the heat, cover with a lid and simmer gently for 45 minutes, adding extra stock if necessary to thin the sauce. Add 21 ounces of canned, drained and rinsed kidney beans and simmer for another 15 minutes without the lid. Season the chili with a dash of Tabasco (if you like it hot) and season well with salt and pepper. Serve with sour cream and a generous handful of grated cheddar cheese.

A red Rioja, Argentinian Malbec or Chilean Cabernet Sauvignon goes well with both these hearty dishes.

TIP: *Freeze your main dishes prior to leaving (for up to 3 months) so they stay chilled for as long as possible.*

SHEPHERD'S PIE
BAKED POTATOES

Hand these out with just a fork and an optional squirt of ketchup or Worcestershire sauce. Each singed crust where the topping has caught the heat makes the potato look as if it has been touched with fire. For variation, mix the cooked, mashed potatoes with a Welsh rarebit mixture (page 106).

SERVES 8

8 large baking potatoes

1 tablespoon olive oil

2 large onions, peeled and finely chopped

3 large carrots, peeled and finely diced

2 pounds ground lamb

3 heaping tablespoons tomato purée

14-ounce can chopped tomatoes

generous grating of nutmeg

1 teaspoon picked fresh or dried thyme leaves

2 to 3 tablespoons Worcestershire sauce

14 ounces chicken stock

3½ ounces milk

4 tablespoons butter, plus a little extra

1 egg yolk

sea salt and freshly ground black pepper

Preheat the oven to 350°F. Put the potatoes on a baking sheet and place in the preheated oven for 1 hour until the skins are crisp and the potatoes are cooked, or cook them in the campfire (see tip below).

Heat the oil in a medium-sized saucepan. Add the onion and carrot and cook on low heat for 10 minutes until soft. Add the ground lamb, turn up the heat and cook until it turns brown. Spoon away any excess fat. Add the tomato purée and fry for a minute, then add the chopped tomatoes, nutmeg, thyme leaves and Worcestershire sauce and fry for a few more minutes. Pour in the stock, bring to a boil then simmer on low heat, covered, for 1 hour.

Remove the potatoes from the oven and carefully slice a "lid" off the top of each one. Spoon the center out from each one into a bowl, leaving a sturdy outer "shell." Add the milk, butter and egg yolk to the potato in the bowl, then season with salt and pepper and mash together. Divide the ground lamb between the hollowed-out potato skins, top with the mashed potatoes and little pats of butter and ruffle with a fork. Place the potatoes back in the preheated oven for another 15 minutes until golden or omit this step if cooking on a campfire and just fold foil around each potato, and scrunch it into a bowl shape.

 *Warming reds such as Argentinian Malbec or Chilean Cabernet Sauvignon.*

TIP: *Traditionally, potatoes were baked in the embers of the fire. Cover in oil and salt, prick them and wrap in foil, placing in the hot embers for 1 to 2 hours.*

SPICY BEAN STUFFED PEPPERS

Different colored peppers have varying flavors—I've used yellow and red for their campfire colors. You can also use pimento peppers with this recipe. For a side dish, allow half a pepper per person and for vegetarians serve two halves as a main course. Add a generous scattering of fresh cilantro or, for an extra kick, a sprinkling of chopped chili and Tabasco.

SERVES 4 (OR 8 AS A SIDE DISH)

2 large red peppers

2 large yellow peppers

1 tablespoon olive oil

1 small onion, peeled and finely chopped

2 garlic cloves, peeled and finely chopped

2 teaspoons ground cumin

1 teaspoon tomato purée

2 carrots, peeled and finely chopped

1 celery stick, finely chopped

14-ounce can red kidney beans

14-ounce can chopped tomatoes

a small handful of fresh cilantro, chopped

1 fresh red chili, halved, deseeded and chopped

sea salt and freshly ground black pepper, to taste

2 ounces grated Parmesan cheese

1 tablespoon chili powder (optional)

Preheat the oven to 400°F. Cut the peppers in half lengthways and scoop out the seeds. Place the peppers on a baking tray, drizzle with oil and roast for 10 to 15 minutes, or wrap in foil and cook on the campfire.

Meanwhile, heat the oil in a large nonstick frying pan. Add the onion, garlic and cumin and cook for 5 minutes, until soft. Add the tomato purée, carrots and celery and fry for 2 minutes, then add the remaining ingredients, except the cheese, and simmer for 15 to 20 minutes until the vegetables are soft and the juice has reduced.

Remove the pepper halves from the oven or campfire and divide the filling between them, making sure each one is filled right to the corners. Wrap them in foil and continue to cook in the oven or campfire for another 10 to 15 minutes. Remove, open the foil and drain the juices.

Sprinkle a generous handful of Parmesan over each pepper. Return to the oven for 10 to 12 minutes, until the cheese melts, or serve immediately with forks, letting the foil act as a bowl. These are really good with the guacamole from page 52 and a little sour cream or crème fraîche.

An Italian red such as Sangiovese matches the spicy flavors in this dish.

TIP: *Try filling the peppers with a spicy chili con carne (page 371).*

CAMPFIRE CORN

CORN FRITTERS Makes 12

Allow 2 per person. Sift ¾ cup of all-purpose flour and 1½ teaspoons of baking powder into a large bowl. Season well. Beat 3 medium eggs and add to the bowl, then mix together. Gradually whisk in ½ cup of milk to make a smooth batter. Stir in 7 ounces of canned corn, 6 finely chopped scallions, the finely grated zest of 1 lime and squeeze of lime juice, 1 to 2 seeded and finely chopped red chilies (to taste) and a large handful of chopped cilantro. Heat 5 tablespoons of vegetable oil in a frying pan. Drop generous spoonfuls of the fritter mixture into the pan and cook in batches for 2 to 3 minutes on each side until golden. Drain on paper towel, and eat immediately.

CORN ON THE COB WITH FLAVORED BUTTER Serves 8

Place 4 peeled and crushed garlic cloves, 1 seeded and finely chopped fresh red chili, 2 teaspoons of sweet paprika, a small handful of chopped fresh mixed herbs, such as parsley, chives and basil, and a squeeze of lime juice in a food processor and season well with salt and pepper. Blend together until everything is finely chopped, then add 1¾ sticks of softened unsalted butter and mix until well combined. Spoon the butter mixture into the center of a large piece of plastic wrap. Wrap it tightly into a log shape, twisting the ends to secure. Chill until firm. Bring a large pot of water to a boil and cook 8 ears of corn (remove the corn silk before boiling) for 6 to 8 minutes until almost tender. Drain and allow to cool. Place ears on individual sheets of foil. Thinly slice the flavored butter and put several slices on each ear of corn. Wrap the ears tightly in foil. Place the parcels on the hot coals for 10 to 15 minutes, turning frequently. Serve in the foil with the melted butter.

CORN CAKE Makes 16 squares

Allow 2 per person. Preheat the oven to 400°F. Grease an 8 x 12-inch pan and line with parchment paper. In a food processor, blend together four 7-ounce cans of drained corn, 1 cup of milk, 4 medium eggs, 5 tablespoons of superfine sugar, 1 to 1½ teaspoons of salt and 10 tablespoons of softened unsalted butter. Once combined, add 1¼ cups of quick-cooking polenta and 2 teaspoons of baking powder and blend until the mixture is just combined. Do not overprocess or it may become liquid. Mix in ¾ cup of aged grated cheddar, then pour the mixture into the prepared pan and bake for 30 to 35 minutes until golden brown. Serve at your campsite with the chili or camping beans (page 371).

FIRESIDE GRUB

These energy-packed snacks are ideal for campfires, or try trail mix (a mixture of nuts, chocolate pieces and dried fruit), also known as "gorp." Or use the cookie dough recipe (page 23), omit the fruit, and use plastic insects to make fossil shapes in the cookies before baking.

HOT CHOCOLATE SPOONS Serves 8

Melt 7 ounces of good-quality chocolate in a bowl. Scoop 8 teaspoons into the melted chocolate, one at a time, so that it comes two-thirds of the way up the spoon. Arrange the spoons on parchment or wax paper to set. To use them, dip into warm milk or hot chocolate and serve with marshmallows.

TIP: *Make these at home and bring them along for a warming fireside treat.*

BANANA CANOES Allow 1 banana per person

Slit the banana skins lengthwise, cutting right through the flesh but without going through the skin on the other side. Fill with pieces of your favorite chocolate and wrap tightly in foil. Cook in the embers of the fire until gooey. Add a dash of rum for grown-ups.

DAMPERS Serves 8

In a large bowl, rub together with your fingertips 4 cups of self-rising flour, a generous pinch of salt, 1 tablespoon of superfine sugar and 2 tablespoons of cold, cubed butter until the mixture resembles bread crumbs. Make a well in the center and gradually add 1½ cups of milk until it comes together, then turn out onto a lightly floured surface and knead until you have a soft dough. When you're ready to eat, break off a piece of dough, roll it into a 4-inch sausage and push a long stick into the middle of it. Place the stick in the embers and toast for a few minutes, until golden. Remove the stick and fill the hole with chocolate spread, jam or honey.

TIP: *Make the dough at home and take it with you to toast in your campfire.*

S'MORES Serves 8

Break up 7 ounces of good-quality chocolate into squares and divide between 8 graham crackers. Thread 16 jumbo marshmallows onto 8 sticks (2 per stick) and toast in the campfire until softened and turning golden. Slide the toasted marshmallows onto the chocolate, and then sandwich another cracker on top.

GAMES AND ACTIVITIES

This is a time to enjoy being away from computers, televisions and phones. Take plenty of flashlights, playing cards, travel games and books, such as a pocket illustrated wildlife or astronomy guide that can be read inside the tent. A game like Pick Up Sticks is portable and light, or make your own version by using wooden sticks from the wild. A magnifying glass and some binoculars will help identify some of nature's wonders. For late-afternoon antics before the light fails, here are a few games and activities to keep kids busy.

MOSQUITO BITES

Give each player a set of small round stickers—these represent mosquito bites (each player should have their own color). The purpose of the game is to subtly "bite" other players by planting stickers on their clothes without them noticing. The person who gets rid of all their stickers first, without being bitten themselves, is the winner.

CRAMBO

One player leaves the group and waits out of earshot. Everyone else comes up with a word. When the player comes back, they are given a word that rhymes with the chosen word. So for "seat," the clue might be "heat." The "guesser" then asks questions without actually saying the word that they suspect to be the answer. The exchange might go something like this: Guesser: Is it a part of the body? Player: No, it is not feet. Guesser: Is it somebody who plays foul in order to win? Player: No, it is not a cheat. Guesser: Is it something you do when you first encounter someone? Player: No, it is not greet. This goes on until the word is eventually guessed correctly. It can be hard for the guesser to frame their indirect questions, but sometimes it's even harder for the other players to work out the word that she or he is getting at. It requires inventiveness and quick thinking from everyone involved.

CAPTURE THE FLAG

Divide players into two teams. Lay down some kind of marker for the center line. Each team takes one half as their territory. At one end of each territory—as far from the center line as possible—a "flag" (a scarf or a bandanna) is laid on the ground. The aim is to capture the opposing team's flag. To do this, players must enter the other team's territory, grab the flag and bring it back to their own side. Players defending their flag are allowed to tag members of the opposing team once they have left their own territory. When a player is tagged, they must drop the flag where they are. They are then sent to a designated "jail" space on the opposition's side, where they remain until one of their teammates stages a "jailbreak" (when a player runs and touches their teammates to save them). Players returning to their own side after a jailbreak are granted "free walk-backs" and cannot be tagged. The game is won when a player manages to bring the enemy's flag into their team's home territory. To make things harder, let teams hide their flags somewhere out of sight at the start of the game. I've seen players have to climb up trees to capture the enemy's flag. Try playing the game at night and replace the flags with glowsticks or lanterns.

KICK THE CAN

A can is placed on the ground in the middle of the playing area. A seeker is chosen; this person takes the can as their base. They cover their eyes and count to 40 while everyone else runs off to hide. Once the counting is complete, the seeker looks for the other players. If they spot someone hiding, they must run back to the can and, providing they get there first, touch it, while declaring that player "in the can." Anyone caught goes to a designated "jail" area. However, if a player in hiding manages to make it to the can before the seeker does, they can kick it in order to release everyone. The game goes on until the seeker puts all of the other players in jail. At this point, the person who ended up in jail first is declared the seeker and a new game begins.

CAMPFIRE SONGS

When night begins to fall and the campers gather around the fire, there's nothing quite like a good old sing-along to bring people together. I have included a few songs that I remember singing as a child around a barbecue with our next-door neighbor strumming his banjo (a favorite being "The Quartermaster's Store"). If someone can play an instrument well and lead the sing-along, this can really add to the atmosphere. Look up the lyrics of the songs below before your trip and make up song sheets to hand around.

GING GANG GOOLIE

This song is attributed to Robert Baden-Powell, the founder of the Scouting movement. All kinds of theories have been applied to the origins and meanings of its nonsense language, but perhaps most important it means that children of all nationalities can enjoy singing it.

ROW, ROW, ROW YOUR BOAT

Fun for younger children, this, along with many other songs, such as "London Bridge Is Falling Down" and "99 Bottles of Beer on the Wall," can be sung in rounds, adding to the camaraderie.

UNDER THE SPREADING CHESTNUT TREE

This is just a short song: "Under the spreading chestnut tree, where I held you on my knee / We were happy as can be; under the spreading chestnut tree." The point is to see how many words in this song you can replace with actions. After you've sung it through a first time as it stands, sing it again and omit "spreading" and instead spread your hands apart. The second time, omit "chest" but pat your chest. The third time, also leave out "nut" and tap the top of your head. Then leave the word "tree" and instead mime tree branches. Then replace "knee," by patting your hand to your knee, "happy" and point to a large grin, and so on. Make it into more of a game if you are a crowd—whoever makes a mistake is out. Start again each time and see if you can get to the end.

THE QUARTERMASTER'S STORE

This song is made up of a verse that keeps changing, followed by a chorus that remains the same (look this up online). You can make up your own lyrics using people's names around the fire, such as "Jim, nice but dim" or using animals and insects: "lice, living on the mice"; "rats, big as alley cats"; "beans, as big as submarines"; "snails, crawling on the nails"; "moths, eating through the cloths"; "bears, but no one really cares"; "scouts, eating Brussels sprouts"; "foxes, stuffed in little boxes" . . .

Many a night I saw the Pleiades,
rising thro' the mellow shade,
Glitter like a swarm of fireflies
tangled in a silver braid.

"Locksley Hall,"
Alfred, Lord Tennyson

STAR GAZING

This activity is best in pitch darkness on a very clear night, and can be exciting for even quite young children. Wrap them up warmly and take them out on a late-night walk in the dark with flashlights. Binoculars are very useful for looking at the craters on the moon and spotting the Milky Way but not for studying individual stars as the binoculars can be difficult to hold steady.

The major patterns in the night sky are easily identifiable when you get to know them. Start with the Milky Way and the Pleiades and then move on to the major constellations and asterisms (often confused with constellations, these are groups of stars that make particular shapes). Learn the names of some of the brighter stars and they will soon become your constant friends.

THE MILKY WAY

Easy to spot, the Milky Way galaxy is a beautiful spiral of stars stretching like a band of hazy light across the night sky. This galaxy contains somewhere between 200 and 400 billion stars and includes the Earth.

THE PLEIADES

The Pleiades is a cluster of hundreds of stars, of which only seven are usually visible to the naked eye. Also known as the Seven Sisters, it is conspicuous in the night sky with a prominent place in ancient mythology. There are wonderful pictures and diagrams of the Milky Way and the Pleiades on the Internet. You'll also find better guidance on how to find them in the night sky than I can manage in this book because it depends on which hemisphere you are in.

THE PLOW (URSA MAJOR)

An asterism, the Plow (or the Big Dipper) is part of the Great Bear and is always visible in the Northern Hemisphere. The saucepan pattern of its seven brightest stars is easily recognizable and it is very useful for locating Polaris (see below).

THE NORTH STAR (POLARIS)

Although not particularly bright, Polaris is important because it lies more or less along the axis of the Earth's spin. In the Northern Hemisphere it appears to be fixed at due north, with all the other stars rotating around it, so it is a very useful aid in navigation.

Polaris

ORION

Orion (the Hunter) is only properly visible during the late autumn and winter months in the Northern Hemisphere. The easiest part of the constellation to spot is Orion's belt, a straight row of three stars that line up with other bright stars, such as Sirius, the brightest star in the night sky. Online star maps will show you how to use Orion to find a number of other important stars.

CASSIOPEIA

This is on the opposite side of Polaris from the Plow and has five principal stars in the shape of a "W."

PRESERVING AT HOME

There's something very satisfying about seeing a row of your own homemade jams, chutneys, pickles or liqueurs glowing on the pantry shelf. I always look forward to the harvesting times of the year, picking fruits like blackberries and blueberries when they're at their best, or at pick-your-own fruit farms, staining my hands in the process. Then returning home to prepare jams and alcohol-based concoctions: it inevitably takes the whole weekend and covers the kitchen surfaces in a sticky mess, but that's all part of the process. Once matured and prettily labeled, your homemade preserves will make lovely presents for friends and family, but equally are something you can enjoy yourself.

PRESERVING TOOL KIT

- **Thermometer**: *a candy thermometer is the most accurate gauge of the setting point (220°F).*
- **Preserving pan**: *wide and heavy based, to allow for even, rapid boiling.*
- **Jars and bottles**: *with tight-fitting lids and tops.*
- **Wax disks, elastic bands and labels**: *for sealing and labeling.*
- **Funnel**: *useful for easily and cleanly decanting liquids into bottles.*
- **Cheesecloth**: *for straining liqueurs.*

STERILIZING BASICS

This is the most important part of preserving—the containers you use must be completely clean and sterile before you fill them, otherwise the contents will go moldy. Remember to sterilize the lids and the tools you work with too.

I: Wash your jars and lids in hot, soapy water and rinse well. 2: Immerse them in boiling water for 10 minutes. 3: Place lidless jars upside down on a baking tray in a preheated oven at 250°F for 10 to 15 minutes. 4: Fill the jars while still warm.

PANTRY SUPPLIES

As well as the fruits and vegetables you've gathered, you'll need some basic ingredients.

- **Pectin**: *used to set jam. Some fruits are naturally higher in pectin than others, so will give a firmer set. Lemon juice is also sometimes used to raise the pectin level.*
- **Citric acid**: *used for cordials, this can be bought in a specialty food store or ordered online.*
- **Vinegar**: *essential for all pickles and chutneys. Keep a variety in stock (red and white wine, malt and cider).*

QUICK STRAWBERRY JAM Makes eight 12-ounce jars

This jam is great for using up the abundance of fruit in summer. The recipe is made with strawberries, but use it as a guide and change the fruits as you wish. Once opened it should be kept in the fridge and eaten within two weeks.

• *5 pounds hulled strawberries* • *2½ pounds white granulated sugar* • *Powdered pectin (as packet instructions)*

Put half of the strawberries in a large preserving pan and crush lightly with a potato masher. Add the remainder of the fruit, sugar, and pectin, then place over a low heat and stir occasionally until the sugar has dissolved. Turn the heat up to medium and bring to a boil for 5 to 7 minutes for a loose jam, stirring to prevent it from clumping, adding an extra 2 or 3 minutes if you prefer a firmer set. Remove from the heat, stir well and use a funnel to pour into sterilized jars. Leave to cool a little before covering with sterilized lids. Store in a cool dark place for up to 6 months.

TIP: *You can use any soft fruit for jam as long as it is not overripe; in fact, slightly underripe fruit is best. Wash the fruit and cut out any bruises, then peel, pit and chop larger fruit where necessary.*

FINDING THE SETTING POINT

There are several ways of checking that the setting point (220°F) has been reached. The best and easiest is with a candy thermometer, accompanied by a saucer test if required. Place a few saucers in the freezer while you make your jam. When the correct temperature has been reached, drop a bit of the mixture onto a cold saucer and let it cool for a moment. If the jam forms a skin and wrinkles when you run your finger through it, it's ready. Take the pan off the heat as soon as you reach the setting point—do not overboil.

GRANNY'S SQUASH CHUTNEY Makes eight 12-ounce jars

This is my granny's recipe, which has been passed down to the family. It's a great way of using up very big zucchini, but you can also use large yellow summer squash if you prefer, or experiment with different fruits and vegetables.

• 4 pounds zucchini, peeled, seeded and chopped into small chunks • 4 medium onions, peeled and chopped into small chunks • 3 apples, peeled, cored and chopped into small chunks • 8 ounces golden raisins • 8 ounces pitted dates, roughly chopped • 2½ cups malt vinegar • 2 pounds soft brown sugar • 1 teaspoon salt • 2 tablespoons ground ginger • 2 tablespoons mixed pickling spices, tied in a piece of cheesecloth.

Put the squash, onions, apples, raisins, dates, vinegar, brown sugar, salt, ginger and pickling spices in a large preserving pan and stir together, then place over medium heat. Bring to a boil, then reduce the heat and simmer gently for 1 to 2 hours or until well blended and thick. Take the pan off the heat, cool and remove the pickling spice bundle, squeezing the liquid from the bag. Spoon it into sterilized jars, filling them to within ⅓ of an inch of the top. Ensure the rims are clean, screw on the sterilized lids and store in a cool place for up to 12 months. Once open, store in the fridge and use within 1 month.

LABELING & PRESENTATION

Taking care over presentation is all part of the fun. Reuse interesting jars and bottles from store-bought produce; just soak off the labels in warm water and sterilize. Glass jars are perfect for pickles and come in many different sizes; buy clip-top or corked bottles for liqueurs, cordials and flavored vinegars. Cover lids with pretty fabric tied with raffia string or elastic bands, attach paper tag labels (page 246) around bottlenecks with ribbons, add stickers or simply write with white glass-paint pens straight onto the bottle.

RED-ONION MARMALADE Makes two 12-ounce jars

This tangy relish is quick and easy to make and goes very well with cold meats and leftovers (page 131), baked Camembert (page 313) and cheese- or haggis-based canapés (page 163). This is best made as you need it, but will keep for a couple of weeks in a jar in the fridge.

• 4 tablespoons olive oil • 4 red onions, peeled and finely sliced • pinch of salt • 4 teaspoons soft brown sugar • 2 star anise • 2 cinnamon sticks • 4 tablespoons red currant jelly • ⅔ cup red wine • ⅓ cup red wine vinegar

Heat the oil in a pan, add the onion and salt, cover with a disk of parchment paper and sauté gently over low heat for 30 to 35 minutes, to soften. Remove the parchment paper, stir in the brown sugar, star anise, cinnamon sticks, jelly, wine and vinegar, turn up the heat and simmer uncovered for another 30 to 35 minutes, stirring occasionally, until thick and syrupy. Allow to cool slightly before storing in sterilized jars with vinegar-proof lids.

ELDERFLOWER CORDIAL Makes 1½ quarts

This delicate summer cordial is wonderfully refreshing in drinks and is delicious on vanilla ice cream as well as in gelatin and fools. It's a British classic, served with sparkling water or sparkling wine, or vodka, mint and soda.

• 20 to 25 elderflower heads • 1½ quarts boiling water • 2½ cups white granulated sugar • 2 ounces citric acid • 4 lemons, sliced, plus their zest

Gently pick over the elderflowers to remove any dirt and stand them, flower side down, in cold water to remove any little creatures. Pour the boiling water over the sugar in a very large mixing bowl. Stir well and leave to cool, stirring occasionally if necessary to dissolve the sugar. When cool, add the citric acid, the lemon slices and zest, then the flower heads. Cover and leave them to steep in a cool place for 24 to 48 hours, stirring occasionally. Strain twice through some cheesecloth into a pitcher and pour through a funnel into sterilized bottles. Label and store the bottles in a cool, dark place, where they will keep for several weeks. Once opened, keep in the fridge in a stoppered bottle for up to one month. You can also freeze the cordial.

TIPS : *The elderflower season is short, from late May until mid-June. Choose a warm sunny morning to get the most flavorful flowers; pick heads away from roadsides and above waist height. • Make the cordial immediately so the flowers don't spoil.*

RASPBERRY VODKA Makes 1 quart

All sorts of fruits and foods can be used to flavor spirits. This version is perfect to use in cocktails or even drizzled over white chocolate ice cream. Blackberries or other fruits are easily substituted, or change the vodka for gin or another clear spirit. Adjust the sugar content depending on the sweetness of the fruit and your own personal taste.

• 14 ounces raspberries • 2 cups superfine sugar • 1 quart vodka

Fill a 1½- to 2-quart sterilized glass jar with the raspberries and pour in the sugar, then top with the vodka. Seal tightly and give it a good shake. Leave overnight, then shake again. Repeat every day until the sugar is completely dissolved. Using cheesecloth and a funnel, strain into sterilized bottles, then store in a cool, dark place for at least 3 months.

TIP : *To make chocolate- or toffee-flavored vodka, pour a little vodka out of a 12-ounce bottle, add a ¼ cup of smashed butter toffees and leave it overnight, or for at least 8 hours. Speed up the process by putting the sealed bottle in the dishwasher on a hot cycle. When done, the toffees will have dissolved. Keep in the fridge and shake before serving.*

SLOE GIN OR WHISKY

Makes 1 quart. Freeze 18 ounces of ripe sloe berries in a single layer to burst their skins, then defrost and place into a large sterilised glass jar. Pour over 9 ounces of sugar and 1 quart of gin or whisky, close the lid, shake well then store in a dark closet, shaking every day until the sugar has completely dissolved. After 3 months, strain through cheesecloth and bottle. Store in a dark place for another year.

INDEX

ACKNOWLEDGMENTS

Writing this book has been an enlightening and thoroughly enjoyable experience but I wouldn't be where I am now without the help and support of many lovely people.

First and foremost I'd like to thank my family for being so understanding and for being the inspiration behind so many of the chapters in this book. In particular, I wish to thank my mother, who has read and reviewed (more than once) every word I have written and who has cheerfully allowed our family home to be taken over for meetings, reviews and photo shoots on more occasions than I can remember.

Thanks to my agent, David Godwin, who got the ball rolling and whose cheeriness and optimism have never wavered.

Special thanks to Sarah Reynolds, my sounding board and friend. Sarah has been an ear to my ideas, an eye to my words, a cook and sharer of recipes, but most importantly a stalwart traveling companion on this literary journey who has stood by me through the highs and lows and never flagged in her dedication.

A huge thank you too to all the Penguins (from Penguin Books), led by Louise Moore, Katy Follain, John Hamilton, Lindsey Evans and Debbie Hatfield in the UK, and Clare Ferraro and Caitlin O'Shaughnessy in the US. I'm not sure they knew what exactly was in store when we started this book but thank you for all your hard work, patience and genuine belief in me and my vision. I also have to mention Sarah Fraser, who tirelessly art-worked all the pages with care. We got there in the end!

David Loftus has been an inspiration with his beautiful photography, in the pursuit of which he went well beyond the call of duty. Amanda Brown organized the photo shoots with meticulous precision and skill and I'm incredibly grateful to all the stylists who spent long hours and days sourcing the right props, along with Katie Cecil, who brought her invaluable stylish flair. Thank you also to the home economists Lisa Harrison, Abi Fawcett and Anna Burges-Lumsden who, with their devoted support team, guided, advised and developed many of the recipes. And not forgetting Sam Duffy for helping me with handicrafts and making all manner of things.

Other special friends have helped me along the way: Rose French, chief recipe tester; Thierry Kelaart, my craft and creative companion; Thomas William Foulser, cocktail confidant of Barts, London; and Ed Pilkington from wine merchants Corney & Barrow. Florist Hannah Bignell, from Ruby & Grace, was generous and inspirational on all things floral, and brothers Simon and Hugo Godwin provided enthusiastic research on historical traditions and games. There are also a number of friends and families who 'celebrated' the chapters with me and brought this book to life.

And finally, thank you to my mentors for their invaluable guidance and support for which I am hugely grateful.